Entered according to the Act of Congress, in the year 1866, by

THE TRUSTEES OF THE

PRESBYTERIAN BOARD OF PUBLICATION,

In the Clerk's Office of the District Court for the Eastern District of Pennsylvania.

STEREOTYPED BY WESTCOTT & THOMSON.

AONIO PALEARIO

AND

HIS FRIENDS,

WITH A REVISED EDITION OF

"THE BENEFIT OF CHRIST'S DEATH."

BY THE
REV. WM. M. BLACKBURN,
AUTHOR OF
"WILLIAM FAREL AND HIS TIMES," "YOUNG CALVIN IN PARIS,"
"THE REBEL PRINCE," &c.

———◆———

PHILADELPHIA:
PRESBYTERIAN BOARD OF PUBLICATION,
No. 821 CHESTNUT STREET.

CONTENTS.

	PAGE
PREFACE	5

CHAPTER I.

DAYS OF STUDY. Paleario's friends—Filonardi—Martelli—Cincio Phrygipani—The poet Mauro—" Our Cæsar."............ 9

CHAPTER II.

THE SACK OF ROME. Charles V. and Pope Clement VII. at war—The Colonnas—The veteran Freundsberg—Bourbon—Rome captured—Pope in St. Angelo—Work of plunder—The Gonzagas—Pompeo Colonna's generosity—Pope in a convent............ 23

CHAPTER III.

WANDERINGS OF A STUDENT. Paleario leaving Rome—Visits Perugia — Lingers at Sienna—Sells his property— Builds family tomb—Goes to Padua............ 45

CHAPTER IV.

ORATOR AND POET. The Bellanti family—Paleario defends Antonio—Wrath of Ottone Melio Cotta—Paleario's Poem on Immortality—Friendships of Bembo and Sadolet—Paleario buys a villa and marries—Vettori—Writes the "Benefit of Christ's Death." 65

CONTENTS.

CHAPTER V.

PAGE

BERNARDINO OCHINO. A zealous young Capuchin—Juan Valdes—Gospel school at Naples—Ochino the popular preacher—Life in danger—Leaves Italy...................................... 84

CHAPTER VI.

SUSPICIONS OF HERESY. Paleario assailed by a monk—Incurs the wrath of certain thievish friars—Goes to Rome—Correspondence—A conspiracy...................................... 97

CHAPTER VII.

THE ORATION OF PALEARIO. Defends himself against Cotta and his accomplices...................................... 117

CHAPTER VIII.

PALEARIO AT LUCCA. Professor of eloquence—Peter Martyr Vermiglio—Burlamachi—Flaminio—Paleario's illness—Letters...................................... 133

CHAPTER IX.

CELIO SECUNDO CURIONI. An old Bible—A young monk—An arrest—New treatment of relics—Celio among the sick—Marries—A monk gets him into trouble—His ingenious escape from prison—Morato—Duchess Renata—Curioni in Switzerland—Olympia Morata—A martyr...................................... 154

CHAPTER X.

PALEARIO AT MILAN. Pleasant letter—Prejudices—Correspondence with reformers—The *Beneficio*...................................... 178

CHAPTER XI.

MARTYRDOM OF PALEARIO. Carnesecchi—Julia Gonzaga—Paleario's book against the popes—Arrest—Trial—Death..... 191

PREFACE.

THE first Protestant scholar, who will have free access to the Vatican, to make researches among the literary treasures, supposed to have been long secreted there, may delve into a rich mine, whose veins run into all the departments of European history. Yet he may be disappointed. The flames may have consumed the best of what is now supposed to exist. It is very certain that there were the elements of a great Reformation in Italy, during the forenoon of the sixteenth century. Italy had a roll of noble reformers contemporary with Luther and Calvin. To Italy was given the Bible in the language of the people; a gospel literature began to spring up on their soil. Mighty men laboured to bring the Italian church back to the ancient faith that existed when Paul preached, Nero persecuted, and Ignatius suffered. Yet how little is known of them! To the memory of one of the Italian reformers and martyrs this volume is devoted.

It is hoped that this book may not fail to be interesting and instructive. The struggles of an educated layman, a distinguished lawyer, and an eminent college professor during the Reformation in Italy, must be worthy of some attention, even if they do not exhibit such brilliant passages of piety as we could desire. The ordinary life of a classical lecturer, who wrote such an earnestly pious book as the "Benefit of Christ's Death," must be important enough to be set forth from such materials as have been preserved from the flames, or the bolts of the Vatican library. A man too, who held a most peculiar position, being intimate with many of the better class of the Roman clergy, personally acquainted with several of the popes, and in correspondence with some of the most advanced Protestant reformers, must present to us a new phase of the Reformation. It is not easy to find in any other part of Europe such a layman as Aonio Paleario. He illustrates the path along which many learned laymen struggled up to the eternal refuge. Our effort has been to present him as he lived and laboured, hated and loved, taught the classics, and wrote gospel truths, suffered for the promotion of literature, endured martyrdom for Christ, and left behind him one little book that had an influence which it is impossible to estimate. We have aimed to do this as faithfully as is now possible, from the records that have been accessible to the scholars of deepest research into the sources of this biography. Paleario belongs to the *Renaissance* quite as much as to the Reformation; but we have not dwelt so much upon his literary, as upon his religious character.

The works chiefly consulted in the preparation of this volume are these—first mentioning those less used—Robertson's Charles V.—Ranke's History of the Popes—

PREFACE. 7

Bayle's Dictionary—History of the Progress and Suppression of the Reformation in Italy in the Sixteenth Century, by Thomas M'Crie, D. D.; Presbyterian Board of Publication*—Aonio Paleario; a tract by the London Religious Tract Society—The Benefit of Christ's Death (several editions of it)—Aonio Paleario, etude sur la Reforme en Italie, par Dr. Jules Bonnet, Paris—The Life and Times of Aonio Paleario, or a History of the Italian Reformers in the Sixteenth Century, by M. Young, London.

The work of M. Young, in two large octavos, presents a series of interesting episodes and biographies, and is full of information upon the times of Paleario. He has given translations of more than eighty letters of Paleario, from which most of the quotations in this volume are taken. These eighty letters show us the strong friendships, the personal troubles, and the literary employments of the reformer, rather than his religious sentiments and experiences. He seems to have been fond of writing letters, and when the inquisitors were searching for evidences of his "heresy," it was natural for his friends to destroy any letters that expressed his strong religious convictions. We have not seen a copy of the "Palearii Opera."

This book will not have been written in vain if it shall persuade its readers to enter more largely into the wealth of biography and history connected with the Reformation, to cherish more gratefully the holy religion for which Paleario was a martyr, to make Christianity more personal

---

* M. Young considers this work as "a mine of wealth," and intimates that his own is but an expansion of Dr. M'Crie's volume.

in their own lives, to exhibit a practical sympathy for those who are now toiling to reform Italy, and to feel the truth of Paleario's famous saying, that the first, second and third ground of salvation was Christ. He is "all in all."

Trenton, N. J.   W. M. B.

AONIO PALEARIO.

CHAPTER I.

DAYS OF STUDY.

(1500–1526.)

ITALY was rich in reformers until late in the afternoon of the sixteenth century; papal Rome threw them into dungeons, drove them into exile, or sent them out of the world by martyrdom. Their labours were not a total loss. Earth knows less of the happy results than heaven, for there has come down to us no full list of Italian names that are written in the book of life. One of these reformers wrote the little volume entitled "The Benefit of Christ's Death," which supplied a great want of the age. From the presses of Venice, Lyons, and Stuttgard it went swift and far through Christendom. In Italian, in Tuscan, in French, in German, in Croatian versions it spoke to the needy hearts of the people. Forty* thousand copies of it were gathering souls for God. They found, what its title-page announced, "*the glorious riches of*

---

* Kurtz says sixty thousand were printed at Venice.

God's free grace, which every true believer receives by Jesus Christ and him crucified."

It won its author the martyr's crown. It too must share in his death and have its resurrection. " The little book," says a late editor, " was too true to Christ and his cross to escape the ban of Rome. It was condemned by the Inquisition. Under their curses and threats it sank from sight, as a stream in Eastern lands sinks before the sun. ' The Benefit of Christ's Death' disappeared." They, who burned authors, also burned books. So completely was it banished from its thousands of homes that Macaulay, following Ranke, said of it, in the Edinburgh Review, 1840, " The Inquisitors proscribed it; and it is now as utterly lost as the second decade of Livy." The historian and the reviewer were mistaken.

A few years since Dr. Thomas McCrie, the Scotch historian, came upon the will of one Thomas Bassinden, a printer in Edinburgh, who died in 1577. In it there was a reference to an English version of the once popular book. This put Rev. John Ayre, of England, in search of it. He found a copy, reprinted it, and awakened such an inquiry that other copies were found, three in Italian. A manuscript copy was unearthed at Cambridge University, which had a touching history. It was made, from the original, by Edward Courtenay, earl of Devonshire, in 1558, while lying a prisoner in the tower. King Edward the Sixth had evidently read it, and written notes upon two of the margins, one of which was prophetic of the book : "Live to die, and die to live again."

Its happy discovery has recalled its author to the memory of the Christian church, which had almost forgotten him. It has restored his influence. Again is it printed by thousands. It is circulating more widely, perhaps, than ever among Protestants; thus gathering the sheaves of a new harvest for Aonio Paleario, who, for three centuries has fully known "the benefit of Christ's death." For this reformer we ask a little space.

Near the river Cosa, among the mountains where the ancient Hernici hunted and fought, stands the old episcopal town of Veroli. On the one side, just beyond the hills, lies the valley of Lake Celano within the kingdom of Naples; on the other the once populous Campagna, stretching up beyond Rome, and now lying around the great seat of Romanism as an immense desert, full of old ruins, overrun with buffaloes, infested with robbers, and yet burdened with entire chapters of the world's history. Among the tribes that tented near the ancient Veroli, the founders of Rome met with their first and truest friends. Here, Pliny says, was the nucleus of the Roman Empire. Here, centuries after, Papal Rome saw born one of the staunchest heroes that rose up against her sins and traditions. He was born on the borders of an immense moral Campagna, filled with the desolations of the true church, overrun with corrupt priests and monks, infested with indulgence-sellers, and holding, buried, ages of cruel history written with the blood of the saints.

In the library of Sienna there is a letter, which asserts that a locksmith came from La Marca to Veroli, and was called La Pagliara. In the same library is another letter written by Ferrante of Salerno, to Paleario, whom the prince offers to assist, not only because of his personal excellence and high standing, but because he is descended from an ancient and noble Salernian house, which had the names of several bishops on its register. It is claimed that both these letters refer to members of the same family; one the father, the other the son. Whether the father was of plebeian or princely family is of little moment; enough for us that his name was Matteo Pagliarolo, softened into Paleario.* If there was some noble blood in his veins, he might have been compelled to keep it warm by labouring in an honest shop. His better honour was in being a good workman. But neither as a locksmith, nor as a scion of the nobility have we aught to do with him; but as the provident husband of Clara Janarilla, whose love he had every reason to return, and

"There are yet other forms of this name. It appears as *Pagliarolo* on the old registers of Veroli, and, also in families now living at Salerno and other places in the kingdom of Naples. There still exists at Veroli a family name Pagliaroli, which claims to be descended from Aonio Paleario. The proper pronunciation seems to be (*a* broad,) Pa-le-ar-e-o.

the father of a son, who alone rescued the family name from oblivion and handed it over to history.

This son, on whom the family fame depends, was born when nearly two-thirds of the twenty-six years, between the birth of Luther and Calvin, had passed away. All that we can gather of the date is from his last letter to his wife, shortly before his death in 1570, in which he declares himself "past seventy years old." If not then a year past seventy, he was born in 1500. He was baptized Antonio, but in later years he changed his name to Aonio, either to gain Italian smoothness, or, as his enemies said, to get rid of the letter T., because it bore the form of a cross. The latter explanation was evidently a slander put forth by Latinus Latino in such wretched verses that a French critic said of them, "They are so frigid, that they would have quenched the flames in which Paleario was consumed."

Love for his parents was his strong motive to filial obedience, but he had not the privilege of loving them many years. They left him an orphan at an early age, with the legacy of a house and small farm. Already had his father been pleased to notice his ardent thirst for knowledge, and confided him to the tutorage of his friend Giovanni Martelli, whose kindness was so essential to Aonio in his orphanage, that he said, long after, "To no one do I owe more than to you." The affectionate son gave early expression to his filial reverence by building an expensive family tomb. We will see, farther on, that he obtained means through Martelli to repair this monument at greater cost than he could well afford.

Veroli had a fair register of bishops dating far back, but of them all, there was no one of a purer life than Ennio Filonardi. He was better fitted for God's work of directing a fatherless boy than most bishops of his time. His warm friendship must have secured to the lad great early advantages. If Aonio was like most other boys, he often wished that he might attain the honours of those, who were high examples in his eyes. Filonardi had risen upon his own merits; why might not some other struggling youth rise in the world? We may imagine that there was enough ambition in the mind of young Paleario to stimulate him in his studies, when he thought that his intimate friend had been born in a small village, of an obscure family, and that by his energy and upright life he had become the bishop of the diocese. He was a man of moderate views on all questions that agitated the public mind. He had no leanings toward reform. Aonio got from him no knowledge of the treasures hidden in the Bible.

It is worthy of notice that in the very year that Filonardi was made bishop, 1503, there was a movement toward reforming the abuses of the church. One of the worst of popes passed away when Alexander VI. died. A cardinal of unusually upright character was elected to the papal chair, who took the name of Pius III. He was convinced that the loud cries for reform must be heeded. If the highest powers in the church did not sweep out the more flagrant corruptions and abuses, new reformers would rise up from among the people, and be more successful than such men as John Huss, John of Wessalia and Savonarola. He called a council for the reformation of existing evils; the hopes of the right-minded were strengthened; but only twenty-six days after his elevation his death was announced. A poet, in his elegy, intimated that the papal chair could not abide such distinguished virtues as those of Pius III.; it was not used to them; it gave him the same black plague which had long polluted it. The cardinals met to elect another pope. They agreed upon oath to elect no man who would not call a council within two years, to reform the church. They elected the well-known military cardinal, Julian di Rovere, and obliged him to take oath that he would fulfil their conditions. He took the title of Julius II. The result was the council of Pisa, held while Paleario was a mere infant, and dissolved by the pope, from whom nothing was to be expected, and who was determined that nothing good should be done. His cruelties and crimes served to arouse the better class of minds to the need of a vigorous reformation. Yet such men as bishop Filonardi were silent. Whatever were their private convictions, they were unwilling to enter upon any new religious movement. They left the work to such coming champions as Lefevre, Zuingli, Luther and Paleario.

The little town, the romantic hills, the kind Martelli, and the genial bishop, had done much for young Aonio; but they did not satisfy his expanding mind. His eye turned across the Campagna to higher institutions of learning. About the year 1520 he went to Rome with no other recommendation than his candour, his youth, and his enthusiasm for study. He probably entered the university, where the study of the Latin and Greek classics was revived. These classics were his admiration, and he devoted himself severely to them. Cicero was his model. He sought to imitate his pure and elegant style. But Paleario must be more than an imitator. A mind like his was not to be satisfied with the mere graces of oratory. He must lay the foundations of his knowledge deep in philosophy. He despised the cavils of the school-men, and sought that better part of science which strengthens the powers, and enlarges the views of the human mind. He studied Aristotle, using his judgment as a fisher employs his net, taking good and bad together at the first; but afterwards reserving the true and rejecting the false. What a lamp the word of God would have been had he known that there was such a book, or that it was meant for him! His diligence in study kept him from evil companions. He chose the law as his future profession, yet theology was his favourite pursuit.

DAYS OF STUDY. 17

While young Paleario was treading the old historic streets of Rome, great events were transpiring in the world. In the papal chair sat Leo X., the papal wonder of his age. No such pope had appeared for centuries. He was the son of Lorenzo de Medici, the magnificent. He encouraged literature; he patronized learned men; he was humanized by his love for the fine arts. Julius II. had exerted himself to adorn the churches of Rome, by employing Michael Angelo and Raphael to paint their fadeless frescoes, and produce the finest specimens of sculpture. But Leo X. exerted himself rather to adorn the mind, to recover the long-lost writings of ancient authors, and to encourage the printing of the classics. Advantage was taken of the pope's disposition to favour learning, and a far more liberal course of studies was adopted in nearly all colleges and universities. Men were beginning to think and search for the truth. Then came the great leaders of the Reformation to direct them to the word of God. Leo was aroused. He invoked the aid of the whole church to put down the new doctrines. If any writings of the reformers fell under the eye of the student Paleario, it was not through the tolerance of the pope, cardinals or clergy.

The court of Leo X. made not the least pretence to the practice of religion. The pope was quite as fond of pagan revelries as of literary pastimes. Though he assumed the title of "Vicar of Christ," an honest-minded student from a quiet village would have been amazed at his want of any resemblance in character to that of the heavenly Master. Leo died in 1521, and was succeeded by Adrian, who resolved upon some important reforms; but who was forced to admit that a pope was most unhappily situated, for he was not free to do any good, however much disposed. His advisers wished him to crush Luther, and reconcile the Germans, without making any concessions or changes. He was told that if "the church of Rome were to attempt any reforms, it would only embolden those who cried out against its abuses, to increase their demands; that it did not become the dignity of the court of Rome to make any change, or own itself capable of corruption or improvement." While the grave questions of reform were agitating all Christendom, Paleario was pursuing his studies, and probably he then for the first time received the idea that any sort of reform was necessary in a church hitherto regarded as infallible.

Six years of study were passing away. It seems that Paleario partly supported himself by teaching, and acting as secretary to some of the nobility. He probably gave lessons to Cincio Phrygipani, a rich young Roman, who became a warm friend. Cincio was not a sedate character; he was genial, generous, full of life, fond of mirth, and strongly tempted by the companions that courted his favours. If Paleario had sought his generous bestowals of wealth, he would have flattered this young gentleman, and he might have drawn largely from his purse. But he sought the highest moral good of one who went often astray, and who might have been ruined had not his mentor felt the greatest anxiety for him, and plainly chided him, or gently persuaded him into the better path. We shall again meet Phrygipani.

Often at the joyous assemblies and revels of Leo X., there was a poetical genius, who drank wine till the Muses came to his aid, improvised verses that kept the whole company in roars of laughter, or sang some old song to the sound of the lyre. He was Mauro, a native of Arcano, who had come to Rome to support himself by his wit, which at least brought him invitations to poetical suppers where wine of a "poetic vigour" was abundant. He had talents which might have placed him above this inglorious occupation. He was successively the secretary to different eminent persons, one of whom was Cardinal Cesarini. He was intimate with another poet, Bernardino Berni. They often changed their wealthy patrons, and, living only for the wants and amusements of the hour, they could thus repeat their store of jokes and recite the same verses to circle after circle with thoughtless jocundity. Years afterwards, when Berni leaned to the Reformed opinions, satirized the abominations of Rome, and sang of the gospel, he lost all favour at the papal court.

We know not what brought Paleario into close friendship with Mauro d'Arcano. Perhaps the sober student sought to lead the poet from his wine-coloured wit to graver thoughts and nobler pursuits. We may be thankful for their friendship. Paleario seems not to have been injured by it, and it supplies us with letters from which we derive most that we know of him for several years. In them we have a glimpse of his social and intellectual life, and the energies of his impulsive nature. At one time he is eager in the pursuit of good; at another indignant over the infliction of wrong; not free from ambition, but seeking earnestly the best things that his age presents to his mind. Remember it is yet only the time of the Renovation (*Renaissance*) with him; not that of the Reformation. He appears as a young man of lofty spirit, large sympathies, an independence that unfits him for being a menial in the houses of great men, and keen sensibilities which "turn at the touch of joy or woe, and turning, tremble too."

His little property gave him but a slender income, and he was dependent somewhat upon the patronage of the great ones of the world, for the world and the church were quite the same at Rome. The nobles and cardinals had generally two or three promising young men in their households as secretaries or librarians. The salaries were a help to students, and they had the use of books which they could not find elsewhere nor afford to purchase.

DAYS OF STUDY.

Mauro recommended his friend as a learned scholar, to a rich noble, who is called in the letters "Our Cæsar." He was probably the Cardinal Cesarini, to whom Mauro had been, or still was, the secretary. It would be the duty of the student to overlook the affairs of the establishment during the absence of his patron. He was soon settled down, the master of a fine library, reading with unceasing diligence, and writing comments on the orations of Cicero. We hear of nothing unpleasant for some years.

But one day the poet was about to leave Rome. Paleario walked with him part of the way, bade him adieu, stood gazing as he rode off, and only lost sight of him when Soracte and the adjacent woods and hills hid him from his view. With a heavy heart he turned back, and met his patron starting on a journey; he must bear the pangs of another parting. He resorted to his friends in print, but books did not banish his feeling of loneliness. He took his pen and gave his thoughts to Mauro, who might forget his restraining influence and turn poetical caterer at some new jocular supper. He described the last look he had of his friend and added: "As I descended towards the river I met *Our Cæsar*, accompanied by a numerous suite; with his usual politeness and munificence, he warmly recommended me to his people, and directed, that during his absence, everything should be at my disposal. Never was there a more illustrious or more affable person. God grant me to behold the return of those whom I have seen depart. On returning to the city it seemed to me a desert."

Little did he think that Rome should soon be more sadly desolated than a desert. But in a later letter to Mauro, he mentions a rumour of alarming war. It is reported that Pope Clement and Charles V., the emperor, have fallen out, that Charles is sending an army against Rome, and that Clement is seeking an alliance with Francis I. the king of France. He writes : "Bologna has taken up arms: the Germans are preparing to fight: if this be the case we are lost. See what a tempest is impending. Do not wait until the combat has begun. Set off immediately. If you can reach Mantua, that will be the safest refuge."

We turn then to the sack of Rome. Whether Paleario witnessed it, and fought to defend the city, we know not; but the event made a powerful impression upon his mind. It must have convinced thousands of the people that Heaven had no special protection for the pope, nor had sent legions of angels to defend him.

CHAPTER II.

THE SACK OF ROME.

(1527.)

CHARLES FIFTH was no Protestant; the campaign against Rome was not a Protestant war. It was papal Rome fighting against herself. There are few events in history in which the hand of God is more plainly revealed. The theme is one of the richest, affording a wealth of biography, a display of shrewd games in politics, a series of hard blows against the papacy, and an array of proofs that the Lord of Hosts was defending his people by drawing their strongest enemies from the principal field of the Reformation.

Charles the Fifth had assembled the Diet of Spires, in 1526, to devise measures for preserving the Romish church. He wished to have the resolutions made at Worms, executed against Luther and his writings. He was about to open a war upon the reformers. But he must first visit Rome to receive a new coronation. The plan was, that he should receive the imperial crown, in the holy city, from the sacred hands of the pope; and in return for this favour, he should give up to Clement VII. the gospel and the reformation. But all at once the pope turned against the emperor, crying out that Charles was taking Ferrara from him, and attempting to enslave Italy. The pope would not endure it. He turned from religion to politics. He formed the "Holy League" with several powers, of which the French king, Francis I., was the chief. He pushed his troops into Lombardy, and gathered the army of the League.

Charles felt injured; he proposed a compromise, and was insulted. His rage was equal to the occasion. He wheeled to the right as quickly as Clement had done to the left. He put the Protestants in safety, and the pope in danger. Instead of marching with the pope against the reformers of Germany, he would march with the reformers against the pope. The evangelical princes, who had their sleeves embroidered with the Latin letters V. D. M. I. Æ., meaning, "The word of God endureth for ever," went home from Spires astonished to find a friend in Charles the Fifth. It was the turning point in the Reformation.

The emperor seized a pen sharp enough to have been pointed by Luther. "He assumed all the airs of a reformer." He wrote to the pope, reproaching him for not behaving like the father of the faithful, but like an insolent man. He was surprised that Christ's vicar should dare shed blood to acquire earthly possessions, a thing "quite contrary to the evangelical doctrine." "Put up your sword, and call a general council to reform the abuses in the church, and to inquire if these Protestants are not more nearly right than we thought they were!" More boldly still, the emperor wrote to the cardinals complaining of the pope, and inviting them to convoke a general council if Clement should refuse to do it. This letter was printed and circulated through Germany, Spain and Italy, and had a wonderful effect in confirming the opinions of the reformers, and showing the people how little the emperor respected the pope. It roused Clement to seek revenge. He saw a storm rising, and looked around for means to avert it.

Rome was in a state of weakness. While the papacy was strengthening its arm for the sword, it received a stab from another quarter. It came from one of the fearful Colonnas. We may share with Gibbon in the regret that the members of this family did not leave the world a history of their illustrious house. It would have been almost the history of Rome during the middle ages.

This family of powerful barons dated its lineage to the eleventh century, when Peter Colonna took up arms against the pope. Its members rose to great influence. All along the slopes of the Appenines lay their immense estates. On them were heaped privileges and honours. They lived like free princes, coined their own money, and increased their independence. They became the safeguards of a long line of popes. But Boniface VIII.

grew jealous of them. In their fortresses throughout the country, they plundered and tyrannized as they pleased. Some of them wrested from a caravan the rich furniture of the pope. They were unrestrained by religion, humanity or justice. They made themselves the masters of Italy, had cardinals in the family, and grasped for the papacy. A bull was sent forth in 1297, against them, denouncing them as "this odious house of Colonna, cruel to its subjects, troublesome to its neighbours, the enemy of the Roman republic, rebellious against the holy Roman church, the disturber of the public peace in the city and in the territory of Rome, impatient of equals, ungrateful for benefits, strangers to humility, and possessed by madness, having neither fear nor respect for man, and an insatiable lust to throw the city and the whole world into confusion." The two cardinals of that house were to be deposed. The estates of all were to be forfeited. Their castles were to be taken from them. A crusade was proclaimed against them. One of their cities, Palestina, was ordered to be razed to the ground, the soil plowed up, sown with salt, and rendered for ever unfit for the habitation of man. Most of them fled. "Degraded," says Gibbon, "banished, proscribed, the six brothers in disguise and danger, wandered over Europe, without renouncing the hope of deliverance and revenge. In this double hope the French court was their surest asylum." Benedict XI. restored them to their privileges and power. Stephen Colonna was noble amid all his misfortunes; the prospect of danger provoked him to avow his name and country, and when asked, "Where is now your fortress?" he laid his hand upon his heart and answered, "Here!"

Such were the ancient Colonnas; their children were true to their lineage. Pompeo, a cardinal of restless, noisy, ambitious temper, was at the head of the family, and was the crafty rival of Clement VII. He saw that the hour of his advantage had come; the troops of the pope were in Lombardy, and Rome was slumbering. He armed the Colonnas, their tenantry and friends to the number of three thousand men, dashed down upon Rome, seized one of the gates, dispersed the papal guards, and sent the pope flying from the Vatican, through a private gallery, into the castle of St. Angelo. It was all done in the name of the emperor, for the family had ever been Ghibellines. The palace of the Vatican, the church of St. Peter, and the houses of the pope's officers were plundered in the old Colonna style. They were about to sack the city, when their ancient rivals, the Orsini, roused the people to a defence of their homes, and compelled the invaders to desist. The pope was helpless; he demanded a capitulation. Moncada, the minister of Charles Fifth, and the secret agent of Pompeo Colonna in duping the pope, made a treaty with Clement. By this the Colonnas were pardoned, but obliged to leave Rome; and the pope recalled his troops from Lombardy, thus weakening the army of the League. The emperor was the chief gainer; the Colonnas, who talked of nothing less than deposing Clement and placing Pompeo in the papal chair, were at the mercy of all parties. Clement drew his troops near him, felt braver, sat in his gorgeous robes, degraded Pompeo from the dignity of cardinal, and censured the whole tribe of Colonnas. Pompeo cited the pope before the Diet at Spires, and appealed to a general council. He posted up his manifesto by night on all the churches at Rome, and spread it throughout Italy, so that it might reach the eyes of as retired students as Paleario. He thus prepared the minds of men for the still more daring insults to the papal majesty which were yet to come. The viceroy of Naples took up the cause of the excommunicated Colonnas, and advanced to attack Rome. But a far greater danger came threatening from the North. The emperor had two armies under two generals whose very names spread terror and alarm. Let us note their marches.

When Luther stood at the door of the hall where the Diet of Worms was to meet, having been gazed at by thousands from the pavements, gardens, windows and house-tops, and when he had everything to fear from his judges, yet feared nothing, an old general tapped him on the shoulder, shook his white head, and said, " Poor monk! poor monk! thou art now going to make a nobler stand than I or any other captains have ever made in the bloodiest of our battles! But if thy cause is just, and thou art sure of it, go forward in God's name and fear nothing. God will not forsake thee!" This valiant knight and veteran in war was George Freundsberg, or Fronsperg—just the man whom the emperor wanted for teaching the pope a lesson on reformation.

"Announce," said Charles to his brother Ferdinand, who bore the old title of king of the Romans, without having any rule in Rome, and who will prove a friend to our Paleario, "announce that the army is to march against the Turks; every one will know what Turks are meant."

The gigantic Freundsberg, who "bore in his chivalrous heart God's holy gospel, well fortified and flanked by a strong wall," was advanced in years, and had given up active service. He looked forward to repose, for his sons had grown up to take his place. Besides, he was of so enormous a size that a new campaign would be quite too much for him. But his son Gaspar, in command at Milan, wrote that all would be lost if relief did not soon come. Parental affection, duty to the emperor, and the prospect of a second conquest in Italy roused him. He buckled on his armour, pledged his wife's jewels and his own estate, sent out recruiting agents, gave to every man the bounty of a crown, told the troops they were going to destroy the power of the pope, and that they must look for pay in the pillage of Italy.

In November he led across the Alps fifteen thousand men, whose feet slipped, heads grew dizzy, and horses sometimes rolled with their riders into the snows. It was but a three days' work.

There was another imperial army waiting in the duchy of Milan, commanded by the Duke of Bourbon, who had forsaken France and come over to the cause of the Emperor. He and his Spanish troops joined the army of Freundsberg in February. He had no money for his weary men, and resolved to march straight to Rome. The soldiers raised a shout at the news. To avenge Charles was the idea of the Spaniards, who loved their emperor; to rout the pope was that of the Germans, who gloried in their Luther: but all of them were quite too eager for pay and plunder.

All at once came strange tidings. The viceroy of Naples had gained a few slight victories; the emperor and the pope were about making a truce; Bourbon was informed that he must stay the advance of his army. As soon as this was known, a frightful tumult broke out. The Spanish troops revolted, compelled the duke to flee and pillaged his tent. They turned to the other forces, and shouted the only German words they knew, "Lance! lance! money! money!" The loud roar was echoed back by the Germans. Freundsberg beat to muster, and calmly demanded if he had ever deserted them. But all was vain; they must have their pay, and they could get it only by war. They again raised the shout for the lance and the money. There they stood, lowering their lances as if ready to slay their officers.

Freundsberg, whom no army had ever frightened, and who was accustomed to say, "the more enemies, the greater the honour," saw these men aiming their murderous steel at him, and lost all power of utterance. He fell paralyzed upon a drum, as if struck with a thunderbolt. The lances were raised, the agitated soldiers fell back. Four days later the general recovered his speech, but his strength was broken. "Forward," said he to Bourbon, "God himself will bring us to the mark." Forward! repeated the lancers. Bourbon had no alternative. It was as well, for neither Charles nor Clement were listening to the terms of peace. Freundsberg was taken back to his castle of Mindelheim, where he died after an illness of eighteen months. Bourbon took the high road to Rome.

Was the "Holy City" prepared for his coming? For twenty-five years there had been loud warnings to Rome. Savonarola had cried aloud and spared not. But she imagined herself protected by an infallible, invulnerable papacy. Clement knew that he had reason to fear; a Colonna had taught him his danger. Fanaticism raised a warning voice. A man of the lower ranks, Brandano of Sienna, a poor emaciated being, went about through the streets, in tattered garments, foretelling the ruin of the priests and of the papal court as the prelude to the reformation of the church. He urged that now was the time to repent. When cast into prison, he persisted in his warning cry. But none regarded him as a prophet, until the day of terror dawned.

The pope heard of the approach of Bourbon. He knew not what to do. He had lately disbanded four thousand men. He asked counsel of the cardinals; they all stood aghast and dismayed. He thought of flying to the sea, of destroying the bridge and waiting for the army of the League, of bribing Bourbon to delay, but nothing was done. At length it was resolved to collect artizans, servants, hostlers and loungers, and organize a guard. Three thousand placed themselves under Renzi de Ceri. The pope asked money of the wealthy citizens: one of the richest of them offered one hundred crowns, so low was public spirit, or so keen was his irony. Clement urged that it was extremely improbable that "the Lutherans" would ever capture the holy city: he doubted not that they were coming only for their own destruction. But still the walls must be defended. If it were consistent with his dignity, he would mount them and set the example. His pleas amounted to nothing. The people shut the gates and pronounced all alarms groundless. Had they not a pope?

On the fifth of May, 1527, Bourbon was at the gates with about thirty-six thousand men; his army nearly starved; the troops disheartened, and overcome with weariness. They rested for the night.

THE SACK OF ROME.

Early the next morning, when the thick fog veiled their movements, they made the attack. The impatient Bourbon seized a scaling ladder, mounted the wall, where friends and foes could see him in his white cloak, waved his right hand, and urged his men to follow him. At that very moment he fell by a blow from an unexpected quarter. The battle had drawn to the spot certain curious spectators, among whom was the eminent and eccentric artist, Benvenuto Cellini, who thus tells his story: "We arrived at the wall of Campo Santo, and here we saw this wonderful army making strenuous efforts to get within the city. Many of the enemy lay slain; near that part of the wall which we approached they were fighting with all their might; the fog was very thick; I turned to Alessandro and said to him, 'Let us return home as quickly as we can, for there is no possible remedy. See, some are mounting and others flying.' Alessandro, much frightened, said, 'Would to God we had not come here,' and turned to go away. But I reproved him, saying, 'Since you have brought me here, we must do something worthy of men.' I pointed my gun where I saw the fight thickest; I aimed at one raised above the others, though the fog did not allow me to see if he was on horseback or on foot. I immediately turned to Alessandro and Cecchino and told them to fire off their guns, and showed them the way to avoid a shot from without. This we did twice, each of us. I cautiously drew near the wall, and saw an extraordinary movement among the enemy, caused by our shots having killed Bourbon. It was he, as I afterwards learned, whom we saw carried off by his men. We then left."

Thus fell the great traitor to France, who had almost ruined his own country. When dying, he desired the fact to be concealed; a cloak was thrown over him, so that the soldiers might not discover their leader's death. Two "Lutherans" first cleared the wall, exclaiming, that God was marching before them in the clouds. The gates were opened, and Germans, Spaniards, and all came pouring in. Renzi was not the man to sell his life dearly at the head of his raw troops, and he cried out, "The enemy is within, save yourselves;" a thing they were prompt to do. The pope, hearing their cries, fled through a covered passage, weeping as he went, lamenting that he was betrayed by everybody, and took refuge in the castle of St. Angelo. From the windows he could see the flight of the Roman soldiers and the butchery of the citizens.

Crowds of cardinals, prelates, courtiers, nobles, merchants, soldiers and women rushed to the chief gate of the castle. The drawbridge could scarcely be shut. About three thousand persons got in; among those who failed to enter was cardinal Cesarini, the supposed patron of Paleario. Then began the famous "sack of Rome." The greedy troops, that had lived for months in wretchedness, determined to make her disgorge the money that she had made from jubilees, pilgrimages and indulgences. Wine-shops and bakeries were soon emptied; churches, palaces, convents, dwellings, banks, tombs —all places where was money or bread—were despoiled. Even the golden ring was taken from the corpse of Julius II., and another from a live prelate, by cutting off his finger.

At first some respect was shown for the pope; the imperialists said, that as Bourbon was slain, they were willing to come to terms; let him pay them three hundred thousand crowns. But when he was willing to treat with them, they changed their minds; they could not control their soldiers. He did not urge the matter, for he thought the army of the League was on the point of delivering him. He fancied he could see their leading horsemen in the distance. But fiercer men—Italians too, the Colonnas and the Gonzagas—were sweeping through the streets, free from all discipline, sacking, destroying and murdering as they went. They fiercely attacked the castle, could not force the gates, put it under siege, and turned again to the pillage of the houses.

There was but one house in Rome exempt from outrage; it was the palace of the Holy Apostles, inhabited by Isabella Gonzaga, the Marchioness of Mantua. She had been there three years waiting for the pope to confer upon her son Hercules a cardinal's hat. He had delayed the gift. Was it because her youngest son, Ferrante Gonzaga, was one of the commanders of the imperial army under his cousin Bourbon? On the very day of the capture of the city the red hat was sent to the palace. Ferrante had warned her of the approach of the army; he and Bourbon had promised that if she could defend herself for two hours, they would protect her. She had invited in several Roman families, walled up the windows and doors, and placed a guard around the palace. On the awful day, a captain of the Italian infantry, ran alone on foot with a small black-and-white silk flag stuck in the crest of his helmet, to the palace to see his sister Camilla, who was with the Marchioness Isabella. The inmates saw him, threw down a rope from the wall and drew him up. To their terror he told them of the death of Bourbon and the capture of the city. Other messengers came from Ferrante, who finally set a strong guard at the gates. For eight days the general pillage went on, and at last the palace was taxed fifty thousand golden crowns as a compensation to the soldiers. This was paid by the nobles and citizens who had made it their refuge. Isabella and her family were exempted from this impressment. It was said that her son Ferrante got ten thousand of these crowns for his share of the booty as captain.

It must be admitted that the German troops did their full part in pillaging. But when food and drink became plenty at their hands, they were less

THE SACK OF ROME. 37

violent and licentious. They aimed chiefly to destroy what papal Rome considered "holy"—images, church furniture, priestly robes and the like. Nothing pleased them more than to turn the papal court into amusement and mockery. They went to St. Angelo and ridiculed the pope. They imitated the priests in comedies and processions. They *played* popery. They set up one of their tallest, best-looking men as pope, in the papal robes and with the triple crown upon his head. They put him in the lead, and marched through the streets wearing red hats, and the garments of priests and monks. They devised frightful music, to represent the pope's band. The burlesque of popery was complete. They acted it in front of palaces and under the windows of St. Angelo. Finally a conclave was formed; the tall fictitious pope resigned the papal office; they went into a new election; a name was proposed, all hands were raised, and all voices shouted, "Luther is pope! Long live pope Luther!" Such were the humours of the Germans.

But the Spaniards did not let the papists off so easily. Clement had called them "Moors," and offered an indulgence to all who should kill them. Their fury was unrestrained. Claiming to be faithful Catholics, they put prelates to death, and spared not the most devout. If a bishop had been paraded about in sport by the Germans, and had paid a ransom to be freed from their jests, the Spaniards seized him, made him pay a second time to be free from their tortures, or took his life on the spot. None could say that the reformers had advised these barbarities. Luther had said, "I would not have Rome burnt; it would be a monstrous deed."

"I tremble for the libraries," said Melancthon; "we know how hateful books are to Mars." The conquerors treated literature and literary men with merciless Vandalism. They carried most valuable manuscripts to their camps, and littered their horses with them. Many scholars lost both their libraries and their lives. Antonio Valdo, a great traveller, and a professor at Rome, was taken prisoner. He saw the labours of years wantonly destroyed; his house was sacked, and his manuscripts used fo cooking in his presence. He was tormented by his captors; but as he could reveal no hidden treasures he was set free. He died of hunger. The fate of Marco Calvi was similar. A vast number of rare Hebrew manuscripts were destroyed. Years after, Paleario expressed his grief to Sadolet, who had lost a splendid library, "for the loss of so many valuable works left us by our ancestors" amid "the destruction of these wretched times."

Two days after the capture of Rome, Pompeo Colonna, the personal enemy of Clement, came to rejoice over the misfortunes of his fallen foe. But his heart was touched when he saw the streets filled with the slain, and heard the groans of women, children and prelates, as they appealed to him for relief. He devoted himself to the work of humanity.

THE SACK OF ROME.

He used his influence to persuade the army to cease from barbarity. He put many citizens in places of safety, fixed the price of their ransom, and when they could not pay it, he advanced the money. His vast palace was filled with ladies, whom he nobly protected from insult, and his doors were opened to all who fled to him for relief. He forgot the injuries inflicted upon him by his enemies, and treated friends and foes with equal magnanimity. A member of the family of Santacroce had killed Pompeo's father in days gone by, but when he saw the noble matron and her beautiful young daughter exposed to violence, he paid a large ransom and secured their liberty. In one act only did he gratify his revenge—he set fire to the pope's vineyard near Ponto Molle. From the heights of St. Angelo, Clement saw the smoke rising, and said to the Cardinals, "Pompeo is only doing what I deserve in return for my having burned his villages in the Campagna."

Clement daily expected the army of the League to drive away the cruel invaders, but no banners appeared. He knew not when the enemy might blow his castle into the air. The lancers muttered beneath his windows, "Death to the pope!" The Spanish captains cut off all supplies in order to starve him into compliance with their demands. He and his cardinals began to dine upon horseflesh, and even upon that of more stupid beasts. Cruel measures were taken against all who sought to carry provisions to the "holy father" Clement. A poor old woman was found carrying some lettuces to him; she was barbarously strangled with a halter and hung up before the walls. Some boys were shot in the merciful act of fastening a few green vegetables to a cord that was let down from the windows.

The air of the city became vile with odours from the gory streets; the plague appeared, making no distinctions between victors or vanquished. It crept into the castle of St. Angelo. The pope began to fear for his life. His pride yielded, his enmity was cooled. He stooped to ask the assistance of his bitterest foe, whom he had deposed from the office of cardinal, and whose ancient family he had excommunicated. He sent a message to Pompeo Colonna, saying that there was no hope for him but in the lance of Achilles, meaning Pompeo, and begging him to come and consult with him. The violent and vindictive Colonna had something nobly generous in his soul. The pope had heaped coals of fire on his head by his very petitions, and it would prove his victory to grant them. He went to the castle. The old rivals were moved when they met. They wept together over the ruins around them. Both blamed themselves for having disgraced their holiest dignity and reduced the papacy to the meanest state of helplessness. This burst of emotion over, they devised means for Clement's deliverance.

The first thing was to raise money to pay the soldiers. But their friends in Rome were moneyless. Clement proposed that the emperor's party should set him free, and then he could borrow funds. The imperialists would not trust his word. He offered to give hostages; the soldiers chose six rich Florentine prelates, relatives of the pope. They were delivered over to the German troops. Days passed, but no money came. The soldiers were enraged; they treated the hostages with cruelty. Pompeo resolved to release these unhappy gentlemen: he bribed the guards, and put them to sleep with drugged wine; the hostages escaped over the tops of the houses, and fled to the camp of the Duke of Urbino, who commanded the army of the League. Clement, not yet released, was in greater straits than before.

Fourteen days had passed since the capture of Rome, when the army of the holy League drew near the city. A vague rumour met the soldiers; they could not cope with the large numbers of the foe; Urbino was not able to kindle in them any zeal for the pope's interests, and they quickly wheeled and marched to a safer region.

Clement feared to trust the emperor. He resolved upon making his escape. Pompeo Colonna offered him a noble Turkish horse. He put on the dress of a tradesman, escaped by night, and took refuge in the convent of Orvieto. Of this place one of his friends wrote, "this town is quite a prison.

People say the pope is at liberty here. A pretty liberty indeed! Want, impure air, wretched lodging, and a thousand other inconveniences, keep the holy father closer than when he was in the castle of St. Angelo. He told me the other day, it was better to be in captivity at Rome than at liberty here." To make it still worse, the ambassadors of Henry VIII. of England, were besetting him in order to gain his consent to the king's divorce of Catherine. The pope refused, and Henry threw off the papacy. Wolsey had said, "this divorce is of more consequence to us than twenty popedoms."

Nothing was now left for Clement but to submit to the terms of the emperor. He was obliged to pledge large money, and remain a prisoner until it was paid—the time proved to be six months; to give up certain cities and fortresses; to pay certain taxes; to renounce every alliance against Charles; to honour the imperial court, and to promise the calling of a general council within a given time.

The reformers gazed with astonishment on this judgment of God in punishing the papacy. One wrote, "Such is the empire of Jesus Christ, that the emperor pursuing Luther on behalf of the pope, is constrained to ruin the pope instead of Luther." The Lord had permitted Charles and Clement to become involved with each, that they might leave the Reformation to win its peaceable way. And in the armies that were in Italy there were men who could do something for the gospel. Many of the followers of the protestant Freundsberg, and many of the Swiss who followed the standard of Francis I. were able to refute the errors of Rome, and to tell the Italians the good news of salvation. Dr. Thomas M'Crie* says, " With the freedom of men who have swords in their hands, these foreigners conversed on the religious controversy with the inhabitants among whom they were quartered. They extolled the spiritual liberty which they enjoyed at home; derided the frightful ideas of the reformers which the monks had impressed on the minds of the people; talked in the warmest strains of Luther and his associates as the restorers of Christianity; contrasted the purity of their lives and the slender income with which they were contented, with the wealth and licentiousness of their opponents, and expressed their astonishment that a people of such a spirit as the Italians should continue to yield a base and implicit subjection to an indolent and corrupt priesthood, which sought to keep them in ignorance, that it might feed on the spoils of their credulity. The impression which these representations were calcu lated to make on the minds of the people, was strengthened by the angry manifestoes which the pope and the emperor published against each other. . . . . The horror hitherto felt at the name of heretic and Lutheran began to abate in Italy, and the minds of the people were prepared to listen to the teachers of the reformed doctrine, who, in their

* Reformation in Italy. Presbyterian Board of Publication, p. 70.

time, were emboldened to preach and make proselytes in a more open manner than they had hitherto ventured to do."

We will see some of the effects which the sacking of Rome produced upon Paleario, who ever after complained of "these wretched times." Perhaps it was this that made him a Ghibeline,* as was almost every Italian reformer who strongly opposed the papacy.

* The Ghibelines took the side of the emperors; the Guelphs that of the popes. "Such was the party-hatred of the two great Italian factions, that they carried their rancour even into domestic habits. At table, the Guelphs placed their knives and spoons longwise, and the Ghibelines across; the one cut their bread across, the other longwise. Even in cutting an orange they could not agree, for the Guelph cut his orange horizontally, and the Ghibeline downwards. Children were taught these artifices of faction; their hatreds became traditional." *D'Israeli's Curiosities of Literature.*

CHAPTER III.

WANDERINGS OF A STUDENT.

(1529.)

Two years after the capture of Rome, Paleario is again in the house of his patron, where he finds his sensitive spirit too high-toned for a dependent position. The patron is jealous over his manuscripts and books, which have cost him large sums in the day when printing is in its infancy. To copy one of them for one's own use, or for sale, without his permission, would be a crime like that of a printer, who should secretly use the press of his employer to obtain for himself copies of a book which the publisher had the sole right to issue. It would be a kind of theft—the *pirating* of a volume. Of this Paleario finds himself charged. It reflects on his honesty; it wounds his honour. He imagines that his distant friends know of his disgrace. He is indignant, and very late one night he takes his pen and drops his grief to the poet Mauro.

"Do you know what disgrace I am in with Cæsar? I am surprised that you have said nothing of it in your letters. The evil designs of the envious have at last found vent. What is it? A trifle which you can easily arrange. I am accused of having in my possession a copy of a voluminous index of the books of Livy, with notes by Cattaneo. In the first place, how could I, in so short a time, copy this volume? And for what purpose? The work is so confused and diffuse, that unless additional labour were bestowed upon it, there would be no advantage. The author is rather to be praised for being the first to undertake this trouble, than for the accuracy of the work. If then they accuse me of having seen the index, and of following, or as they say plagiarizing the method of arrangement, mark the injustice of these men. Before this book fell into my hands I had nearly finished my commentaries on the Orations of M. Tullius [Cicero.]* Verily, on no account would I usurp the praise due to another; I never even dreamt of such a thing. Induced, as you know, by the handsome reward offered by a munificent personage, I cheerfully devoted nights of labour to this work. I cannot imagine how any one can be so foolish as to believe me capable of appropriating to myself the labours of another. Muzzio, an excellent man . . . has been of great use to me, and has shown, not only by words but by actions, that nothing is more ungenerous than to wage war against the innocent. Thus did this courageous man take up my defence. What harm, said he, if a scholar has taken such a copy? Suppose even that

* Hence he could not have used the Index discreditably.

he has transcribed it? Is this so great a crime that the patron should reproach him with angry countenance and threatening words, and say, 'I will take further measures: you shall not go without giving security. The library was confided to you; you received the money: give security and go where you please.' How contemptible this appeared to me, and how indignant I felt, I need not say. Had you been here you would have burst forth. Cincio Phrygipani, a most courteous and modest young noble, did not fail me on this occasion. When he saw the predicament I was in, he voluntarily came forward and offered security. Is this then the reward of all my vigils? I make you responsible for the glaring wrong done me. But you will say, all this is done unknown to Cæsar. I would rather die than be exposed to such treatment. Shall I remain in Rome after being so grossly insulted? No, never!"

Dr. Thomas Chalmers was once private tutor in a family where he found a most ungenial home. He wrote, "It is impossible to be upon a good understanding with people disposed to regard me in so inferior a light as they do. I don't know what it is to act the part of an underling, especially with those with whom, I am sure, elsewhere I would be at least upon a footing of equality." Their custom was, when company came, to dismiss him to his own room and then serve him with supper. But he adopted a mode of relief. When the servant entered his room with "the solitary repast," he declined it, saying, "I sup elsewhere to-night." The patron charged him with an unseemly spirit, saying, "Sir, the very servants are complaining of your haughtiness. You have far too much pride." The reply was to the point; "There are two kinds of pride, sir; there is that pride which lords it over inferiors, and there is that pride which rejoices in repressing the insolence of superiors. The first I have none of—the second I glory in." The young tutor was afterwards treated with proper respect.

Paleario had quite similar feelings when charged, not with pride simply, but with plagiarizing. Though cleared of it, the affront roused his former dreams of study and independence, and he resolved upon a new course of life. In a calmer mood he writes a wiser letter to his friend Mauro:

"None lay aside their anger more quickly than those in whom it is easily kindled. On the 13th, when the night was far advanced, I wrote you a letter full of complaints. Scarcely had morning light appeared, when I regretted having done so; for though the indignation which guided my pen was just, yet, as you know, such are my feelings toward you and my unwillingness to offend, that I am disposed to bear everything. You cannot oblige me more, than by taking care that Cæsar* is in-

---

* He afterwards wrote, "You have done a kind act in restoring me to Cæsar's good opinion. You consider your career bound up with mine."

formed that those whom he left in the city are neither handsomely nor liberally treated by his people [stewards and other officials,] while I have behaved to them in the kindest manner imaginable. I wish to dismiss from my mind what has been said and done against me. * * * * Though you would believe me without an oath, yet I have sworn, that you may not imagine I am under the influence of anger if I now follow out the plan of life which I had laid down from my boyhood. So earnestly do I thirst after philosophy and those studies to which, before the capture of Rome by the Spaniards, I had devoted six years, that having laid them aside for two years past, I now ardently desire to resume them. From the avarice of those whom it would not be proper to name,* there are no professors of philosophy at Rome. I hear that literature flourishes in Tuscany; there is nothing to prevent my going straight to Sienna, unless I first visit Perugia, where my friend Ennio [Filonardi] is vicelegate. I long much to see him, for he is greatly attached to me, and the philosophers of Perugia are said to be by no means despicable. If the inveterate barbarisms, with which commentators in false Latin have disfigured that branch of learning, do not prevail there, I can nowhere be happier. * * *

* Clement VII., notwithstanding his talents for business, was universally disliked for his bad faith, his treachery and his avarice. Literary men and professors had been robbed, killed or driven away by the imperial army and the pope was unwilling to expend any-

"I have entered thus fully into my plans, because I foresee that there will be many remarks made, such as, 'So he has left Rome! Oh, what inconstancy!' Many will not scruple to insinuate, especially to Cæsar, that indignation has been the cause of my departure. Some will say that I do not myself know what I wish: I beg you to answer them until the event shall speak for itself. But you will say, 'Do you then abandon the (Roman) court?' Yes, I shall indeed leave it, for what can be more base than to settle down in the prime of life, without employment, a mere drone and idler, in inglorious ease at Rome.

"The most eminent philosophers, in order to add to their knowledge, have visited, on foot, barbarous lands. Shall I, to dispel my ignorance, shrink from mounting on horseback and traversing a part of Italy? If God had granted me a rich and ample patrimony, the first thing I should have done would have been to travel, not only in Italy, France and Germany, the most cultivated provinces of Christendom; but even through the whole of Greece, where there is scarcely a foot of ground exempt from the power of the Turks. Such a desire ought not to appear to good men either frivolous or reprehensible; while our studies and our affairs at home are in so gloomy a condition, travel cannot be mean or ignoble to a prudent and sagacious mind. As

thing upon institutions of learning. This fact had its influence upon the destiny of Paleario.

when there is smoke and a smell of burning in the house, those who stay in are more to be blamed than those who go out; so young men are to be commended wherever they may go in search of light. . . The road is not sufficiently secure, and the courier, Fabio, will set out for Perugia to-morrow, or the day after. I will go with him."

Thus, rejecting the assistance that came through insult, braving the charge of fickleness, detesting idleness, and decided in character, Paleario left Rome. No cardinal could tempt him with a clerkship. With an independent step and high intellectual aims, he set out upon a journey of about seventy miles up the Tiber, to Perugia, where he arrived in the winter of 1530.

One reason why the Duke of Urbino did not hasten with the army of the League to drive from Rome the legions that sacked it, was, that he lingered at Perugia to overthrow Gentili, and place Orazio Baglioni in the government of the city. The pope was not long in undoing this business, and he seems to have sent thither Ennio Filonardi as vice-legate or governor. To this friend and fellow-townsman Paleario went, and met with the kindest reception and largest hospitality. Ennio invited him to abide in his house, and offered him a place of honour in the university. The guest looked about him, admiring the beautiful situation of the old Etruscan city, the invigorating air, the rich country, which even winter could not render gloomy, and the ancient oaks that stood in forests near the classic lake of Thrasymene. He almost breathed the local traditions of Hannibal and Fabius, who had, long ago, measured arms in the neighbourhood, and he might have talked of the citizen Pietro Perugino, the master of Raphael. He turned his eye to the university, saw that its ancient glory had declined, found the classics neglected, and felt disgusted with the "barbarisms" of the schools. He met fine-looking men and beautiful women; but if these only were the present pride of the city, he could not remain. He was in pursuit of knowledge, and he had come to the wrong place to find it. He afterwards wrote, "You need not ask how everything had been prepared for my reception while I was in Perugia. Ennio Filonardi wished me to stay at his house; if I had consented he would have procured my appointment to an honourable post in the college of young students; he promised me his influence and authority; nothing was wanting on his part. I never knew a better man, either for his upright life, or for his zeal in giving assistance. But as this college is full of barbarisms, my first object was to leave as soon as possible."

Sienna attracted him. There is a tradition that it was built by the Senones, as a city of refuge for their old men. Founded in humanity, it became an asylum for Christianity. In the reign of Diocletian, a man named Ansano, fled from the heathen persecutions at Rome, and introduced the religion of Christ into this ancient city. In later years a retreat was found there by Paleario, who introduced a new style of oratory and literature, and who will tell us more of its situation, its people and its schools.

"I came to Sienna," he writes, "on the 27th of October (1530.) The city is seated on the brow of a beautiful hill, surrounded by a fertile and abundantly productive country; but it is corrupted by party-spirit, and almost exhausted by factions. The greater part of the nobility, who are in general the only patrons of literature, live scattered in villages and hamlets; so that when the nine Muses, so to speak, are banished and discomfited, we cannot wonder if there are no illustrious philosophers, no orators or poets in the State. The inhabitants of Sienna, as well as the Tuscans in general, are of acute and vigorous intellects; their women are handsome; the young men, since the academies*

---

* The academies were not schools, but literary assemblies, in which learned men conversed or debated on such topics as antiquities, poetry, philology, and the sciences. They met on fixed days of the week, at each other's houses, or at the princely villa of some liberal patron, where they supped, and afterwards adjourned to the garden or vineyard. Often a summer night was almost entirely spent in these discussions. Paleario was just the man to take delight in these literary evenings; and Sienna was noted for them. It stood second to Florence in this respect, having several such academies, that became so celebrated as to attract the notice of Pope Leo X. He invited some of their members to perform their comedies before him. One of them was called the Intronati, a name given to it by the genial Marcello Cervini, born near Sienna, and a warm friend of Paleario. Cervini was made pope in 1554, to the delight of all good

have been established, take delight in works written in their mother-tongue. The progress which the Italian language is making has this advantage, it diverts the attention from the Latin and Greek languages, which are acquired only by labour, which of itself is so formidable an enemy to study, that very few attain more than a superficial knowledge of literature. I wish to leave, for I feel an inexpressible desire to prosecute my studies in philosophy; but persons of distinction have hitherto retained me in their castles and villages. Their affability is great, their liberality still greater, and their splendour almost regal; were I not so wedded to study, nowhere could I remain with greater pleasure."

It had been agreed, when Paleario left Rome, that his young friend Cincio Phrygipani should go with him to Padua, pay the expenses, and aid him in purchasing a library. But the rich youth had many temptations, and a short memory of his promises. He delayed, sent no money, and even neglected to write. Paleario need not be delicate about reminding him of his pledges; he had a right to do it; he

men in Italy; but he lived only twenty-two days after he assumed the papal robes and the title of Marcellus II. "The *Intronati* Academy was chiefly occupied in polishing and embellishing the Tuscan language, and to this day," says Mr. Young, "the people of Sienna speak a purer and more harmonious dialect than the rest of Tuscany." Paleario could appreciate its freedom from "barbarisms." To his last days he speaks of having to "fight the barbarisms." He probably heard men contend, as they did in the Sorbonne of Paris, that *ego amat* was better Latin than *ego amo*.

had depended upon them. In his letter to Cincio, he is not fawning for a gift, but urging his claims to what had been promised. He writes to Cincio:

"Do not expect me to write you what I think are the duties of a young man of intellect and noble birth. Our daily conversations, if you have not forgotten them, are admonition enough; if, however, as I rather fear, they have passed out of your recollection, or if, listening to other advice, you have changed your mind, my letters will not persuade you to come to us, more particularly as I hear that you have neglected your studies. . . . After having deceived us with hopes, you keep us, who are longing so much for your arrival, still in expectation. If indeed, I had ever imagined you could do without me, I should have been on my guard, and prepared not to suffer so much pain in case of being deprived of your society. Who so happy as I when you promised to come? Who so grieved at this last news that Livio brings? Will you not really come? If I am not mistaken you will not. Are you so given up to the pleasures of Rome that you cannot tear yourself away? Do not allow yourself to be turned aside by the advice of companions. You share our opinions and follow the same studies, of which they are the bitter enemies. It is due to your own nobleness and greatness of mind to reflect how you have promoted our wishes, and to remember your promises. When we came into Tuscany, we brought with us as much money as your generosity bestowed; if you had come yourself we should want nothing. I beseech you, if we should be obliged to go to Padua without you, to take care that we are not left unprovided.

"You have a great inheritance; (may God prosper it!) your family is small, you have an excellent heart, and aspire after great things. What is there so heavenly and divine as to assist another in every emergency? What so Roman, as to sustain a great and an old friend? What so like yourself as to receive and heartily entertain scholars? We are in need of your generosity to continue those studies which are dearest and most attractive to you; we want to purchase a library of Greek books, and complete a collection of Latin authors. These last cost a great deal, and it is exceedingly difficult to procure Greek books. You who are of a noble race, richly endowed with the goods of fortune, and highly gifted with talent, should consider yourself as born to supply our want."

Cincio regarded this as the importunity of love, rather than of literary avarice. He was not offended; he had money, his friend had not; therefore the urgent plea was reasonable. It was made in the name of philosophy; Paleario could not yet plead in the name of a true religion. Paleario prepared to set out alone for Padua, and sent forward his bedding, books and baggage, when a letter from Cincio revived his hopes. He replied with true Italian fervour.

"Oh, most delightful and much desired news!.. You ought not to make us wait for you more than a month. Though you write as if it were an affront to doubt of your arrival, yet I am tormented with some doubts on account of the persons by whom you are surrounded. .... You will reside with us. You will live in the society of schools, students of the Belles Lettres: you will reap great profit from your intercourse with companions of superior minds, and still greater from association with older men, well furnished with learning. You will derive also from study that delight which it has always afforded you, and even more, for then you will have no other amusement. At Padua there are poets, orators, and distinguished philosophers; wisdom is there gathered as in a house, where Pallas herself presides over the Belles Lettres. Nowhere can you better gratify your insatiable thirst for reading and hearing lectures. Upon this however I need not dwell, for I know the eagerness of youth, when they have taken a thing into their head. ... I thank you for your generous offers and promises, and see that nothing can be greater than your affection for me. For the present you need not trouble yourself about money." Paleario had borrowed funds, and was about to sell his property at Veroli. There were sacred demands upon him other than those of philosophy.

His mind reverted to his native town, and to the ravages of the army that had lately passed over the country of the Hernici, burning the villas, and leaving behind them those three terrible woes, desolation, famine and pestilence. The spoiler had been at the tomb of his parents. Two friends insisted upon his return to Veroli. He replied, with his heart turned to his mother's grave:

"I wish indeed I were with you. Nothing is more delightful to me than the recollection of my dear country and love for my friends; but such is the desire of travelling which has taken possession of me, that it seems as if I should be forever deprived, not only of the country where I was born, and which even on your account is dearest to me, but of any other, if such there be, which may hereafter bind me by the ties of wife and children. I never hear it said that in France and Germany literature flourishes, but I wish immediately to fly thither. . . . .

"After the capture and sack of Rome by the Spaniards, and the ravaging of Latium, what presents a greater spectacle of devastation than the provinces to which you recall me. These things often make me resolve to quit my country. To these considerations, I might add the unfriendly disposition of my companions, who have tormented me ever since I was a boy; corrupt and wicked youth, who as they grew up, showed they had no enemies so great as themselves. They, to say nothing of aught else, (I cannot write it without tears,) have dared to destroy a part of my mother's tomb, a most excellent woman of rare virtue and modesty; may Heaven defend her ashes! Now it is your duty, who have religiously fulfilled all the claims of friendship, in return for the marked regard I have ever shown you, to collect together the relics of my beloved ones, wherever they are scattered, and put them in an urn. The expense will be my care. I entreat you to do thus much to gratify my filial affection. I wish that in that part of the sacred edifice, where my mother's tomb was, a large stone be placed, with the following inscription:

TO MATTEO PALEARIO AND CLARA JANARILLA,

HIS WELL-BELOVED PARENTS;

AND TO ELISA, FRANCESCA, AND JANILLA,

HIS DEAREST SISTERS,

AONIO PALEARIO, A VOLUNTARY EXILE,

CONSECRATES THIS MONUMENT.

"I have written about this two or three times to Maria, daughter of my mother's sister, but she is either overwhelmed with grief or declines writing. However this may be, let me know, so that if I am ever in favour with the Muses, I may consecrate those dear to me in every kind of monument. Farewell."

Whence the means for this noble object? It appears that Paleario had a confidential servant, or business manager, named Pterigi Gallo, who was something of a man in his way. He was ordered to sell the house and land, if need be at auction. His master had written to Cincio. "I am willing to give up everything rather than renounce the study of philosophy. I shall get rid of my servants, furniture, house and land, and all that I possess." But Gallo listened to the advice of persons on the spot, and felt wiser than his master, whose interests he had very much at heart. They thought the traveller should return to his home. He delayed the sale. Paleario, impatient to go to Padua, could not brook the delay, nor the opposition of his servant to his wishes, and his reply was thoroughly Italian. He wrote to Gallo:

"You drive me mad. Is it thus you despise my commands? What I desire most, you attend to the least; thus I pay the penalty of my sins. As usual, I am foolish enough to think that what I would not do myself, no one else would attempt. Why ask advice of others when you know my opinion? I prefer Tuscany to any other part of Italy, and when I can devote myself to the repose of study, I shall choose that part of this country which is the most remarkable for the purity of its air, and the courteousness of its inhabitants. After the sack of the city . . . . what is there in Latium but an open plain, air, and solitude? I wish to sell my paternal estate. The house is honoured by a new successor. Corsini will arrange about the garden and the farm. Basil and Alexander will require something; my furniture was good, the library by no means an ordinary one; this shall be their share. You have now received your directions, see that you execute them faithfully. . . I write to you in Latin, because you do not understand Italian well, and because I think there is more point in the Latin tongue."

Gallo understood the point, and the next we hear is, that the good old friend Martelli makes an offer for the house. Paleario accepts, giving him more time for the payment than was asked. Again his filial heart prompts him to make a generous outlay upon the family tomb. He wishes that he might re-visit his native dwelling, and with tenderness he writes to Martelli, his father's chosen friend, " I desire first and foremost that all the world may know that I hold you most dear, and next, that my friends may enjoy it. With three-fourths I shall take care that the tomb be repaired, so that if these relics of my dear ones can feel anything, they may take a kind of pleasure in it. . . . . As I cannot do so, I am most happy that you will dwell in my house. If I were there we should spend whole days together. Do you think I have forgotten that, when I was a little fellow, my father took me to you every day? and how he used to rejoice at having found a man to whom he could safely confide his children? Your kindness has been essential to me from my boyhood. To no one do I owe more."

Meanwhile, he did not get away from Sienna; disappointments blocked up the road to Padua. Cincio did not answer his letters, nor make his appearance. The plan of going to the city of "congregated wisdom," in company with a rich and studious young noble, had failed. He had been on the point of starting alone, but some wealthy and influential citizens earnestly persuaded him to linger. One of them was Antonio Bellanti, who was unconsciously winning a friend to defend him at a future day. They kept Paleario with them for a year, delighting in his company, relieving him of the idea of dependence, entertaining him with free hospitality at their villas, putting their libraries at his disposal, and offering him every facility for writing the letters we have just read, and for drowning his annoyances by plunging into the deep studies of philosophy. Not yet does he give up Cincio; he hopes to win him to a sober life. He has already written to Gallo, with no little irony in his pointed Latin, a message to be delivered:

"When you arrive at Rome, go and salute Cincio Phrygipani cordially from me, say how well I understand, from his many letters, that he has no need either of my entreaties or exhortations. I fear, however, that his crocodile tears, so hard to press forth, will extinguish his ardour for study. But I have fulfilled the duties of friendship, and have given this young man both sound and faithful counsels. Incite him, however, as much as you can by word of mouth. I am very desirous to withdraw him from Rome, and from the envy which follows, as the shadow does the body, all who live under the eyes of their fellow-citizens. I have always, from his childhood, hoped that he would become a man of high integrity and ancestral virtue. I am greatly attached to him, and hope he may accompany you to Tuscany. We will set out for Padua on the 26th of September, (1531.) Oh, what sad intelligence of Lorenzo Carolo! Was he carried off by a fever? in so few days? . . . What will become of his mother and his most unhappy sisters? I can write no more for tears."

Paleario went to Padua, where the eminent poet, linguist and lecturer, Benedetto Lampridio, received him with kindest attentions, either to revive a former friendship, or to acknowledge the brotherhood of congenial scholars. The student sat at the feet of the sage, enraptured with the vehement eloquence and sonorous voice of the orator, when he lectured on the Greek and Roman classics. The emotions of Paleario led him to say, extravagantly, that "a single lecture from Lampridio is worth all the magnificence and popular glory of Rome." Then to enjoy such elating oratory for nearly twelve months must have been regarded as worth all his estate at Veroli, whatever Gallo might think to the contrary. Add to this the privileges open to him in the university, to which students flocked from all Europe, and he must have revelled in literature. He was prepared for an unexpected effort at Sienna, to which he was called, at the end of a year, by the urgent entreaties of Antonio Bellanti, who was in grievous trouble.

CHAPTER IV.

ORATOR AND POET.

(1532-1542.)

THE earthly destiny of Paleario turned upon his friendship for the Bellanti family, into which he was led by the failures of the rich, young Cincio. The amities of this ancient house, which were so delightful, seemed to doom him on through a troubled life to final martyrdom. Therefore there is an interest in this family. We need not prove their lineage from Bellanda, a celebrated warrior in the time of Charlemagne; they bore his lion on their shield. They were of French origin. Their six estates, their intelligence and their integrity insured some of them the highest civil offices in the Siennese government.

A child of this family was blind when five years old, but the sightless Petrini learned to play on all kinds of musical instruments and invented the Angelica, now fallen into disuse. He became a lawyer, a philosopher, a distinguished patriot, always on the side of liberty, a theologian of great ability, and a professor of law in the universities of Sienna and Pisa. He whispered his free thoughts in the ear of his son Antonio, who rose up against Rafaelle Petrucci, the self-constituted lord or tyrant of Sienna. The better class wished Antonio to assume the guidance of the state, but the opposite faction was too strong for him; it declared him a rebel, drove him into exile, and went on as their wrangling predecessors had done for centuries. The banished patriot took with him a son, Antonio, thirteen years old, and his wife, Ugurgeria, a very superior woman, held up as an example to matrons, for religion and excellence of life. On his deathbed he made this child swear to be faithful to his country; never to put up with insults from the senate, but not to rebel against its authority. Little did the good mother dream, that in fulfilling this oath her son would be in danger of losing his life, and that Paleario would defend him: nor, that in her old age, this same Paleario would get into trouble with the monks for protecting the rights of her grandsons.

Young Antonio returned in due time to Sienna, became exceedingly popular, dwelt in his villas or his castle on the borders, entertained such scholars as Paleario, and was elected tribune of the people. There were still in the city, as restless, crafty and lawless men as in the time of Dante, who remembered his exile there, and introduced several of the Siennese characters into his "Hell" and "Purgatory," but none into his "Paradise." He says,

ORATOR AND POET.

> "Was ever race
> Light as Sienna's? Sure not France herself
> Can show a tribe so frivolous and vain."

Then with keen irony he excepts from this charge certain young spendthrifts, who sold their estates, built a palace in which they lived in common, and indulged in the utmost luxury. Among other extravagancies they shod their horses with silver, and forbade their servants to pick up one of the costly shoes if it came off. Of course they ended their gay career in poverty and wretchedness. Every class of turbulent spirits abounded; they were always tending to anarchy; nothing but tyranny could keep them in order. Paleario will describe some of the most factious, who formed two conspiracies; the first against his friend, the second against himself.

Antonio Bellanti was not tyrant enough to keep the envious and rapacious under an iron sway. They conspired against him; they accused him of bringing salt into the city, or removing it to his villa, contrary to law. The Saline laws were extremely severe; whoever transported salt from one country-house to another, or into the city, was condemned to lose all his property, and even his life; the estate was awarded to the accusers and the witnesses. Antonio was wealthy; there were many greedy for the spoils; they would enrich themselves by appearing against him. The penalty was terrible, the danger imminent. In his trouble he summoned Paleario to his aid; he knew that he could depend on his fearless exposure of the evil plot.

Paleario came from Padua to employ his talents as a lawyer and orator, in preventing six barrels of contraband salt from utterly destroying his friend. He appeared before the senate. Osma and Cova were the judges. They sat in the house of Spannochi. A third-rate man, Ottone Melio Cotta, was present to bring up the reserve corps of accusers, and to seek his revenge on the lawyer if the client should be cleared. Paleario sifted the evidence. He proved the covetousness and falsehood of the accusers. He showed that they had suborned witnesses. They alleged that there was one witness whom they could not obtain—a servant of Bellanti, who had been detained in the country by force, at his master's order, lest his evidence should be overwhelming. Paleario showed that this witness had been sent into Sienna, where he was seized by the conspirators, thrown into prison, and tortured to make him betray his master. But the poor fellow was proof against all their cruelties. One witness had been imprisoned by Bellanti for debt; he had told the accusers that he would swear to anything if he could be freed from his burdens; they made him a citizen of Orbitello, which protected him from being sued for debt, and then they promised him an estate of the accused if he would convict his liegelord. These were specimens of the accusers; we mention them because men of this class were on this very spot, laying a train of enmity against the defender of Bellanti. There was one last and most convincing argument; it was the fact that Bellanti had lent a large sum of money to the Senate, and he was to be repaid in yearly portions of salt. It was a part of this salt that had been removed.

Paleario made an eloquent appeal to the judges, not to condemn an innocent man, whose ancestors had been the support of the state, and who was himself an example of distinguished patriotism. It was evident that Bellanti would be absolved by the judges. But the conspirators were not content to rely upon the witnesses already advanced; they must bring up the reserve corps, armed with new weapons. Cotta opened with a new charge—that of Bellanti's having a castle dangerous to the republic. To show how Paleario disposed of this adversary, we quote a paragraph from an oration, which he made nearly ten years afterwards at Sienna, when defending himself from this same Cotta and his faction. He said:

"When Antonio was accused, Osma and Cova induced the Senate, who were assembled in the house of Spannochi, to absolve him unanimously; for I had proved, in the clearest manner, that the witnesses were unworthy of credit. The justice done to this worthy man so annoyed Ottone Melio Cotta, a great man in the opinion of the vulgar, (who measure greatness not by a man's mental gifts or moral qualifications, but by the extent of his riches, and the position he holds in the state,) but a bad, violent and arrogant man, according to the estimation of those who do not follow the opinion of the crowd. When he saw that all present were disposed in favour of Bellanti, he began to shake his scanty locks, as the dragon does his mane, and to roll his eyes on me with fiery glance; then getting heated, in his agitation he shifted his mantle from shoulder to shoulder, and began with his natural subtlety to speak Spanish, partly to prejudice against me the brave Spaniards who were present, and partly that I might not confute his objections; but not being quite ignorant of that language, I understood all that his wicked tongue uttered against Bellanti. He said that Bellanti possessed a well-fortified castle, which was dangerous to the republic, especially as it was continually kept open, and might be used as an asylum for the ill-disposed. At such language, seeing the impression it made on Osma and Cova, I cannot express to you, O senators, the virtuous indignation which burned within me. I granted that he owned a castle built by his uncle, and showed that it was useful to the republic, because, being situated on the confines of the state, it might serve as a point from whence to make sallies, and carry the war into the enemy's territory, or to send succour or provisions. I did not see how such things could be hurtful to the state, unless, indeed, the very existence of a virtuous and strong-minded man, and the interests of his well-educated family be injurious. I contended that these accusations sprang from envy and malevolence on the part of Melio Cotta; that the falsity of the accusation was evident, because the enemies of Bellanti, who had moved heaven and earth against him, had never touched on this point. Would they, do you think, have overlooked a circumstance of such importance, and grounded their accusations on six barrels of salt, if they could have convicted him of so capital a crime as that of receiving into his castle men denounced by the Senate as enemies of the state?" Bellanti was absolved. This brilliant success of Paleario riveted the mutual friendship between him and Bellanti, and established his reputation as an orator. Its further results will appear hereafter.

This affair being happily ended, Paleario again turned his thoughts to Padua. He wrote to Lampridio; "I thought that no one loved me more than you did, so many and so great were the favours you bestowed on me during my visit to Padua; but now I fear I am almost forgotten." His mind was soon relieved by a letter from the learned Pietro Bembo, one of the most remarkable men of his age. He had attained high scholarship, corrected the Aldine* edition of the classics, become secretary of

* Issued at Venice, (1494—1514,) from the celebrated press of Aldo Manuzio, whose learning and industry were such a benefit to literature. In twenty years there was scarcely an ancient classic that had not been published from his press. Erasmus said, that if Aldo had his wishes fulfilled, the learned would soon have books in

Leo X., gone on confidential missions, fallen into the snares of wealth and beauty, forgotten his vows to the church, lived twenty-two years with the captivating Morosina as his wife, (too small a matter for scandal!) educated his children with great care, removed to Padua, formed a splendid library, laid out a botanical garden, kept his villa free to learned men, who sought him from all quarters, written poetry, and was engaged upon the history of Venice when Paleario was at Padua. It was Bembo, who thoroughly knew the papal city, and who said in terms which may be mildly translated, "Rome is a vile cess-pool, full of the wickedest wretches in the world." Paleario received from him a letter worth quoting.

"In your letter just received, I observe, what I never doubted, your great regard for me. Lampridio and I often speak with admiration of your kind and admirable disposition, the agreeable fruit of which we enjoyed when you were at Padua. This, by your absence we have lost, and it would indeed be a privation, if you did not make it up by frequently writing to us. We have been rather ex-

---

every language and on every subject. He projected the idea of printing the old Testament in Hebrew. He taught Greek, besides constantly working with old manuscripts, attending to his press, and writing extensively. When over-worked he used to say, "I suffer willingly, if I can but do good to others; while I live I will persevere." He did not, by any means, make a fortune; his mind was superior to grieving over his losses. He died in 1513, still busy at his press. He founded an academy at Venice.

pecting to see you instead of your letters; not only because you had promised to come, but on account of the frequent reports of Sienna being in arms. Your quiet and studious habits have nothing in common with factious spirits. There can be no attraction there for you, if we except those excellent persons whose reputation you have so carefully defended with your eloquent oration. What can you in the midst of arms? You are surrounded with assassins. . . . *The books you have begun to write on the Immortality of the Soul,* not only require but demand completion."

We have italicised the words which give us a hint of Paleario's first work upon a Christian theme. A poem on the soul's immortality had been in his mind; he had talked with Bembo about it. He went to Padua and finished it. The next thing was to find a publisher. We find him now in intimate correspondence with another of the great Italians of the age, Jacob Sadolet. They had met at Veroli or Rome. Sadolet drew the eye of Leo X., a quick discerner of merit, who made him a papal secretary along with Bembo. He was then made bishop of Carpentras, in Dauphiny. Under Pope Adrian he was not appreciated at Rome. He started for his bishopric, a mule carrying his bed and baggage. After his departure, a scholar at Rome wrote of him, "I think if the custom of putting on mourning when we are sad were still kept up, not fewer than twenty thousand persons would put it on as they did for Marcus Tullius. Every good man seems to think, that with him goodness and virtue leave Rome." He was again at the papal court under Clement VII., and laboured to persuade the pope to defend the city, or to flee. But all was in vain; he left twenty days before the capture, and lost one of the finest libraries there collected. He sought consolation by serving the church at Carpentras, relieving the poor, comforting the afflicted, protecting the oppressed Jews, encouraging young men to study, and providing teachers for them. Such a bishop was rare in those days. He was known as the "father of his people." Francis I. made large offers to draw him to his court. Had he gone, he might have attracted to him young Calvin, then a student in Paris. Long after he held correspondence with Calvin. He wrote to "his dearly beloved brethren, the magistracy, council and citizens of Geneva" an affectionate letter, to caution them against the reformers, and to persuade the "wandering dove to return into the secure ark of the true church." None of them could answer the powerful appeal; they gave the task to Calvin. He made it a "six days' work," and wrote such a reply that it left Sadolet little hope of success. Both the letters were elegant, courteous, eloquent.

It is related that Sadolet was so impressed with the reply that he had a great desire to see Calvin. Passing *incognito* through Geneva, he inquired for the house of the celebrated reformer, expecting to be directed to some magnificent palace. A poor, insignificant house was pointed out to him; he knocked at the door, and Calvin came to open it. The traveller was astonished at such simplicity of life; it was not after the Romish style. They talked freely and long together. The visitor was convinced that Calvin had not left the church of Rome for the sake of riches or advancement. Sadolet desired to see a great reform in the papal church, but he was not a leader. There was not in him the stuff that martyrs are made of. But if free inquiry had been allowed in the Romish church, there can be little doubt that he would have gone farther in the advance. He was averse to superstition; he was opposed to persecution. He was more nearly a reformed Christian than any man that had probably yet crossed the path of Paleario, from whom he, one day in 1536, received a kindly letter, in which was the following:

"Do not be surprised, if being a good deal perplexed on the question of the immortality of the soul, and obliged to draw from philosophy the greater part of my arguments, I fear the outcry of certain individuals, and thus hesitate not to call on you, the valiant defender and promoter of this kind of studies, to befriend and advocate my cause. . .
As a proof of my regard and veneration, I have sent you my books, such as they are." Perhaps he sent them in manuscript. A few days after he wrote again: "These letters are accompanied by

my writings on the immortality of the soul. Though they are scarcely worthy of being read by so learned a man, still I flatter myself that your name being mentioned in terms of affection in the second book, may in some degree prove my regard for you. . . Gryphius* can easily add my poem to those of other authors who have written on Christian subjects. I scarcely dare hope to obtain this favour, if you do not send him a letter of recommendation to accompany the work."

We may learn the general character of the poem from the letters of Sadolet. To Gryphius he writes: "I received a few days ago Paleario's book on the Immortality of the Soul; a poem which interests me greatly, both from its exalted title, and the epic form in which the author has treated the subject. I sat down eagerly to read it, anxious to see if the work corresponded to the sublime title with which it is adorned. I found, to my great delight and unspeakable admiration, a subject too lofty even for the highest talent, treated with so much seriousness and emotion, and such elegance and harmony of style, that I can say I have not read any work of our times which has afforded me more delight. . . . It is all written in good and accurate Latin, and shows evident marks of great

---

* Sebastian Gryphius, the famous printer at Lyons. The art of printing had become corrupted; he was chiefly instrumental in restoring it. He procured new and beautiful types in Hebrew, Greek and Latin. One of his greatest achievements was the Latin Bible in two volumes, printed in 1540, with the largest type ever used.

diligence and discernment; brilliant passages also may be found strikingly conspicuous for classic taste. But what I appreciate more than all the rest, are the Christian sentiments and the pure and upright religious opinions it contains. The veneration towards a beneficent Creator, and the feelings of piety found here, are not only calculated to instruct the ignorant, but are suited to fan the flame of devotion, and direct the mind towards pure religion."

To Paleario he wrote: "It took me three days to read your poem. The judgment I have formed of your work is this. Few have treated the subject, either in our own day, or that of our forefathers, with so much elegance, and none with more erudition. What I specially admire is, the poem is not loaded with forced and specious arguments, or images drawn from mythological subjects; your reasoning is based on true and holy principles of religion. As the mild and gentle expression of a man's countenance is a sign of an upright and well regulated mind, so the piety which shines forth in your writings commands admiration of your learning and good feeling." After all, the poem would hardly prove so charming to readers in our day. Mr. Young says, "The curious mixture of Pagan and Christian imagery in this singular poem, is highly illustrative of the state of learning and opinion in Paleario's time, and brings us into close acquaintance with the character of his mind. While we admire his lofty conceptions and aims at divine knowledge, we must, at the same time, lament to see his flagging wing so often brought down to earth. Though we perceive that he had studied the Scriptures, and was to a considerable degree imbued with their light, he was not yet free from the dominance of human authority: fear of consequences obliged him to clothe, in the form of hypothesis, the distinctive qualities of the gospel, and thus he leaves us in the dark as to his real opinions. But he had gone too far to recede; he was struggling towards light, and soon we shall find him basking in the perfect liberty and love of the gospel."

He rejects the doctrine of purgatory, and of any recovery for the soul after death. He represents the Son of God as sent down from heaven to take away our sins by the sacrifice of himself, and strives to paint in glowing imagery the end of the world. Gryphius published the poem. It made the author generally known. Some of the most eminent scholars and philosphers sought his acquaintance. The best result was, that, having committed himself to freedom of investigation, he was led more deeply into the study of the word of God. It would be interesting to know how, when and where he first came upon the Bible.

The charms of the literary society at Padua could not make the new poet forget that he had friends at Sienna who loved him as a lawyer. The hearty hospitality and social excellence of the Bellanti family inclined him to think of fixing his abode near to them. He first went to Rome to see his friends, especially his townsman Filonardi, now the governor of St. Angelo. On his return he spent some time at Volterra, where he met Marco, a venerable bishop, who seems to have expounded to him the way of life more perfectly. Shortly after, in a letter to young Paul, a nephew of Sadolet, he refers to this good man and the "Christian tone of his discourse," and he complains of certain men, who "stifled all divine wisdom, by which we live and attain to light and tend towards heaven; good men can never approve this. There are some at the present time, who, like the owls, delight in darkness and groan at the approach of light. It would be useless to require them to cease from their folly. Your uncle was among the first to oppose this system. . . Virtuous men can scarcely breathe in these days. We retain a shadow only of Christian devotion, and for a long time past we have had no real piety." The light was dawning.

Paleario was some time at Colle, a small, old city near to Sienna, built on a high hill which was crowned with the picturesque ruins of an ancient castle. It had its bishops and its most hospitable people, who showed all attention to the visitor without, perhaps, suspecting that he was a philosopher, poet and orator, but they did suspect that he was looking for a home and for some fair one willing to identify herself with his happiness. He had read of the villa of Aula Cecina, whom Cicero defended, and now he could purchase it. Three miles from Colle, conspicuous among the hills, lay Ceciniano, with no carriage-road thither: he went on foot or on horseback to see it. The retirement and healthful air were great attractions to a studious man. He bought the villa, some of the leading inhabitants of Colle, probably, advising the purchase. From one of these families he took a wife, Marietta Guidotti, most worthy of being commemorated.

He was now thirty-four* years of age, as he tells us when giving an account of himself to Filonardi. In his letters, he says that he "desired nothing so earnestly as to lead a Christian life." He speaks of frequently visiting a near neighbour, a retired bishop, Luca Joannino, "a good man, who, after his daily devotions, employs his time in reading works on theology, and in agriculture; he takes great delight in improving his fertile and pleasant little farm; says he is a true Christian; and though he has been employed in public offices, he is so devoid of ambition that he thinks nothing so delightful as a villa of his own, even though not very elegant." One evening he was supping at the house of the bishop, who, "to add fresh gusto to the meal," introduced a book upon marriage—perhaps relating to the marriage of the priests, a subject much dis-

---

* The date of his marriage, however, is about 1537, as gained from other sources. This would fix his birth in 1503. It is not possible to harmonize the dates.

cussed at that time; perhaps, treating of domestic life, a theme quite likely just then to interest Paleario. The guest then met with an annoyance, which he thus graphically described: "Just as I had eagerly begun to read it, I was disturbed by some foolish visitors, who spoke of nothing but grain. I never remember hearing more loquacious talkers, nor have I ever seen more self-importance on such trifling topics. I returned to Ceciniano quite disgusted, and sat down to read attentively the book which I had brought away. . . . You cannot be blind to the good which this pamphlet may produce." The price of grain was not a trifling topic to the rustic visitors; the good bishop was doubtless more patient than the philosopher.

Paleario was led into a warm friendship with the celebrated Piero Vettori, professor of Greek, Latin and elocution at Florence. In a large letter he says of his own affairs, that he had bought a villa, " that I might bury myself in the library I proposed purchasing; but it did not turn out as I wished. . . I bought Ceciniano dearer than I intended; though they tell me I have made a good purchase, I am so oppressed with debt that this villa only distracts me from study. When freed from this perturbation and uneasiness, if it please God ever to free me from it, I shall return in right earnest to the study of your distinguished compositions." He invites Vettori to his villa, there to find " a man who will never leave you a moment, so eager is he to enjoy your delightful society." Thus, it seems that the plans and hopes of Paleario were not sustained by his purse—a fact that he was not the first scholar to discover, nor the last to lament. There was need for his excellent Pterigi Gallo to give his wise management to the little farm.

Before Paleario had left Padua, he received a most sacred charge. Antonio Bellanti, knowing that his days were short, visited him, committed his two sons, Fausto and Evander, to the guardianship of his former defender, and left Padua to die. The children found a father in their father's dearest friend. He managed their property, superintended their education, and defended their rights.

The happiest years in the life of Paleario were passing. He could say, "nothing yields more peace, consolation and hope than theology." All his studies tended to the Holy Scriptures. He evidently studied the so-called "fathers of the church." Perhaps some of the writings of the reformers fell in his way. Study was not all; he taught private pupils, most probably at Colle, walking or riding over the narrow path that led thither. It cannot be proved that he taught publicly at Sienna; he, however, applied for a professorship there; we shall see how he was defeated. The archives of Sienna show that he occasionally engaged in the practice of law. It must have been about this time (1542) that he wrote his most important work; he must keep it a secret; he dare not seek the advice of

Bembo, who was now a cardinal, nor of the gentle Sadolet, who was not brave enough to advise a man to send so much gospel truth into the world as to raise the cry that he was a reformer—a restorer of the ancient things. Palcario must hide the fact that he was writing of the "*Benefit of Christ's Death to believers.*" The book appeared anonymously. Its authorship was ascribed to several eminent persons of the day—Valdes, Ochino, Morone, cardinal Pole. But there were persons in Sienna on the hunt for heresy, and ready to detect the hand of the quiet dweller at Ceciniano.

In writing this little volume of positive truth, there were, doubtless, certain great errors of the papacy ever crossing the line of his thoughts. He resolved to put them in a volume by themselves and refute them. Hence the work written and kept secretly in manuscript until he saw the dangers of his arrest at the close of his life, and entitled "A Testimony and Accusation against the Popes." He was also meditating a letter to the reformers of Germany and Switzerland. Of these writings we hear more in his later years.

CHAPTER V.

BERNARDINO OCHINO.

(Born 1487. Died 1564.)

DANTE sang of "Branda's limpid spring," a beautiful fountain erected by the ancient Branda family, to furnish Sienna with water. Not far from it in 1487, was born a child, who was one day to offer to the people of that city the water of eternal life.[1] His father, Tomasini, an obscure citizen, named him Bernardino; to this was afterwards added the name Ochino, or Ocello, because his home was in a district which had for its ensign a white goose (*oca*)[3] on a green field.

A more devout Romanist seemed never to have been born. In his earliest years he imagined that religion consisted chiefly in self-infliction and misery. In order to be under the strictest, severest rules, he enrolled himself among the Franciscans. When a branch of this order became still more rigid in their rules of "holy living," and were called Capuchins, he entered this new brotherhood of monks. With the cowl on his head, and the scourge in his hands, he sought to lash the old Adam into holy subjection. He was very zealous. He thought he could add to the severities of his mendicant order. He introduced the "forty hours' devotion," which consisted in holding an image of Christ crucified for forty hours, and spending the whole time in gazing upon it. The idea was to have an unbroken meditation upon the sufferings of the Saviour; the error was in leading men to trust in this outward act, rather than in Christ for salvation. Formality took the place of faith.

He afterwards wrote, "Being now persuaded that I had found what I had been seeking, I said to Christ, 'Lord, if I am not saved now, I know nothing more that I can do.' In the course of my meditations I was often perplexed, and felt at a loss to reconcile the views on which I had acted with what the Scriptures said about salvation being the gift of God through the redemption wrought by Christ; but the authority of the church silenced these scruples, and in proportion as concern for my soul became more intense, I applied myself with greater diligence and ardour to those bodily exercises and mortifications which were prescribed by the doctrine of the church, and by the rules of the order to which I had submitted."

Ochino began to have a saintly reputation. He preached with an astonishing eloquence and fervour. Crowds came to hear him. The rudeness of his dress, the austere manner of his life, the suffering depicted on his countenance, and the earnestness of his speech excited curiosity, and drew the

tion of the multitude. Princes, great men and women, not a few, looked upon him as a most extraordinary man. He was invited to preach in almost all parts of Italy. The highest honours were paid him wherever he went. Yet he went or foot even when fine carriages were offered him, and in the most magnificent houses, seated at luxuriou: tables, he observed the strictness of his rules. He ate of only one dish, and that sparingly; thoug' offered the finest wines, he drank nothing but water Most monks in his day, might have profited by his example of temperance. Rich couches we provided for him, but he wrapped his coarse clo. around him and slept upon the ground. Thus his corrupt times, he acquired a high reputation sanctity.

The gospel shed new light upon him; perha when making his journeys, he met with the writii of the German reformers, which began to be cir, lated in Italy. As he had been trying to refo the cloister, he now thought of reforming the chu He soon groaned under the monkish yoke, e sought spiritual liberty. He compared the relig of Rome with the Christianity of the gospel, ; saw the amazing difference. Popery was a perv 'on; Christ alone was the Saviour. He tells t he became convinced of three things; *Fir* Christ had wrought for his people a perfe 'ousness; *Secondly*, that religious vows o 'nvention were not only useless, but hurtfr and wicked; *Thirdly*, that the Roman church, though calculated to fascinate the senses by her external pomp and splendour, was unscriptural and abominable in the sight of God. In 1536 he went to Naples, where he met a remarkable layman, whose influence was to be felt in all Italy.

Juan Valdes or Valdesso, was a Spaniard. He and his twin brother, Alfonso, were men of high birth and education. They may have known Cardinal Ximenes, a man of a master-mind, who was ambitious of two things—great learning and great power. He laboured for two objects, which seemed in conflict with each other; one was to perpetuate popery by means of the Inquisition; the other was to complete his splendid polyglot edition of the Bible. It is a singular coincidence that he was finishing this celebrated edition of the Scriptures the very year (1517) that Luther was beginning his war against popery, and directing the attention of all Europe to the word of God. The brothers Valdes became acquainted with some of the German reformers, and wrote volumes that put their lives in danger. They were favourites of the Emperor Charles V., who seems to have made Juan a knight. The eyes of the Inquisition were fixed upon them, and Juan found an opportunity to leave Spain.

Pompeo Colonna, the viceroy of Naples, died in 1532, and the emperor appointed Don Pedro Toledo in his place. Juan Valdes became his secretary. The viceroy made himself a terror to evil doers;

the secretary pursued a more excellent way. He assembled his friends, many of them from the court, and the best society of Naples, and set before them the gospel. He did not preach, but he expounded the Scriptures. These friendly meetings were held in some secluded garden or tower, where the bigoted Toledo was not likely to molest them. Before the interpreter were gathered many of those who were to shine as reformers in Italy. Within the four years that he lived, he gave sound instruction to the renowned Peter Martyr, to Julia and Vittoria Colonna, to Carnesecchi, who was to lay down his life for his divine Master; to Flaminio, the friend of Paleario, and other eminent personages, some of whom we shall meet as we advance. One of them was the Capuchin friar Ochino, who fixed his keen eyes on the lay teacher, and listened with astonishment to the doctrines of grace. He was an Apollos, unto whom a Priscilla was expounding the way of God more perfectly. Some think that he was converted through the agency of Valdes.

While the layman was teaching privately, the friar was preaching to thousands in the church of St. Maggiore. The other churches were left almost empty, and the whole population flocked to hear friar Bernardino, as he now boldly denounced vice and luxury, and then softly spoke of the compassions of Christ. Charles V. during his visit to Naples, often listened with delight to his persuasive eloquence, admiring the natural orator rather than the gospel which he proclaimed. It is said that the emperor declared, "That man would make the stones weep!" During the whole of Lent, after the departure of Charles, he continued to preach, and introduced as much Scripture doctrine as he could venture to announce. But the viceroy Toledo did not admire this new style of preaching, and gave ear to the monks who whispered that Ochino was tainted with Lutheranism. The case must be examined, and therefore he was forbidden to declare the love of God to sinners, until he would give from the pulpit his views on the points under suspicion. He defended his opinions so skilfully that his reputation increased. Valdes and his disciples attended his preaching. Thus Naples had the first school, if we may so call it, for training up ministers and martyrs.

In 1538 the Capuchins elected the popular preacher to fill the office of vicar-general of their order. He visited the convents on foot, and exhorted the friars to a more sincere faith and practice of the gospel virtues. But he was urged to appear again at Naples, where he was heard by vast crowds in the cathedral of St. Januarius. Great numbers were shaken in their belief of Romish infallibility; unlearned artisans and women, who in that age were not expected to inquire into the truth, ventured to converse upon the New Testament and to compare one verse with another. The celebrated Vittoria Colonna, Marchioness of Pescara, was being qualified for employing her pen, her poetry, her influence and her friendships in the extension of the gospel.

The strange Bembo, now a cardinal, was at Venice in 1538, and sent the entreaties of that city to Vittoria, asking her to persuade Friar Bernardino to go thither and preach the Lent sermons. Bembo was eager to hear him. He enjoyed the privilege, for the next year, he wrote to the Marchioness in terms that engage our kind judgment of the aged cardinal. He said, "I own that I never heard any one preach more profitably, or in a more holy manner. I no longer wonder that your ladyship likes him so much. He speaks quite differently, with more charity and love, and in a more Christian manner, than any one, who in my time has mounted the pulpit, and he sets forth better and more joyful tidings. Every one is much delighted with him, and I think when he goes away he will carry the hearts of the whole city with him."

These "better and more joyful tidings" were new to Bembo, who perhaps had never opened a copy of the word of God. He sought spiritual advice. He wrote to Vittoria, "I speak to you, as I did this morning to the reverend Friar Bernardino, to whom I laid open my whole heart and thoughts as I would to Jesus Christ himself, by whom, I think, he must be both accepted and beloved. I never conversed with a more holy man. . . . I am resolved to stay here as long as he does." Again he wrote: "Our God, from whose compassion we receive all things, confers on me so much grace, that I can respond to the confidence you have in me. Our Friar Bernardino, for mine I shall for the future call him as well as yours, is actually adored in this city. Both men and women exalt him to the skies by their praises. Oh, what a treasure he is! How he does edify us." The cardinal wrote to the powers at Rome, entreating them to forbid Ochino to fast during Lent, and oblige him to eat meat, "so that he may last longer, for the honour of God, and the edification of men; for if he continues to treat himself so harshly as he now does, he cannot hold out long." It appears that Bembo, now sixty-nine years of age, was ordained a priest; he laid aside his literary studies and began to read the Scriptures and the fathers with great diligence.

It may be that Paleario was among the learned men who gathered at Venice to hear this first great preacher of his day. He had also an opportunity nearer home. Ochino preached at Sienna, his native city, in 1539, with such acceptance that the public authorities took measures to secure his ministry for a longer time. It is pleasing to read from these records that the "eminent counsellors" issued their decree to this effect: "remembering how good and profitable for the salvation of souls, the Rev. Friar Bernardino Ochino of Sienna is, who preached so useful a discourse this morning in the great hall of the council: in order that the people may hear him, the illustrious gentlemen and the captain of the people are entreated to invite him to preach another day either in the cathedral or in the public town-hall, so that a greater number of persons may be present: and [it was decreed] that four gentlemen go and see Friar Bernardino and entreat him not to leave Sienna: and that letters be written to the pope, if necessary, for the fulfilment of the wishes and commands of the citizens."

After all this display, we might imagine that the good friar would ever share the protection of the "illustrious council." Yet we find him preaching the gospel so earnestly that his life was endangered. He was passing through Modena in 1541, and not intending to preach; but the people would not let him depart without a sermon. When conducted to the cathedral, he found that there was not even standing-room for all who wished to enter. The most eminent personages were there, waiting for the truth. He laid the foundations for an extended reformation in that city, but the papal power afterwards sought to demolish the spiritual temple of God. At Venice again the voice of the friar was heard. He knew that he was narrowly watched: he was prudent and somewhat restrained, until one of his friends, Terenziano, a pupil of Valdes, was thrown into prison on account of his religious opinions. This roused the gospel orator; and in a sermon before the Senate he exclaimed, "O sirs, what remains for us to do? To what purpose do we waste and consume our lives. If in thee, O most noble city of Venice, queen of the Adriatic, those who announce to you the truth are here imprisoned, confined in houses of correction, loaded with chains and fetters, what place then remains to us, what other field free for the truth? Would to God we might but preach the truth freely! How many blind eyes would be opened, and how many, who are now stumbling in the dark, would be enlightened!"

This strain of eloquence thrilled the magistrates, but even Venice dared not be independent of Rome in matters of religion. The papal nuncio heard of the friar's appeal to the Senate, suspended him from preaching and reported the case to the pope. But the Venitians had the courage to protest; they so beset the nuncio that in three days' time, Bernardino was allowed to re-appear in the pulpit. But he felt as if a sword was hanging over his head, and a word of suspected truth might bring it down upon him. He was soon cited to appear at Rome. He knew not what to do. The danger was great; he would expose himself either to make a denial of the authority of Scripture, or to suffer death for refusing to obey the church. He must decide the question which all the Reformers had to settle, whether to obey the church or Christ? Ochino sought advice, and finally met Peter Martyr at Florence. They had listened together to the teaching of Valdes; they were filled with the same spirit and placed in the same peril. Martyr advised him to obey the words of their Master, "When they persecute you in one city flee unto another." This decided the point; they resolved to leave Italy, not in company lest they should be discovered.

Ochino hastened to Sienna to bid farewell to his friends. Here he was exposed to an arrest, for he wrote to Muzzio, "Twelve men surrounded the convent of the Capuchins near Sienna on the vigil of St. Bartholomew, with the intention of taking me, but having gone on before, I escaped, though they followed me to Florence." He lingered a little at Ferrara, and then started for Switzerland. Thus departed from Italy, a man of fifty-five years, who was exchanging honours for the brand of heresy, leaving admiring crowds for strange faces, and becoming an exile and a wanderer. The Inquisition lost a victim; the gospel still retained a powerful reformer. It was related by the annalist of his order, that he was attended by three monks, and, on reaching the summit of the Alps, he turned to take a last look of Italy. He burst into tears and poured forth an affectionate adieu to his order and to his native land. We might follow him to Geneva where he preached to the Italian refugees; to Augsburg where he lectured with his usual eloquence on the epistle to the Romans, until Charles V. drove him thence; to England where he again preached to his exiled fellow-countrymen; to Zurich in Switzerland, where he gathered the banished

Locarnese about him to hear the word of God: and to Moravia where he died of the plague at the age of seventy-six years. And there we might shed a tear, that in his later days, when infirm and brokenhearted, the eye of his faith became so dimmed as to lead him into some errors from which he would have recoiled in his earlier life. He had married, and it is supposed that his wife, a French lady of rank, died in their wanderings, and that his children perished with him by the plague.

We shall hear of him again from the lips of Paleario, who lamented his flight from Sienna, and who closed a letter to Calvin, saying; "Farewell, good and faithful minister of Jesus Christ! I commend to you our fellow-servant, Bernardino Ochino. In whatever you assist him, you assist Christ." Ochino wrote back a letter to the magistrates of Sienna, in which he gave his religious opinions and said, "the salvation of the true church and the ruin of the kingdom of anti-christ, depends on one article alone, and that is living faith in Christ. . . . I have begun, and hope to go on publishing, in Italian, a summary of those things which are necessary for the Christian, that you may have no excuse before God. You will say, that my works are forbidden to be read. . . There is nothing in the substance of my sermons but the very passages of Holy Writ. . . God will conquer, through the blood of the martyrs shed throughout the world. . . Oh, how happy I would be, my dear Sienna, if you would purify yourself of so many ridiculous, pharisaical, tiresome, pernicious and foolish fancies, invented by those who pretend to be saints; but who are an abomination before God. Take the word of God and his gospel in the sense in which it was preached by Christ and the apostles."

CHAPTER VI.

SUSPICIONS OF HERESY.

(1542.)

AFTER calm, a fearful storm; this was the experience of Paleario. As his letters describe the rise of his troubles, it is best that he should speak for himself. He felt compelled to seek protection from his enemies, and first appealed to head-quarters. He wrote to a certain Tommaso [Badia?] the pope's *maggiordomo*—master of the sacred palace at Rome, and, fearing that false reports had been made by his adversary, he sent a narrative of the facts.

"A few years ago, the inhabitants of Colle having loaded me with honours, I bought the villa of Aula Cecina, in the territory of Volterra; Ceciniano, being within its limits. Two philosophers came to visit me; men of great learning and profoundly versed in that science, of which the principal scope is the investigation of nature. I gave them a friendly reception; after dinner the conversation turned on some points which Aristotle has treated in an obscure manner. The next day, attracted, I suppose by the similarity of our studies and the powerful ties of friendship, they returned after dinner to see me, and begged that I would explain more fully some points in my poem on the Immortality of the Soul. In complying with their request, I was obliged to bring in many things relating to theology, a science in which I have always taken the greatest delight. Finding myself engaged in a discussion with men of great talent, one of whom lectures on dialectics, and the other devotes his time to the study of the peripatetic philosophy, I treated with considerable care the arguments arising out of the subject.

"About this time there came to the city (Colle) to preach, a man of a bold and subtle nature. To excite exasperation, he began by boasting that he was writing against Thomas Vio of Gaeta, as he had discovered a great many errors in his books; but not finding much credence given to his assertions, he announced that he was going to publish a work against the opinions of the Germans (German reformers.) Attracted by these reports, and knowing that the sight of a man's countenance is a great help towards forming an opinion of his character, I accosted him politely; but on questioning him I soon found the depth of his peripatetic philosophy. I found him altogether ignorant of this science, though eager for wordy disputes about new things; he knew nothing of Greek and Latin, and was but little versed in the Italian language, which is both witty and elegant. I inquired among his friends what he had written against the Germans. A facetious man then exclaimed, that there was a robber in the town; that he had made a bad compilation from Eckius, Rochester, Marcello and Lancellotto; and among these plagiarisms I discovered the disagreeable fact that the excellence of these books had been, by his means, greatly obscured and sprinkled with barbarisms. I laughed at this account, and discontinued to attend his daily discourses. It was reported to him that I made game of his writings. Do you think this fierce, ambitious, arrogant man could contain himself?

" With a changed countenance, and in the greatest agitation, he presented himself early the next morning to preach. Complaining of being injured, he wept, and entreated the citizens, and excited the populace against me. Taking advantage of the discussion I had held with the two natural philosophers, he taxed me with infamy, and accused me of a capital crime, (heresy) formed a conspiracy with partizans of the same cast, not only for alienating from me the citizens, but for rendering me odious to the excellent [Cosmo I.] prince of the most flourishing state of Tuscany.

" Persuaded that silence would not put an end to the injurious language which he poured forth in public, I, almost for diversion, wrote in two days a defence, in order to teach this man something of himself, to impress him with a dread of being exposed to the learned, and to convince him that his vulgar loquacity would meet with no encouragement. . . . I believe it to be a fact generally acknowledged, that no two things are more closely connected than ignorance and arrogance; hence he thinks himself at liberty to do whatever he pleases. I thought this part of the apology would not be unacceptable to the citizens, and I hoped to regain those whom his clamours had alienated from me. I sent the apology to Piero Vettori, an excellent citizen of Florence. . .

"When my adversary heard this, and had read my defence, of which I had sent him a copy, his courage suddenly fell. Meanwhile, some excellent persons in the city besought me to be reconciled to him. I went to him with the utmost urbanity. He took my hand, apologized for the insults he had offered me, and threw the blame on hasty moments of anger. I accepted the excuse, and with Christian compassion laid aside all rancour, cancelling every feeling of aversion and hatred. I threw into the fire the copies of the apology which I had resolved to send to some persons, that there might be no trace of our enmity. He returned to his friends. I no longer suspected anything, had no communication with him for two years, and laid aside the questions in dispute.

"While I imagined that all was now at rest, behold letters came from my friends, informing me that the fury of my adversary was again kindling, that he was uttering threats, circulating dishonour-

SUSPICIONS OF HERESY.

able reports, and in his sermons calling me by the vilest names, and promising to publish in his book, written in bad Latin, some letters full of slander against me. He had suborned persons to calumniate me at Rome."

Paleario had been aided by Francesco Ricci of Florence, to whom he wrote, "You have by your influence distanced him (the accuser) for the present. I shall try in future to have no more to do with these gentry, and perhaps *I shall suppress the theological commentaries* in prose, and the orations and the laudatory verses which I have begun to write, until this weapon [the Inquisition] be torn from the hands of wicked and ignorant men, who cannot bear this most holy branch of knowledge (theology) to be illustrated by the graces of oratory, and who, for their own gain, would prefer to leave it buried in obscurity, rather than see it set forth in high places for the benefit and consolation of the souls of men." This monk was silenced for a short time; but on returning to his convent, he found such encouragement that his courage revived, and he plotted new schemes of revenge. The conspiracy gathered force from another circumstance.

The grandmother of the Bellanti children, who were under the care of Paleario, was aged and feeble. Certain monks went every day to her house, perhaps as her confessors, or to administer some superstitious rite of the Romish church. She did not suspect their tricks, and either by fraud or robbery they carried away all the large sum of money that she had in keeping for her grandsons. It was an abuse of their office which was almost beyond belief; but on searching, the bags were found torn open, and not a farthing left. The wooden-shod* monks were cited to justice; Palearico assisted in pleading the cause of the children whom they had robbed. Nothing was gained, for the monks swore, with their hands on the crucifix, "as if they had wooden fingers," that they were innocent. They were of the sacred order, and there was no redress. They escaped punishment, and ought to have been satisfied. But they were enraged against Palearico, and entered into the conspiracy.

A greater champion than the monks appeared. Palearico was in the senate at Sienna when some important document was being read. Ottone Melio Cotta and Belida tried to divert the attention of the senators. A severe sentence was passed upon these turbulent citizens. Belida uttered his reproaches upon Palearico. Cotta asserted, that if Palearico continued to live, there would not remain a vestige of religion in the state, because, one day when he was asked what was the chief thing that God had given to men in which they could place their salvation, he replied, "Christ." What was the second? "Christ." And the third? "Christ."

* *Lignipodas*, so called from their wearing wooden shoes. It will appear from Palearico's oration, that their names were Pansa and Siano.

"No one," wrote Paleario to young Fausto Bellanti, "was found in so good a cause to rise on my behalf. Your uncle was absent, but had he been there I should not have hoped much from him. I cannot tell you how completely I have been deserted by him in my distress. By a serious remonstrance he might have either retarded or repressed the violence of my adversaries. He could have appealed to the archbishop, his near, neighbour, with whom he is very intimate. . . While your father lived, I could count on him; now he avoids my society. He is either spoiled by the increase of his patrimony, for we all are more humane in poverty, or perhaps he is alienated by Cecilia, whose words are for him the dictates of an oracle." This Cecilia was some low chatterer to whom Paleario seems to refer when he nobly says, "I have long desired not so much to revenge myself on certain persons as to cure them."

Paleario went to Rome. He knew that the dangers were alarming. Heresy was a crime, a capital offence. He knew that he might be proved guilty of what some called heresy, for it was really Bible truth. He had declared that Christ was "all in all." He had written commentaries. He had written a book showing forth the benefits which Christ had procured for mankind by his death. In his conversations with his friends he had grown eloquent when dwelling upon the Saviour's mission and character, and his readiness to receive sinners.

It was not the church that prepared men for Christ; it was Christ who prepared them for the church. These were the grounds on which he would be accused. He sought some relief, or a brief escape, by going to Rome. There he met Filonardi, and Cincio Phrygipani, who were warm friends to him in his distress. Poor Mauro was no more. He had been again in the service of Cardinal Cesarini; had fallen from a horse while hunting, and died of a fever, leaving behind a high opinion of his talents and a deep regret for his death. Another long-known friend was there, Bernardino Maffei, a young man of great promise and irreproachable life, for whom the red hat was waiting to deck a head of but thirty-six years. He was so intent upon kind offices that Paleario wrote of him, "This excellent man leaves nothing undone which can contribute to my consolation or assistance. Knowing that from my earliest youth, I have devoted myself to those studies which have brought him no small glory, he reads to me an historical account of his collection of ancient coins. We frequently prolong our reading till the night is far advanced. I also profit greatly by his generosity, for he wishes me to consider all that he has as mine. In the increase of his prosperity, he has not forgotten his early friendships."

But separated from his family and friends, Paleario could not be at rest. He could not possibly foretell the result of the conspiracy against him. Pope Paul III., incited by the fierce Cardinal Caraffa, had recently given the Inquisition new powers to apply tortures and to put heretics to death. And what charges were the conspirators about to bring forward? Some light was thrown upon the accusations by a letter from the young Fausto Bellanti, who said,

"On the 16th of February [1542?] before daybreak, the servants of Placido brought me a letter, by which I learned that a great movement and a most inconceivable conspiracy was forming against you by some wicked men. Both my mother and that excellent woman your wife wished me to write and tell you not to stir, but to stay where you are, till this mystery is solved. We do not know the ground of the accusation, nor the names of the accusers. It is rumoured that on account of calumnious reports about your religion, persons of importance have been excited against you. My mother thinks that the monks have conspired against you, on account of your hatred of the superstition by means of which they have exhausted the funds of our family. You assisted us in pleading our cause (against these monks,) and no wonder they are enraged. This is my mother's opinion, and I do not deny that these rogues may have some hand in the disturbance, though I cannot think these paltry fellows have originated a matter of so much importance. *This conspiracy takes its rise in higher quarters.* . . . I have a presentiment that those Senators, whom you displeased in the affair of the salt, have not forgotten it.

"Egidio, who interests himself in all that concerns your honour and dignity, has found out, as far as he can, that your cause will come on very soon. If this be so, you have everything to hope, for Sfondrato, and F. Crasso will bear witness to your integrity, devotion and piety: two men of such superior character and weight are worth a hundred thousand others. They are so highly approved by the Senate and by the people of Sienna, that, by their authority and influence, they can do more than any one else. . . . If necessary I shall employ an advocate; I will find the money and be ever ready to defend you at the risk of my life."

To know who were the two men of weight just named, we must make a note of affairs at Sienna. There had been a new uprising of the factious element; the pope had sanctioned it to turn the allegiance of the city from Charles V. to Francis I. The emperor sent his councillor, Granville, (afterwards the enemy of William the Silent in the Netherlands,) to Sienna to re-organize the government. He was soon joined by F. Sfondrato, who was appointed Governor. Crasso assisted him as Prætor, and afterwards took his place. We turn to Paleario, sitting in Rome by a winter fire, and replying to Fausto Bellanti. He had summoned to his aid the consolations of Christ. He says:

"After dinner, while we were sitting by the fire, your packets of letters were put into my hands. After reading them I became somewhat more tranquil, but I do not feel re-assured; not that I think those excellent men, Sfondrato and Crasso will fail me, but with all their good will, they cannot promise more than that which you know. . . . The conspirators gather in crowds, and the more bitterly a person speaks of me, the more religion he is thought to have. . . . But, however miserable my condition may be, Christ will ever be to me the only object of holy hope and veneration. If we can succeed in being allowed to confront the witnesses, we shall gain the victory. These men, made up of falsehood, will never stand the fire of my countenance. You will perhaps, think I speak with too much confidence. If they appear, I will make them repeat their testimony without giving them time for preparation. It is wonderful how easily liars forget. . . . The Hernici (at Veroli) expect me, but the distance is great, and the road not very secure, for the forest is infested with banditti. . . . Take care not to mention any of these things to my wife, lest her fears should be increased. She is already sufficiently anxious about me, for I hear that she is the most miserable of women. I must tell you that, to my great grief, she cannot bear our unhappy lot with any strength of mind, and passes whole days in tears. She is continually thinking of what may happen, as is natural to a faithful and prudent woman. God has hitherto protected me from evil. Console her in my name; if she is gone to Colle, and if you go to the castle of Mætiano, entreat your mother to go to her; if there is no brighter hope, let her invent something to divert the poor thing from her misery. . . . .

"If any misfortune befall me, I recommend my children to your care; receive and protect them as if they were your own. If my life were to be prolonged, dear Fausto, you would have to render me many services; render them instead to the children of him, who, in defending your substance and the reputation and life of your father, did not shrink from drawing on himself the enmity of powerful men, and who, to serve you when infants, abandoned both country and friends and changed his abode. I commend to you, my children, O Fausto! and remember what I say; you are not only to imitate, but to surpass me. When, a few days before his death, your father left Padua, he commended you and your brothers to my care. His words are so deeply fixed in my memory, that they have never been effaced. Death itself would not, I believe, extinguish the remembrance of that most dear friend's recommendation."

The exquisite tenderness thus revealed will not fail to be noticed by the reader. There was yet a glimmering hope that justice might be secured for Paleario, even at Sienna. He learned that Sadolet, now a cardinal, was to pass through Sienna at a certain time; might he not go thither and meet him? He resolved to go, as if he went from Colle, thus concealing the fact that he had been at Rome, unless questioned on the point. And here Pterigi Gallo re-appears. Where he is we cannot discover, but Paleario knows that he has no stauncher friend, and thus writes to him:

"Certain *Joannelli*,* the dregs of the populace in Sienna, have brought an accusation against me. May God help me, for they are greater enemies of Christ than the Parthians. I might avoid the danger, but do not choose to do so, that I may not appear in the wrong. Innocent as I am, I do not fear the result, nor am I so fond of life as to seek to preserve it contaminated by a note of infamy. I am in great hopes of putting an end to their envious dealings, if I can but be allowed to speak in reply to those evil-intentioned witnesses. The archbishop, Francesco Bandini, will be my judge; he is the brother of my friend Mario, and though once very friendly towards me on account of our studies, is now greatly alienated through these furious men. They are not aware that I am in Rome. . . . It is of the greatest importance to me that I should go to meet Sadolet at Sienna, as if I went from Colle. . . I am obliged to run many risks at once, and fear lest I shall not be able to overcome them all. It is just at this moment that I need your activity and fidelity. As soon as you have read this, make

* Probably some order of monks.

haste, get ready, mount your horse and fly. Let your affection for me spur you on."

Even this good spur did not bring the prompt Gallo in time. Paleario set out, stopped at Viterbo, and then met Fabio, the same courier who had attended him to Perugia twelve years before. This carrier of confidential letters must have been remarkable for something better than the loud snoring, of which Paleario speaks in a curiously graphic account of his night at the inn. It affords us a glimpse of the humble way in which learned men travelled. A land-proprietor, who is also highly educated, and is intimate with two or three cardinals, is lodging at so humble a tavern, in no mean city, that he shares the room of the courier. He writes to Gallo: "After supper we returned to rest in the same room; but he (Fabio) snored so loudly that I could not sleep. I therefore occupied myself in reading, with the closest attention, the letters 1 had received the day before from Tuscany. I perceived that my enemies are trying to implicate me in a new trial, while I am busy with the first, so that I may never get free. . . . Do not delay carrying the packet (sent by Fabio) to Bembo; you often spoke to him at Padua—why should you fear? Bembo has had an increase of fortune, but his amiability is not diminished. All will be well if your courage, fidelity, and solicitude do not fail you. Remember how often you have begged God that some opportunity might offer for you to prove to me your faithfulness. I was never in such need of your exertions as now. The Filonardi are at Rome; their zeal for my honour and safety are remarkable. Go every day to see them. Go also to Cincio. It may be difficult for you to go to the other friends, on account of your maidenly bashfulness, against which I should say a good deal if my light were not going out."

Paleario avoided the snares at Sienna, passing around it one morning before daylight, and reached the suburban villa of Bellanti, whence he sent word to Gallo, " Tell our friend that I was unwilling to mention my adversary by name, because I was not sure whether all that had been told me was true. If, in consequence of our reconciliation, he does not mean to injure me, I should esteem it my duty not only to refrain from injuring him, but even not to offend him. In fact, injuring and offending are much the same thing. Whoever molests us is our adversary."

Noble spirit! We conclude that if he sometimes used severe language, there was reason for it and truth in it. Imagine now that he has met Cardinal Sadolet, and received from him honest advice, and we are prepared for Paleario's letter to the archbishop Bandini, on whom much depends in a trial for heresy. To avoid repetition we condense a few of the most important passages: " I had determined not to write to a man of your exalted position until the close of the suit got up against me, lest my first letter should contain something annoying—for sometimes when a first painful impression is made, it is never afterwards effaced. My adversaries, who employ the shadow of piety without the substance, have changed my resolution. I do not think they have learned from Christ to hold me up to public obloquy. For six whole months they have been solely employed in gathering materials for the iniquitous accusation. Though in my writings there is nothing to offend any pious man, yet they have moved heaven and earth to find in them subjects of suspicion. No one was ever so holy as to be secure against the suborners of false witnesses, and the malicious diligence of accusers. . . Was not Christ himself, the holiest and most innocent, treated in like manner? Has anything been left untried to alienate from me Sfondrato, the father of your country, and Crasso, the powerful head of justice? What more? Have they not almost deprived me of your favour? Not to speak of old injuries, what shall I say of the reports now spreading through the city?

"A few days ago that most holy man, Sadolet, paid you a visit. I came to salute him. He warmly recommended me to you, and bore witness to the nature of my studies. You appeared to be prejudiced against me, and received the recommendation coldly. Though somewhat agitated by this, I answered with modesty and politeness, and threw the blame on those who had unfairly reported the matter to you. I had hardly reached the church of the Virgin, when I was told that my adversaries were busily talking about me in the public square, some saying that I had been silent from shame, others that Sadolet had severely reproved me for my words. Both these assertions were utterly false. Could I dare to remonstrate with my venerated archbishop? The accusers were not present; if they had been they might have heard more than would have pleased them.

"The very day that I came to Sienna, Ambrozio Spannochi came to me, took me by the hand and said 'O, my dear Aonio, I heartily congratulate you. Envy will not gain the day. You have a most excellent person as your defender.' After being seated, he told me that four of the noblest Senators had been sent to you, as if by the Senate, to inquire about my studies and manner of life, and that your answer was so liberal and friendly, that he was certain nothing would be wanting on your part to secure my triumph. Hence I made you a visit, being ever mindful of benefits received. I think it a Christian duty to lay aside all ill-will, on the slightest sign of kindness either of word or look.

"Is it not an honourable thing for Sadolet to testify, that at Rome I had spoken to him about those (matters) now called in question, and that my opinions did not differ from those which had always been considered the soundest? Even supposing

there had been some reproof on his part, could anything be more gentle than his admonition? He, who had authority to command, only entreated me not to be studious of new things. I answered that I was not desirous of novelty, for I thought there was nothing in the world more ancient than truth. . .
I verily believe these wretches are now sorry and ashamed of having raised such a storm against me, who do not acknowledge anything to be holy or right, either in my words or writings, except it be approved by the catholic and apostolic church. This sentence, full of heart, energy and piety, I depose as a sure testimony before you as a most holy man, and as the best sanctuary I know of; from whence if occasion require, I can recover it at pleasure to overcome the wickedness and humble the audacity of my enemies."

Thus we have seen the accusation preparing against Paleario, and himself preparing to meet it. He had once defended Antonio Bellanti; he had proved himself superior to the monks in learning and piety; he had studied the deep things of God in the Holy Scriptures; he had written what the ignorant called heresy; he had confronted the robbers of an aged lady who thought that her spiritual consolers were honest men; he had declared that Christ was first, second and last—the alpha and the omega in our salvation; these were the offences which rendered him obnoxious in the sight of his accusers. Add to this the fact that he was not a native of

SUSPICIONS OF HERESY.

Sienna. He had everything to fear. The law condemned all heretics to the flames.

Three hundred desperate men, incited by Ottone Melio Cotta, were banded together in oath to crush him. They went to the archbishop, and had he been a Pontius Pilate or Herod, Paleario would have been burned without a hearing. The noble layman knew it all. Not a stone had been left unturned. Suborned witnesses might win their case—they did against the Lord of glory. What should Paleario do?

He might flee. He had a fresh example before him. Bernardino Ochino had just escaped from Sienna, saying, "I see by their manner of proceeding that, in the end, my accusers would examine me, (by torture) and make me deny Christ, or kill me. If I had crucified Christ they could not have made more noise. I decide on going away. If St. Paul were in my place, I think he would do likewise." But Paleario had not been such an avowed reformer; he had not broken with papal Rome; he was not a preacher, and, perhaps, he thought that as a lawyer he could make an effectual defence. He sat down to the labour. He pryed into the secrets of the conspiracy. He prepared himself to overthrow and confound the witnesses. He wrote an oration which would hold comparison with those of Cicero. If not delivered in the senate, it is nevertheless worthy of careful study. It shows us the man and his times. It was regarded as so important, that this very speech was brought forward, nearly thirty years after, as a strong proof of his heretical opinions. Let us hear him speak for himself, with all the energy and argument of a man fighting for his life.

CHAPTER VII.

THE ORATION OF PALEARIO* IN HIS OWN DEFENCE, BEFORE THE CONSCRIPT FATHERS OF THE REPUBLIC OF SIENNA.

(1542.)

"WHEN in years past, Conscript Fathers, my enemies (notwithstanding my innocent life even from infancy) circulated reports against me, I did not suffer myself to be greatly moved by them; because in those miserable and wretched times, when human and divine rights were utterly confounded, and good men were left neglected in obscurity, I deemed myself happy to be despised by those men, in whose approbation I could take no pleasure without sharing in their ignominy. I then consoled myself with the thought that I only shared the common lot, and that perhaps my sufferings might in some sort comfort my friends, who were oppressed by the same evils. But now by the blessing of God and the compassion of the emperor Charles V., the republic is restored, and excellent judges are prepared to defend those who are engaged in the very studies which they pursue.

* A few paragraphs are omitted, and an occasional sentence is condensed.

"I will not heap rude epithets upon my adversaries as they have done upon me; but will bring them to the presence of illustrious men, capable of overawing malevolent and envious minds, who easily know those in the city that are given to evil speaking and are unrestrained in lying. For, methinks, it must be a severe punishment to them to be seen by you in their true colours. . . .

"I came into Tuscany three years after the sack of Rome, when the whole of Latium was a prey to the disasters of war, and the province of the Hernici was wasted by plague and famine. I had heard of the happy state of this part of Italy, that it was occupied in useful studies, and adorned with the love of literature. As soon, however, as I set my foot in your territory, I found that your country had not escaped the calamities of the times. I did not find here the philosophers I so ardently sought, nor the poets and orators of whom I had heard. They had either been silenced by sickness, or put to death by cruel men. The youth of the country were factious and eager for change; the old, inflamed by party spirit, thought of nothing but cruelty.

"In this dismal state of things, two young men shone conspicuous for their talents and character; Carlo Bartolomeo and Bernardo Buoninsegni, united together by friendship, similarity of studies, and congeniality of disposition and principles. Finding it impossible to be useful to the republic, they devoted themselves to those pursuits which impart truest consolation; when we apply ourselves to them, present evils lose their sting. These young men detained me for a whole year, just as I was on the point of leaving Sienna. As an inducement to stay, one of them offered me the use of the books which his learned father had collected; the other introduced me to the most distinguished persons who lived in their villas and castles. Among these was the excellent Antonio Bellanti Petrini, who was accused by those who sought to destroy the glory of a most ancient family, and the property and good name of a distinguished man. You know, O senators, with what peril, and with how much devotion, I defended your fellow-citizen. This was the beginning of all my troubles; the very circumstance I had hoped would procure the good will of the citizens, raised me up enemies. If men are so cruel towards me for having defended one of their own citizens, in what way ought they to punish him who spoiled and oppressed the friends of the people of Sienna? Are you not surprised that a person whom you sentenced to imprisonment for having amassed an immense fortune by blood and oppression, should find defenders among the chief persons of the state. I do not say this to irritate you against any one, but to make you comprehend that he cannot be a virtuous man who hates me for having defended an excellent citizen. . . .*

* Part of this paragraph already given in Chapter IV.

"I doubt not, O conscript fathers, that the cause of Ottone's enmity will appear to you very slight. I almost fear lest you should think I am inventing, and falsely accusing him; more especially as he has the reputation of being religious. As you behold him, his purple robe, and the air and bearing of his person, and discern in his countenance an excess of pride, I entreat you to observe the vanity of his mind, his arrogance, his ostentation and ferocity. Never was there anything like it. If he were asked, who among the senators is most distinguished for wisdom? may I die if he, speaking out his real sentiments, would not say, Ottone. Who stands highest in rank and honour? He would reply Melio. Who is most worthy? the answer would be Cotta.*

"No wonder then, that when I boldly defended an innocent man, he considered the little heed that I gave to his dignity and excellencies, as a crime almost equal to high treason. And when, last year, the young men were anxious to recommence their literary studies so long suspended, and entreated the eight, the directors of the college, to appoint me as professor of eloquence, what do you think? It roused the implacable wrath of Cotta against me. Is it likely that he would let slip so good an opportunity for doing mischief? You know that from a child he has been infected with party spirit; op-

---

* Ottone Melio Cotta, supposed to be the same as Orlando Marescotti.

posed as he is to literature, he is yet clever and sagacious in business. His heart is not directed to that kind of religion which consists in a devout worship of God, but to a superstitious reverence adapted to deceive mankind. . . .

"You, O Cotta, think yourself perhaps a Christian because you wear on your scarlet cloak the sign of Christ crucified, even while you oppress and destroy with cruel calumnies the innocent living image of Christ. Whoever persecutes with wicked intent, is far from the religion of Christ. Do you think your conspiring against me, who have never done you the smallest injury, can be pleasing in his sight? When you accused me falsely, did you learn this, think you, from Christ? When you went daily to the palace of the directors to propagate lies against me, you perhaps thought it was equal to going on a pilgrimage to Jerusalem or to the Virgin (at Loretto.) Did it occur to you that Christ the most innocent of beings, was attacked by similar devices? O wonderful piety! Most admirable religion! If this be the worship you pay to Christ, no wonder that to commemorate his death, you crucify the innocent. The will indeed would not be wanting, if it were lawful to do what your violence, pride, and anger suggest. . . . You begged the directors not to confer a professorship on me because I was a heretic. This new appellation I reject. You added most impudently that I had adopted the opinions of the Germans, and offered to bring ample proofs of your assertions. The directors assembled in the morning to consult about the professorship. Scipione Gabrielle, formerly my devoted friend but now alienated from me by the arts of this wicked man, made a speech not much to my advantage. He almost pronounced the name of Ottone, when he said that Cotta wished very much to be chosen. It was not enough for Ottone to injure me; he wished me to know that he was a candidate. Why? That I might throw myself at his feet, and when I met him in the forum, to tremble and keep silence and say to myself, this is the man who was so terrible to Bellanti and me, and to whom the council of the eight pay reverence!

"How I wish, O Cotta, you knew my character as well as I know yours. You asserted that I was infected with heresy. Tell me, how many years have passed since Bellanti's cause? Why? Do not ask. How many years? Ten. What then? In the affair of the salt and the castles, was there any mention of religion? Indeed there was not. During these past ten years have I ever exchanged a word with you? In reply you will say that it does not become a senator to allude to any private conversation in a public affair. I know that you great men do not like to be entangled in private discourse. Then have you, by chance, read anything that I have written? You will say, what do I care for your writings? But you ought at least to pay some regard to the light of truth and the holy testimony of God. . . . You said that I had adopted the opinions of the Germans. Do you think the Germans are all tied up in a bundle and that they are all bad? . . . There are indeed in Germany many great theologians, nor is there any other nation in which opinions are so various and so much confused. Thus, in saying that I agree with the Germans, you really say nothing. Do you call Œcolampadius, Erasmus, Melancthon, Luther, Pomeranius, Bucer and others who have been suspected, Germans? Verily I do not think that any of our theologians are so stupid as not to understand and to acknowledge that in their writings there are many things highly worthy of praise; written with great gravity and truth; copied partly from the early fathers, who have left us salutary precepts, and partly from Greek and Latin commentaries; who, though not to be compared with those great men, are nevertheless worthy of attention. . . . If I have taken the fathers for examples, why cavil because I agree with the Germans? If they are followers of holy men, why may not I follow them? . . .

"I call my slender means golden poverty, and in it I truly rejoice. On no account would I exchange it for the splendour and magnificence of these men. My patrimony is small, but my conscience is clear; the furies do not agitate it by day, nor alarm it with burning torches at night. Let them be crowned with diadems, clothed in purple, and enthroned in chairs, with carpets spread under their feet. I, with my three-legged stool will retire into my library, and feel content with a woolen robe to protect me from the cold, a handkerchief to wipe my brow, and a couch on which to repose.

"Thou, O adorable Christ! the author, preserver and liberal dispenser of thine own gifts, hast granted me to despise these things, and given me sufficient firmness of mind to speak, not according to my own sense or will, but according to truth. Do thou please to grant me piety, modesty, temperance, and all else that shall please thee and thy followers.

"As to the Germans, I approve some things, and disapprove others. To say nothing of other points, I praise the Germans for having, in our times, adorned Latin literature. . . The study of divinity lay hid in the cells of idle men, who, pretending to retire to the woods for the purpose of meditation, snored there so loudly that we heard them in the towns and villages. To the Germans we owe the revival of Hebrew and Greek learning. . . . . .

"Now, O conscript Fathers, I can vouch for the truth of the following statements concerning my adversaries. When they began to devise mischief against me, they met late at night in the subterranean church of St. Sebastian, where superstition had attracted a great number of those persons called *Joannelli*. Three hundred of them, incited by Ottone, swore on the stone altar that they would not light the lamps in honour of the saints until they had effected my ruin. In this holy place confectionery and wine were distributed. In this conspiracy, O Ottone Melio, if it be true that this was the beginning, what part did your tongue perform? I cannot positively affirm that this was the exact spot where the conspirators met, for some say that they assembled in the convent of the Franciscans; but of this I am sure, that you, Cotta, are the author, and that they met under your auspices; and that twelve persons were chosen out of the three hundred, as accusers and witnesses. Those selected from the first class were priests of little note; from the second the Capuchins were chosen; the third class, by far the largest, furnished an Ottone Melio Cotta!*

" These persons went in a body in the afternoon to the archbishop, who lived in the suburbs; they made so much noise on the way, that the women ran to the windows to see if anybody was being led to execution. They were quarreling among themselves; some of them were of the opinion that as soon as the witnesses were heard, I should be burned without a hearing. . . . The archbishop, who was taking a little repose in his villa, heard the clamour, and sent a servant to let those noisy persons in. Alessio, a most ridiculous man, having supped once with the archbishop, looked around with a confident air and began to speak. He set forth such a display of calumnies that the archbishop told him they

* The names of those from each class are given in the original.
11 *

seemed to be a collection of trifles. This bold, bad man insisted that an accusation, signed by three hundred persons, could not be a trifling one. The archbishop replied, 'Alessio, there are six hundred persons who accuse you of being a very sharp usurer, and confirm their assertion by an oath. I have, however, paid no attention to their accusation. Have I done right or wrong?' The impostor grew confused; to deny would be useless, and to confess very disagreeable. The others cast themselves at the feet of the archbishop, entreating him in the name of religion to allow them to act according to law. This being granted, they bore witness against me. . . . .

"Now-a-days all are rushing to the bookseller's, and piles of books are sold at auction. What is the meaning of this? The study of the liberal arts is deserted, the youth are wanton in idleness, the young men wander about on the public squares. By whose advice? Inquire, Conscript Fathers, inquire. Alessio Lucina boasts of being an enemy of all poetry, an impudent and ignorant man, who believes every one to be a poet who can write bad verses. This impostor deceives the youth with the arguments of Bernia, who points out the sad deaths to which the great poets have been exposed; as though all the principal orators had shared the fate of Sardanapalus, or as if the deaths of emperors were not notorious. But as this bold inept man calls himself a theologian, I will ask him; How did those holy men die, who were witnesses for Christ? How did Christ himself die, the best and holiest who ever walked on earth? . . . . . . What shall I say of Pansa and Ciano? Rapacious creatures, who having been cited in court by me last year for appropriating money, have thus taken their revenge. Innocence may be attacked, but cannot be convicted of crime; there is nothing which can excuse robbery. It is infamous that two such monstrous hypocrites should be wandering about at will to exhaust families of their wealth. My having denounced these men by name, has made all the other Capuchins my enemies. They are like the wild swine, if you attack one, all the rest will come upon you.

"I wish you to see, O senators, that these things are facts. I have here the accusation, the list of witnesses, the names of those who signed. From these we find the accusation was not in support of religion, but religion was a mere pretext for the accusation. Thus you may understand the light character of the accusers, the want of integrity in the witnesses, and the impudence of those who signed.

"In it (the book) I spoke of that order and series of things which has its origin from eternity; of the kingdom established by God before the foundation of the world, of which Christ is the only head, author and governor; of the abrogated law and of the heavy yoke of bondage; I said as much on this point as these wretched times would permit; not indeed all I wished to say, for to enter fully into the subject places one in peril. These are hard, sour men, by whom not even God, the Father of our salvation, nor Christ the king of all people, can be praised.

"*It was made a subject of accusation against me, that in this same year I had written in Italian on the great benefits which mankind had derived from Christ's death.*.* I said that from him, in whom the deity resides, and who so lovingly shed his blood for our salvation, all (believers) may expect peace and assurance of the good-will of heaven. I affirmed, on the authority of most ancient documents, that . . . all, all guilt was wiped away from those who turn their hearts to Christ crucified, with full faith in him, trust in his promises, and confidingly rest on one who cannot deceive. This doctrine appeared so bitter, detestable and execrable to these twelve—I will not call them men, but inhuman hearts, that they judged the writer to be worthy of being thrown into the fire. If I am called to undergo this punishment on account of the testimony deposed, for I consider it rather as a testimony than a book, no one will rejoice more than I shall. *These are not times for a Christian to die in his bed.*

* This settles the question whether he wrote *a* volume on the Benefits of Christ's death. That it is *the* volume now passing under that title is now clearly established; his description of his book agrees with the contents of the one which we possess. Having been originally published anonymously, it was during the life of Paleario ascribed to various persons.

It is a small matter to be accused, dragged to prison, beaten with rods, hung with ropes, and sewn up in sacks; but we ought even to be roasted in the fire, if by this method the truth may be brought to light. . . .

"By means of these rude, ignorant men, Bernardino Ochino has been lately accused; a man whose hard and abstemious life was worthy of the highest admiration. He, seeing that you were not disposed to exert yourselves in his defence or protection, has thought it best to fly. At this moment, I say it with sorrow, your fellow-citizen is driven from Italy, and has become a solitary wanderer in countries far distant from our Tuscany. What shores, woods or cities will not feel honoured wherever he sets his foot? What sort of people will they become, think you, where he makes a protracted stay, and where they can profit by the society of a man who unites great talent with extreme benevolence! No place is so rugged or so barbarous, none so uncivilized as not to be moved by his eloquence. . . I meditate within myself upon how much Italy has lost. In the principal towns he was honoured with the highest applause; immense crowds listened with admiration to his extraordinary and heavenly gifts; this is the man whom exile will reduce to a miserable state of life. . . .

"We come to the trial. Seeing that the witnesses travestied every circumstance by their falsities, I entreated the archbishop that the witnesses might repeat their depositions in my presence. It was at last granted. But they would not appear. Volaterna, in producing the accusation about *the book on the death of Christ*, repeated the evidence. It was found to be false. What followed? Nothing. I for having exalted Christ have been often accused, have been summoned to justice, expelled and all but condemned to death. Volaterna suffered no punishment for his wickedness. The accusers though challenged by me would not appear; the witnesses who had deposed contradictory evidence, took to flight. For security they remained in Cirsa's castle, but still in your territory. . . . If I had either said or done anything, they could have proceeded against me according to the decrees of the pope; why then am I not to be allowed to call them to account according to the laws of the emperors? (Paleario then states the law by which his accusers might be brought to trial for their malicious accusation and their suborning of witnesses.)

"Great are the consolations, O conscript fathers, which I anticipate from your equity. This has sustained me in my unhappy circumstances. It is impossible that your wisdom should not take into consideration that the good inhabitants of Colle, who have honoured me with the most flattering letters, have flocked here in great numbers. Do you not read on their brows and in their eyes an intense desire to defend their fellow-citizen? I should not have spoken so long in my own behalf if they had not earnestly entreated me to do so. Many of them are descended from those who, for five hundred years have defended your fathers by arms, and given them refuge in your civil wars. In their name I ask an amicable return for their good offices by granting me protection.

"There are here two brothers Fausto and Evander Bellanti, excellent, upright young men, whose affectionate looks move me to tears, while they themselves cannot refrain from weeping. They are distressed because in defending their father and family and in saving their property, I have drawn on myself a hatred so terrible as to lead me to destruction. More than once have they promised to show me their gratitude, and now they see the time come through you to express it; they intercede for me even with tears. . . . and you too, my wife, why are you come, clothed in deep mourning, to throw yourself and your children at the feet of the senators? Oh my life, my light, my soul, return home and educate your children. With Christ as their surety they will not want for a father."

If this oration was not formally delivered, it was nevertheless circulated, either in manuscript or in print. Sadolet, to whom Paleario had shown the beginning of it, approved the defence, and said that it was "dignified and of thundering eloquence." It is printed among his works, but there is no trace of the trial in the archives of Sienna. We know that he was absolved, but how must still remain a mystery. It has been supposed that the change in the government was favourable to him, or that through the influence of Sadolet and the Archbishop Bandini, the accusation was quashed. But it is important to notice that he claims to have a book upon the "Benefits of Christ's death," and that the study of theology was the head and front of his offending.

CHAPTER VIII.

PALEARIO AT LUCCA.

(1546–1555.)

PALEARIO had gained his cause; at least the persecution against him was arrested for a time; but he retired to his villa writhing under disappointment. The chair of Philology had been refused him. He must seek some employment for the support of his family. His land had not been profitable, and his trial, like all strifes, had not paid expenses. His mind was intent upon animating young men with the love of study, and to be a teacher would be his great delight. A friend at Rome, who was not satisfied with the professors there, applied to him to take the superintendence of his son and educate him, but Palcario's private lessons had been suspended; he was not disposed to resume them. The monks would busy themselves in ferreting out his "heresies;" if he had a professorship he would be above their reach. Four years after the conspiracy against him, and at the time when he was almost in despair, he received an invition from the senate of Lucca to fill the chair of eloquence, and to become the orator of the Republic.

This was partly due to Cardinals Bembo and Sadolet, who were performing their last good offices in his behalf. It was the closing year of Sadolet's life, 1546, and his last letter to Paleario was intended for the eyes of the senate of Lucca. After approving his oration in his self-defence, as we have seen, Sadolet gives a caution in regard to religious writings. He wrote feelingly, for his own works* had been condemned at Rome. Did he refer to the "Benefit of Christ's Death?" Had Paleario written to him about certain works of the reformers that Paleario had been reading in the shade at Ceciniano? Sadolet wrote, "As great inconveniences have arisen from those, who have passed judgments upon authors contrary to the clemency and equitable customs of our ancestors, the pope has done wisely in appointing a very learned and moderate man [probably Tomaso Badia] to examine all works on sacred subjects. Bembo and I have recommended you to his favour; he told us that he had received last year, from you, a very courteous and pious letter, and he both professed and promised to exert himself in your behalf. . . But I, in Bembo's name and my own, not only exhort but entreat you to listen to persons who love you sincerely; for we live in times when more is thought

---

* Sadolet had published some essays, sermons and commentaries, the chief of which was a Commentary on the Epistle to the Romans. Tomaso Badia had prohibited it on account of its leaning to Pelagianism. The pope, however, removed the censure.

of the calumnies circulated against us than of our real opinions. Employ yourself in compositions which rather incite, than controvert the course of your thoughts, which is so well known to us. You are going to take up your abode in a city, which I hear has excellent laws and morals; therefore, to be agreeable to the inhabitants, why not apply your mind to what has been written on morals by the whole family of Peripatetics; but which have never been properly commented on in Latin? I need not tell you what will be the consequence, for you must see it yourself. There are some who are much opposed to writers... In short, provide for your own tranquillity."

There were men who were disposed to allow him no tranquillity, and to prepare thorns for him at Lucca. One of them was Maco Blaterone, (the babbler) who had already annoyed him greatly at Sienna. This Maco had failed so completely there as a professor of Latin, that he had gone to Venice, where he found himself represented in a most ridiculous light on the stage. The satirist Aretino had given him a large place in a comedy, and Maco hastened away with chagrin and in despair of imposing upon the Venitians. After some wanderings he appeared at Lucca, where he began to defame Paleario, as an old rival of his who ought not to be tolerated in that city. But Paleario, resting in one of the castles of Bellanti, took measures to refute the slanders of this adversary. Maco attempted to persuade the Dominicans at Rome to silence him; but he had friends among them who stifled the accusations. In a letter to Visconti, governor of Sienna, his intimate friend, he says, " Tell the Lucchese I am a good Christian, and ready even to die for Christ, if circumstances require it."

Paleario prepared to bid a temporary adieu to his household, his villa, his friends in the Bellanti family, and to the annoying monks of Colle, and to engage in a new mode of life. Lucca was the capital of a small but flourishing republic, which began to reckon among its inhabitants a greater number of converts to the reformed faith than, perhaps, any other city in Italy. This was chiefly owing to the labours of a man to whom we give a little attention.

In Florence dwelt Stefano Vermiglio and his wife Maria, who had mourned the loss of several sons, and vowed to consecrate the next one to Peter Martyr of Milan, whose life had been taken by the Arians, and to whom a chapel in their neighbourhood was dedicated. They hoped thus to preserve their last surviving boy, who was born in 1500, on the 8th of September, the day that Titus captured Jerusalem, and, as they imagined, the birth-day of the Virgin Mary. They supposed such remarkable coincidences were presages of the child's future greatness. Thus began Peter Martyr Vermiglio.

His tender and sensible mother taught him Latin, and was pleased with his quick perception, his wonderful memory, his eagerness for study, his engaging modesty, and his tendency towards a religious life. Among his companions were two, who afterwards became devoted friends of Paleario, Francesco Ricci, and Piero Vetori, the wonder of his age. The parents were not pleased, however, when Peter, at the age of sixteen, entered the Augustinian convent at Fiesole, for his only sister followed his example and entered a nunnery. The monks were delighted, for they hoped that his talents would add renown to their order. They gave him the privilege of the large convent library. They paid unusual attention to eloquence, and the Scriptures were diligently read and studied. The young monks, who had good memories, learned to repeat whole books of the Bible. This store of Scripture, added to his thorough education, was to Peter Martyr an excellent preparation for the work of his life.

He passed three years of convent life at Fiesole; about eight more at Padua, learned the Greek language, won the degree of Doctor of Divinity at twenty-six, and began to preach in the convents and lecture on the Scriptures. Every spare hour was devoted to sacred literature, so that, with the little help he could find, he mastered the Hebrew language and easily read the Old Testament in the original. He was appointed Abbot of Spoleto, and surprised certain luxurious incumbents by his reformations. Some convents and nunneries under his charge had reached such a depth of iniquity that they were the detestation of the whole town; he advised, punished and entreated until order and formal piety were restored. At the risk of his life he reconciled the factions, who had long disturbed Spoleto.

After three years of such labour he was appointed prior of a convent at Naples, a position of great value and dignity. He began to see the abuses in the church of Rome. Just then a copy of Bucer's commentaries* met his eye. It opened to him the Gospels and the Psalms in a new light. Shortly after Zwingli's "True and false Religion" fell into his hands. These and other such works led him to desire a return to the simplicity of the Christian faith and practice. He conversed with others, who were seeking the truth, especially Marc Antonio Flaminio, the poet. He went to hear the expositions of Juan Valdes, and at length received the great and joyful tidings of salvation in an honest heart. He must have listened to the persuasive eloquence of Ochino, and soon he felt impelled to declare the truth. He began to expound the first Epistle to the Corinthians in his convent. His brethren, and several bishops came to hear him. The audiences

---

* This work was published under the feigned name of *Arezzo Felino*, a common custom then in Italy, so that the publishers might circulate more widely the writings of the reformers. It was read with great favour, even by bishops and cardinals, until it was discovered that Bucer was the author, then it was cried down as a bad book and suppressed.

increased, and those who did not attend his lectures were considered very indifferent Christians. Some of the first nobles of the land began to inquire earnestly the way of eternal life, among whom was Galeazzo Caracciolo, a hero in the faith.

The envy of the monks was excited; they whispered about that his doctrines were heretical. His sermons were reported to Don Toledo, the viceroy, who forbade Martyr to preach. But the prior refused to obey, and appealed to the Pope. There were powerful friends at the Roman court, such as Cardinals Pole, Bembo, and Hercules Gonzaga, whose mother had received his red hat, as the reader will remember, the very day that Rome was captured. They had the prohibition removed, and Martyr continued preaching. But he was seized with a dangerous fever, and on his recovery was made vicar-general of his order and sent to travel through Italy.

After promoting various reforms, he was appointed prior of a convent at Lucca, which gave him episcopal authority over half the city. Here he acted as a thorough reformer, and directed his attention to the education of young men. He chose professors well versed in the Scriptures, on which he himself lectured daily. He preached every Sunday to the people. He gradually drew together a congregation, who advanced in the knowledge of the truth. Persecution began. One friar was thrown into prison; the nobles gathered, forced open the doors, carried him out of the city, and told him to flee. The good man broke his leg, was captured and sent to Rome. Measures were taken against Peter Martyr; plots were laid; spies were at work; his friends advised him to make his escape, and he quietly went to Pisa. There he concealed himself a short time, but met in secret certain Christian friends and nobles, to whom he administered the Lord's supper after the simple and touching manner of our Lord. He went to Florence where he met Ochino, and thence he crossed the Alps into Switzerland. Of his reception at Basle, he said, "On our arrival, we were most lovingly received by Bucer into his house, and remained with him seventeen days. His dwelling seemed to be a home of hospitality, he is so accustomed to entertain strangers, who travel for the gospel and the cause of Christ. He governs his house so well, that in all these days, I could not once perceive any cause of offence, but found many occasions of edification." Bucer obtained for him a professorship of theology. We will not follow him further; his later useful career belongs mainly to the history of the English Reformation.

The infant reformed church at Lucca was permitted to worship God in secret and in peace for a few years. But Rome threatened to establish the Inquisition in the city to root out heresy; the authorities so dreaded this monster of tyranny that they forbade all conventicles, all correspondence with heretics, all discussions on religious subjects, and all books that condemned the Roman Catholic religion. Thus Lucca was placed under the power of the pope.

These rigours caused an attempt to free the cities of Lucca, Pisa and Florence from the dominion of Duke Cosmo, and unite them with Sienna in a republican league, and also to restore the church to its ancient liberty and sanctity. It was a political effort for reformation, somewhat similar to that attempted at Geneva before Farel and Calvin went there with the true reforming power of the gospel. The prime mover was Francesco Burlamachi, a noble, whose intentions were good, but his policy wrong. He hoped to see Italy freed from the papal yoke, and civil and religious liberty restored. He was Mayor of Lucca in 1546, and had his plans laid to surprise Pisa. But one of his party took some offence, and in revenge laid the whole plot before Duke Cosmo. The senate of Lucca, fearful of being suspected as his accomplices, arrested him, tortured him three times; but he made no important revelations. He was condemned to death; the poor mangled prisoner was taken to Milan and beheaded. "Thus fell a noble victim to national independence."

It appears that during this same year, 1546, Paleario went to Lucca. There was a reason in the existing troubles for his saying, in his first oration to the senate and people, "Even your present vigilance is deserving of high praise; how often in the night, while engaged in study, do I hear the guard in the fortress challenging the sentinels." The eloquence of the new orator was satisfactory to the Lucchese. A part of his task was to make short speeches twice a year, and rouse the citizens to deeds of virtue and patriotism. He was to be what the press is to us, an agency in forming public opinion. The subjects treated by Paleario were such as these: eloquence, the republic, a defence of the best studies, justice, temperance, happiness, fortitude, prudence, civil discord. These orations were afterwards published.

We must read his letters if we would learn something of his life. He feels his loneliness and writes to his young friend Lilio; "After your departure and that of our Giuseppe, [a poet,] nothing could please or enliven me, and I fell into such a languid and torpid state of mind, that every one was astonished to see the cheerfulness, which you used to admire, all gone. Both mind and countenance were changed. The only person who could at all revive me by his amiability and sweet disposition, was your cousin, Martin Lilio. . . His illness gives me so much anxiety that I feel as if I was either ill, or going to be ill. His mother, his engaging wife, and his excellent brother, beg and entreat me to go and live with him. Here I am in my apartment, without wife, children or servants, and without money. For, as you know, I was obliged some months since to go to Colle, by a long and dusty road, [to visit them,] but now, in consequence of the heavy rains so deep is the mud, that I will not allow these unhappy creatures to take such a journey on my account. Your father and all your friends assist me in my necessities; though I am content with so little that I feel myself as rich as Crassus. In your letter I see that you are reading the Epistles of Paul, and that Flaminio, your friend and mine, is leading you to the study of theology. May God reward him, who, to make you truly happy, is teaching you the sum and substance of true life, the chief crowning point of all study. . . By no means withdraw yourself from the city, (Rome,) that is the house of Flaminio."

Cicero had written an oration in defence of L. Murena; Paleario wrote one against him, and sent it to the celebrated jurist, Alciati. The great lawyer replied, saying, "I am rejoiced that this art (eloquence) has been so gloriously revived by you. . . Arise, thou most learned man, and bring us back to our ancient eloquence, and restore to civil law its true dignity."

Marc Antonio Flaminio was one of those gentle spirits that formed a link between the reformers in the Roman church, and those who had broken off from it. He had met Paleario in Florence in 1537, when, perhaps, their strong friendship was formed. Though he yielded to his father's wishes in studying philosophy, yet this was not his favourite pursuit. The Scriptures were his chief delight; the Psalms his daily food. He wrote a paraphrase on thirty-two of them. When he began a Psalm he could not leave it unfinished, however far the night was advanced; morning light often found him sleepless over the songs in which David celebrates his rest. His health failed, and he went to Naples. He had read some of the writings of the German reformers, but now heard the word of life from living lips. He joined the little companies, who sought a retired place, and heard Juan Valdes talk of things divine. The balm was found for his troubled spirit. He was able to say, "I acknowledge no other master than Jesus Christ crucified." When his little work was published, men read the gospel in the Psalms. His poetry became more and more inspired with the love that he bore to his only Master. He wrote an "apology" for Paleario's work on the "*Benefit of Christ's Death*," and was supposed, for a time, to have aided in writing the original treatise. He, with his friend, Cardinal Pole, an Englishman, must have had a happy influence upon Paleario. Flaminio died in Rome, at the house of the cardinal, who buried him in a church belonging to the British nation; thus proving his love to the last. Paleario wrote of the event, "I had not yet recovered from the wound I received at the death of Sadolet and Bembo, and this last blow grieved me the more, because if his holy life had been prolonged, he would have relieved me from great annoyance . . . When I recall his courtesy, his greatness of mind, his activity and piety, I am soothed; this is my consolation and relief." Lilio, who had read the Pauline Epistles with him, seems to have been one whom he led into the truth, a matter of joy to Paleario.

Another subject claims our notice. Among the writings of Paleario, is a "Letter of Paleario, the servant of Jesus Christ, to Martin Luther, Philip Melancthon, Martin Bucer, Calvin, and all the Swiss and Germans who invoke Jesus Christ." It was written in 1542, about the time of his first trial for heresy, to notify the reformers of what was going on in preparation for the Council of Trent. In his mind the project was a noble one; it should be a kind of religious parliament, where all parties would be allowed to speak their opinions freely, candidly, fearlessly. But he was anxious lest the reformers should be out-generaled and defeated. He perhaps wrote from Rome. He refers to pope Paul III. and his party, and says, "These persons make every exertion that nothing may be omitted which can be devised against you. The pope himself, not very robust at his age, does not devote even the night to repose. He has many counsellors. Sometimes he consults lawyers, or men of experience and shrewdness; and also, if you please, dishonest men. At other times he summons sophists, theologians or philosophers, who delight in contention. . . . He reminds them that in this council the majesty of the church of Rome, the fortunes of all the bishops and of the chief pontiffs are at stake; he presses them to spare neither labour nor diligence to be acute in discussion against you. He has increased his party in the college (of cardinals.) Thirteen were admitted yesterday; two more are in prospect. Do not ask whether this excited our indignation, who were willing to die for Christ? What is this but an unlawful mode of favour, bribery to corrupt the council?" Paleario exhorts the reformers to be united and to stand firm.

The council was delayed; the papal party was in no haste; it did not assemble until 1545; its sessions were held at intervals during the next eighteen years. Paleario must have anxiously watched its deliberations, and deeply lamented the defeat of the Protestants. What is remarkable is, that its last president, Cardinal Morone, was afterwards charged with heresy, and thrown into prison on suspicion of Lutheranism. Among the charges were these: "*Inasmuch* as he said to a certain prelate that the Council of Trent ought to retract its opinions on the article of justification, and that he would do so.

"*Inasmuch* as he keeps by him, and reads the writings of heretics and gives them to others to read.

"*Inasmuch* as he took great pains to distribute a little book entitled *The Benefits of Christ*, and gave orders to a heretical book-seller or one suspected of heresy, to sell as many of such books as he could, and give them freely to those who could not pay and he would repay them."

The acute inquisitors could not convict him, and they declared that he should be set free. But he at first declined to leave the prison, wishing to draw from the pope a concession that the arrest was unjust. The wary Paul IV. would not publicly declare that Morone had been wrongly accused. The prisoner remained in his cell until the pope died in 1559. The cardinals permitted him to sit in the conclave that elected Pius IV. At his death in 1566, Morone was very nearly elected pope, but unfortunately the fierce inquisitor Alessandro was raised to the papal chair.

It would seem that Paleario's little book had been quite extensively circulated in Rome. In 1549 it was put in the Index of prohibited books, the highest of papal honours, unless burning be more glorious.

Paleario's family did not join him the first year of his professorship, but so tender-hearted was he that he could not be happy long away from them. They were coming, and he was to get their baggage through Pisa. His experience at the custom-house is described in a playful letter to a friend, in which he explains how it was that he did not call to see him in Pisa, "My business was with the customhouse officers; to satisfy them I was obliged to return to Lucca the same day that I went to Pisa, and I was afraid if I spent any time in visiting my friends, I should be overtaken by the night on my journey. . . . The rain coming on, I had to take a journey of three days, by a very bad and muddy road to prevent my wife from losing her female ornaments. They had been detained because the boxes were not plumbed. . . . You know well the great influence of a wife, so you must not be angry with your friend who was overheated, and in a shabby travelling hat attending to business."

Palcario and his pupils seem to have kept up a lively correspondence after their painful separations. As a specimen of their mutual affection we make the following quotations. The young Gadio, who had hoped never to leave his teacher, was at home. He heard that Paleario was coming to visit him, and he wrote to him: "This made me exult with joy. The villa Pancrazio, which I think you must have seen, is about four miles from Rome. Lay aside, for a time, the idea of town life and banish all literary occupations. Remember that for a long time past you have given up all recreation. Set off at break of day and fly to us as quickly as possible." Paleario replies: "While enjoying as much leisure as my continual warfare with the barbarians, and my public efforts in transporting Athens to the foot of the Appenines, will permit, I received your invitation. I should have been with you, if my friend Eutychus and his wife, a superior woman, had not previously engaged me and my wife to go to their villa of Graguani. I must defer my visit to you. Take all possible care of your health, that when I come you may not only be able to take two or three turns with me under the portico, but to wander round the farm, and accompany me to the neighbouring villas, and prolong our supper and our conversation far into the night."

To a friend who had invited him to visit him at Rome, he replied, "If it were not to see you, I have no desire to go to Rome. I cannot express the disgust I feel at the pomp of the Roman court, and how extremely I dislike those, who despise both God and man, and live such lawless lives. We had hoped that the censures of the bishops would have restrained the passions of such men. If this ever takes place, religion, justice and temperance will revive: if not, it will be a long time before you see me in Rome."

Again we find the wife of Paleario at Colle, in considerable peril during the birth of a child. He is at Lucca dangerously ill, and so anxious are her relatives that one of them, Guidotti, is sent to comfort him. The messenger thus writes back: "The sun was rising when I left the town of Colle: I reached Lucca before the evening. Pterigi had arrived before me, which increased Paleario's fears that his wife was dead. When I came, my horse bathed in sweat and my boots covered with mud, he was so greatly terrified on seeing me, that he burst into tears, exclaiming, 'Oh, my life, my light, the desire of my eyes!' He was suffering from fear and a pain in his side, and tossed himself from one side of the bed to the other, clasping the pillow: he would not believe either Pterigi or me, when we told him his wife was alive. . . . I said that I had come at her request to take him to her as soon as his health would permit. This seemed to soothe him a little, but he could not lay aside his alarm, and was all the time afraid that we were deceiving him. I am sure that our arrival increased his illness. We remained with him till the night was far advanced without any diminution of the pain or fever. Wearied out we went to bed. About the third watch, the servant says, he told her to bring him ink and paper, as he wanted to write something. Not having closed his eyes all night, a little before dawn he had his bed carried up stairs to the room where the portrait of his wife hangs. He fell asleep. When we were looking for something else, we found a sheet of paper on which was written in a trembling hand the following verses:

> 'If Christ were not my hope and stay,
> Whom thou in life hast followed close,
> Disjoined from thee I ne'er could live.
> He promised and he'll faithful prove
> To raise thee up to life and light:
> This feeds my soul with sweetest love.
> Meanwhile, dear wife, Aonio hastes
>   To meet thee in Elysian fields.'"

After his recovery he prepared to leave Lucca, disappointed in his literary career, borne down by pecuniary cares, and fearful of persecution. His well-known religious opinions most likely exposed him to the enmity of the priests. In his oration at the close of his fifth year at Lucca, he made certain utterances which were quite certain to rouse opposition. He alluded to the folly of those, who, searching for unbroken contemplation, have foregone all the decencies and comforts of life, and taken up their abode with the beasts of the desert, and have tortured themselves with cruel torments, under the mistaken idea of living near to God. He declared that nothing was so delightful as the study of divine things. So ardently does he desire the joys of heavenly contemplation, that he asks the senate and people of Lucca to consider his advancing years, and choose some younger man as their orator.

One can see that the shadow of disappointment rests on his spirit. His heart turns homeward. He has already given directions about certain improvements and buildings at his villa. He fears that they may run him into debt. His daughters are soon to be married; his sons must be educated. He says, "Do not let us sacrifice these dear children, nor let the builders take our all." Again he writes to his confidential man of business: "I can no longer bear the heavy air of this country. I feel, my dear Pterigi, that I have lost my health. I grow worse every day; neither diet nor medicine does me any good. I have a great difficulty of breathing, which sadly depresses my spirits. This arises either from the disease itself, or from the loss of those excellent men who died a few years ago, Sadolet, Bembo, Flaminio and Sfondrato, true pillars of defence for me, and protectors of my writings... I have a great desire to fly to you, for I cannot express how irksome study has become to me. We will pass whole days at Ceciniano enjoying the sun with Lampridio and Fedro, my dear children, and we will walk about with our wives and visit the neighbouring villas.... Let the garden be kept in order that we may live on vegetables, for the expenses of the town have exhausted my resources. The country will furnish us with herbs, snails, eggs, fish, chickens and thrushes. If we want to make a more sumptuous repast, your dish of cheese and salt fish will be royal food; if it is difficult of digestion, we will work in the garden to fatigue ourselves and assist our digestion. So get ready, and see that there be at the villa a handsaw, an axe, a wedge, a pick, a rake, a spade; and, until we are quite well, we will plant trees for the future generation."

With broken health and depressed spirits he turned for consolation to his quiet home. There, says Mr. Young, "in the society of his wife, surrounded by his children, he proposed to carry out his plans of improvement. But the want of funds, no doubt, prevented their execution. The water still trickles over broken and shapeless stones, and the walk, traditionally called Aonio's walk,* offers no beauty to attract the lover of the picturesque. But the air is good, the retirement perfect, and we may picture to ourselves the family group assembled on a dewy morning, or on a hot, sultry evening watching the glorious sunsets which are so frequently to be seen in Italy. We may imagine Paleario himself rising at early dawn, and see him with flowing hair and head bent down, perambulating his domain. Filled with thoughts of immortality, indulging in philosophical reveries, he lifts both thoughts and eyes to heaven, and while gazing on the splendour of the firmament, he tastes the luxury of divine contemplation." There is much work still in store for him, and his leisure will not be of long duration.

* The present proprietor of the villa is very proud of its former inhabitant, and still points out Aonio's walk. It is interesting to note that in 1561, Pietro Cipolla petitioned the town council of Colle for "permission to put up a commemorative stone on the house inhabited by the illustrious *Letterato* Aonio Paleario." By a vote of eleven, only one opposing, it was agreed upon, and the record reads thus: "Considering that it is always commendable to perpetuate the remembrance of persons of note in the history of literature, the council declares that they have no objection to the fulfilment of the request to put up a flint stone on the door of the house of Cipolla, with the following words: AONIO PALEARIO LIVED HERE." Since then another house in Colle has been pointed out as the one in which he lived a part of his time.

CHAPTER IX.

CELIO SECUNDO CURIONI.

(Born 1503. Died 1569.)

ONE of the friendships of Paleario brings us into acquaintance with a man whose adventures and narrow escapes were of the most romantic character, whose sufferings and exile throw a glory upon his Christian faith, whose children furnish a most pathetic record of family griefs, and whose learning made him a great accession to the reformers of Switzerland.

Celio Secundo was a native of Piedmont, and took the name of Curioni from the old castle of Cuori, which had belonged to his ancestors. He was the youngest of twenty-three children, eighteen of whom were in their graves. His father, Jaconimo, owned large estates; his mother, Carlotta, had been maid of honour to Bianca, duchess of Savoy, and had been accustomed to the ease and luxury of a court. His parents died when he was nine years old, leaving certain property to be divided between their five children, and also to him the family home, with some neighbouring farms. But the best legacy of all, and the only one that he really enjoyed, was an old family Bible, written on fine parchment, illuminated with gold, and coloured in a beautiful miniature style.

A servant was his first teacher, but he was afterwards sent to a grammar school where he made astonishing progress. His aunt Maddelina gave him a home in her house at Turin, where he studied under superior masters. He applied himself to the study of civil law, of which Francesco Sfondrato was professor. Soon he heard no little severe talk about the books and opinions of the Reformers. Hearing them condemned as false and heretical, he felt an eager curiosity to read and judge for himself. This was not difficult, for he had friends in the Augustine convent, who were zealously studying the new writings. He first read Luther's book on "Indulgences," and his "Babylonish captivity of the church:" then Zuingli's "True and false religion," and Melancthon's "Common Places." These writings made such an impression on his mind that he resolved to go to Germany.

Two young men, Camillo and Guarini, agreed to set out with him. The eager youths were not very prudent, and as they travelled along they talked so unguardedly about religion, that Boniface, the cardinal bishop of Ivrea, had them arrested and imprisoned in separate towers. Curioni was shut up for two months in a castle, and it was only through the good offices of some friends among the nobility that he was released, with a severe reprimand and a prohibition from conversing on such subjects. If his friends had such an injunction laid upon them, when set free, they did not long heed it, for they became ministers of the gospel.

Boniface saw that his young captive had superior talents and wished to secure him to the church. He sent him to the convent of St. Benigno, as a better school than German universities, so that he might enlighten his mind and confirm his faith. But this was the last place to produce such an effect. The convent boasted of having certain rare bones and relics which attracted crowds of people to their shrines. Curioni was disgusted at such superstition. He could not restrain his indignation, and he privately uttered his sentiments to his companions. He went farther. To one particular young friend he spoke of Melancthon's "Common Places," advising him to read them. The young man, accordingly took the volume, and started out one day to walk near the river, where he might read it without detection. When he had left the gate of the town, he was horrified by meeting a beast, like a dragon, pouring flames from his mouth. The timid youth, knowing that he was forbidden to read the book and fearing to give account of himself to his prior, was so frightened that he took refuge in another convent near at hand. He told what he had seen and read. The friars, who very likely had contrived the whole affair with the aid of phosphorus, declared that the monster had appeared to him because of the awful book and its religion, and persuaded the credulous boy to give it up to be burned and to retract his opinions.

Celio was quite as credulous, but less confident in the friars, and thought the apparition was a Satanic vision. But he laid the blame, not on the new books, but on the old relics. He had learned to value the Bible, and was doubtless surprised not to find it used at the convent. He resolved to teach the monks a lesson and then leave. He watched and learned where the keys of the relic-box were kept, took them and secretly opened it; he laid hold of the superstitious treasures and threw them away. In their place he put a Bible from the library, with these words written upon it—*this is the ark of the covenant where the true oracles of God are to be found and consulted; these are the veritable relics.*

So cautiously was this done that it was not discovered until a certain saint's day, when the relics were to be carried in solemn procession. Then the box was opened and lo! they were gone. The friars were not disposed to consult the Bible, nor could they vent their rage upon young Curioni, for he had escaped to Milan. He travelled through Italy for some time, and then being persuaded by several leading families, he settled at Milan, where he taught for several years. He was there when Freundsberg and Bourbon combined their armies for the capture of Rome. The next year Di Leva the Spanish general held Milan for the emperor.

Young says, "Di Leva, after fleecing the inhabitants to the uttermost farthing, was reduced to put a heavy tax upon bread and flour: every loaf was stamped with the Austrian double-eagle, and none but the rich could enjoy the luxury of eating bread. On this occasion it was jocularly said that the emperor to his numerous titles had added a new one, that of *baker*." The Spaniards plundered the people, and then came the plague with all its horrors. One tenth of the inhabitants were dying. Curioni saw his friends hurrying from the city, but his courage and benevolence led him to devote himself wholly to the good work of relieving the sufferers. He gave all he had to spare to the poor. A noble family, the Isacchi, who had retired to their villa in the neighbourhood, gave him a home, and he went unceasingly from house to house consoling the mourners, helping the sick, feeding the starving and burying the dead. The city became like a desert; many left even their nearest relatives unattended.

Still tenderer sentiments sprang up in his heart and in his home. He was deservedly esteemed worthy of Margarita, the pearl in the house of his protector. After the plague had ceased, and the marriage been celebrated, he looked about for some quiet spot in Italy, where he might dwell unmolested by the priests for his religion, and undisturbed by the armies that were devouring the land. He found it at Casale, where he passed several years in quiet domestic happiness. Having heard that his two only brothers were dead, he was advised by his friends to return to his country, and obtain his share of the property, which had been taken possession of by his sister Martha and her husband. They and other relations treated him kindly until they found that he came as the heir of his brothers. Then they contrived a suit against him as a heretic, and drove him from the district. He then went to Moncalier, five miles from Turin, where he had passed a part of his childhood, and his father had left him a house and some land. He did not remain idle; he gave lessons to the sons of the surrounding families. His admirable method of teaching, with his learning and his engaging manners, won him the affections of pupils and patrons. His zeal for the truth was not extinguished, nor his indignation at the ignorance and impertinence of the priests.

One day he went to Castiglione to hear a Dominican monk preach. It was asserted in the sermon that Luther's doctrines found favour in Germany because he allowed every kind of licentiousness, and taught that Christ was not God, nor born of a virgin. Such gross falsehood was not to pass without correction. Curioni obtained permission of the friar to make a reply, and addressed him: "You have advanced great things against Luther; if Luther has indeed written what you assert, can you point to the book or the page where such doctrines are taught?" Without waiting for a reply he opened Luther's commentary on Galatians, which he held in his hand, and read the very opposite of what the monk had asserted. The audience, with the nobles at their head, were indignant, and loudly expressed their displeasure of the falsehoods that were thus exposed. Some of them had arguments very erroneous, but yet more convincing to an ignorant friar; and they advanced and struck him with such violence that his rescue was owing to the interposition of the governor. All this was reported to the bishop, who set out with an armed force, went straight to his house, took Curioni prisoner, allowed the soldiers to sack and spoil the premises, and carried his innocent captive to Turin.

The name of Curioni was not likely to secure him favour in that city, for the affair of the relics was laid up against him; nor was it forgotten that he had once left there for Germany. Menaces were not spared; he was regarded as such a heretic that no proofs were necessary. Nothing less than burning him to death was proposed as the deserved punishment. But there were chief persons in Turin who highly esteemed the prisoner; Bishop Aventino knew it, and he must not offend them. He set out for Rome to consult the pope, ordering Curioni to be safely kept. The assistant bishop had him removed by night to a walled fortress; his feet were put in the stocks, and two guards placed over him.

He was not cast down; he resolved not to deny his faith. Being ingenious, he meditated an escape.

A gleam of hope appeared when he found, by remarks of the guards, that he had once known well the locality of the fortress. If he could once get outside of the prison walls, flight would be easy; but that would have seemed to many an impossible thing. In a few days his feet were swollen from the weight of the irons; he entreated the guards to relieve one foot at a time. This was done; he then contrived to make a false leg with rags, or with part of his clothing stuffed into his stocking, and fastened to his right knee. He then begged that his other foot might be released. In the change he managed to put the false leg into the stocks, by covering it with his long cloak, and have irons put on it. Thus his limbs were free. On the same night, when all were asleep, he got through a window on the landing-place, and was soon out of danger.

His escape was imputed to magic. Not willing that the Christian name should lie under such an imputation, he published a dialogue, in which he gave a full and true account of the affair. He tells his friend Lucio, in the dialogue, that before he left his prison he prayed that God would assist him, and he made a vow. His Romish friend says, " a vow of poverty, pilgrimage, or such like." "No," replies Curioni, "I vowed to devote myself, and all I possess, to the service of Jesus Christ our Redeemer, and I prayed that I might not live according to my own desires; but be drawn by the

Spirit towards him, and be used in his service as a chosen vessel for his glory."

Many of the citizens of Pavia were in the habit of spending their summer in the quiet village of Sale. There they met a man of such cultivation and talent that they wondered why he lived in obscurity. He was Curioni, who had failed to secure his property because he was a "heretic," and had retired with his family to this secluded town, hoping to spend his days where he might worship God under his own vine, and have none to make him afraid. These Pavians insisted on his accepting a professor's chair in their city, and thus be of service to their young republic. He went, and for three years distinguished himself and gave honour to the university. Students flocked to his lectures, and so high was his reputation that the Inquisition dared not arrest him. But at length the pope ordered him to be removed. The republic protested, but was obliged to give up its brightest light and ornament. Curioni wandered about for a time, and took refuge at Ferrara, where he formed the acquaintance of some others of those interesting characters which the Italian reformation produced.

We cannot, in this volume, trace the rise of the gospel work in Ferrara, nor dwell upon the influence of the duchess Renata, her cousin Margaret of Navarre, her instructors, Le Fevre and Calvin, and her friend Madame Soubise. As Renata (Renée) was the daughter of Louis XII., and the wife of

Ercole, duke of Ferrara, her court was a refuge and meeting-place for both French and Italian reformers. But in 1536 the pope was jealous of the French influence, and Renata had to dismiss her Christian attendants and scholars, who had come with her from France. The gross Rabelais "feared that she would suffer much" because she was "served by Italians." The pope had blundered, for she only exchanged one protestant influence for another even more powerful. The all-wise Disposer of events was bringing pilgrims to her palace with the love of God in their hearts.

Among the learned professors of literature at Ferrara was Pellegrino Fulvio Morato, a native of Mantua. When he was publishing his exposition of the Lord's Prayer, in 1526, he was probably quite as anxious for its welfare in the world as for that of his new-born child Olympia, who was to become the "marvel of her age." Seven years afterwards he was obliged to leave Ferrara. It was whispered that the cause was, a book written by him favourable to the reformed opinions. His scholars deplored his absence, and at first refused to learn from any other master. It seems that his family were left behind, for a friend wrote to him soon after, saying, that he had just become the father of a little daughter—probably the third, Vittoria—and that the writer had "held her at the baptismal font."

For six years Morato was a wanderer. He met

Curioni, whose life was, like his own, imperiled on account of the true faith. He seems to have dwelt for a time at Vercelli, got a house, brought his family into it, and enjoyed leisure and study. There Curioni visited him, probably spending a vacation from his professorship at Pavia. Morato invited him back, saying, "Nowhere, I think, can you be more comfortable. Your place as our guest is now empty, and above all, our library, where you can enjoy the pleasure of being quiet, silent, unknown and forgotten. . . When you reach the end of your journey, be sure to write to us how you are situated, and send us any writings that you can collect, which you may esteem conducive to a good and happy life, and particularly whatever contributes to the demolition of the stronghold of perfidious impostors and deceitful rulers (the priesthood and the papacy.) Do this, I entreat you, again and again. Farewell, thou chosen instrument for the glory of God." Had this daring letter fallen into the hands of the inquisitors, Morato might have been the first modern martyr of Italy, and Curioni the next, for he had imparted to his friends a new store of the heavenly treasures.

Morato returned to Ferrara about the year 1539, from which time his life is eclipsed by that of his remarkable daughter Olympia. Study was her absorbing passion. At twelve she knew Greek, Latin and much of the highest philosophy; best of all she had the knowledge of the gospel. The Duchess

Renata, hearing of this "prodigy of talent," invited her to court as the preceptress of her daughter, the princess Anna. The teacher was thirteen, the pupil eight years of age. They pursued such studies as belonged to the universities, and read the Scriptures together in the Greek language. It has been said that Paleario was at one time their instructor, but there is no evidence yet discovered that he was ever at Ferrara. He knew, however, of their studies and expressed his admiration of what was being done at the court for learning and for the gospel.

Curioni joined the Morato family at Ferrara, about the year 1541, when he was driven from Pavia by the order of the pope. Their tastes, their studies, their religious opinions and their kindred experiences were bonds of the most endearing union. It was not prudent for Curioni to remain long in this refuge, nor for the Duchess to protect him, or the pope would be waxing wroth against all parties concerned. She gave him letters to Lucca, hoping that he might live there unnoticed by the Inquisition. Morato grieved over his departure, and wrote to him as one "who has, I doubt not, been sent by God himself for my instruction and edification. Nor do I think that Ananias, Paul's teacher, taught with more holy admonitions or Christian discipline when he invited him to Christ, than you have taught me. Nothing assuages my grief so much as to believe that I belong to Christ, and that he does not reject me. For at the moment when I was in the greatest difficulty, forsaken on all sides, in the greatest danger and colder than ice itself, behold, you were sent by God and returned straight to us, passing by many greater men who would have desired to have you as a guest. Formerly, indeed, when I had leisure, which from my avocations rarely happened, I snatched some moments from the needs of my ill-conditioned body and my increasing years, to read, or rather devour something of John and Paul, or other holy Scriptures. But your living voice and mighty spirit, which have kindled a spark in so many and fanned the flame in others, has so vividly roused, moved and warmed me that I now know my darkness and I live. Not I, but Christ in me, and I in Christ. In a word you have brought me from famine into plenty, and from cold to heat. Now I no longer vegetate, but feel that I am fervent and full of life, and even able to make many rich by imparting to them the treasures which you have bestowed upon me."

Curioni was honourably received by the senate of Lucca and appointed professor in the college. Before the end of the year (1542?) the pope requested the senate to have him arrested, and conveyed to Rome. They were unwilling to deliver up the innocent, and suggested his escape. As there seemed to be no foothold for usefulness in Italy, he left his family and went to Switzerland, the asylum of the persecuted. He bore letters of recommendation from the Duchess of Ferrara. Through Calvin and Viret, he was appointed director of the protestant school at Lausanne, and prepared to settle in that city. He returned cautiously to Lucca for his wife and children. Having made the arrangements for taking them away, he went into an inn at Pescia to get some refreshment. Just as he had seated himself an inquisitor and his gang, who had tracked his route, appeared at the door, saying, "In the name of God and the chief pontiff, you are my prisoner."

Curioni was astounded. He rose from the table with a knife in his hand, probably unconscious of the fact that he was thus fearfully armed, and intending to deliver himself up. The officers, seeing a large man thus coming toward them, were seized with a sudden panic, and retreated into a corner. He, who had great presence of mind, walked deliberately out of the room, rushed to the stable, mounted his horse, and was away like the wind. A violent storm favoured his escape, and he gratefully acknowledged the hand of God in his deliverance.

Curioni was a teacher for four years at Lausanne, whence he went to Basle, then called the "Swiss Athens." Eminent literary men persuaded him to remain, secured him the professorship of eloquence, and he began the brilliant career which, for twenty-three years made him a light of the reformation. He refused tempting offers from kings and princes, and even the pope pretended to overlook his heresy, and tried to win him back to Rome by the most splendid offers of patronage. But he had at last found his quiet haven, and he continued to teach the foreigners who flocked to his lectures, and the young men whom he received into his family.

Olympia Morata left the court of Renata in 1548, to attend upon her father in his last illness. For some reason she was not received again by the duchess, and this surprising alienation added to her grief for her father's death and her mother's feebleness. But her sorrows were sanctified to her heart, and she resolved to live and die an avowed believer in Christ. She wrote to Curioni, "Oh, how I needed this trial! I had no taste for divine things, or for the reading of the Old and New Testament. If I had remained longer at court, it would have been all over with me and my salvation."

She devoted herself to her invalid mother and her younger sisters, redeeming a wonderful amount of time for study and devotion. At the age of thirteen she had written an elegant "Apology for Cicero;" she had continued to write essays and poems, and now, when dependent upon her own exertions, she may have had plans for winning her way in the world by her pen. But she was interrupted in her studies and her dreams. A young German, who had studied under her father, and taken his degree in medicine, filled with admiration of her talents, and touched with pity for her misfortunes, offered her the best affections of his noble heart. She looked upon Andrew Grunthler as a firm Protestant, of good birth and fortune, a superior scholar, whose literary sympathies would accord with her own, a protector sent by merciful Heaven, and a guardian for her mother and family. They were married; he set out for Germany to secure a professorship; she felt lifted above the petty spites of the court, and while writing him the tenderest letters, gave the sympathies of her great heart to a poor sufferer in the hands of the Inquisition.

It was claimed by the earliest historians that the first[*] modern martyr of Italy was Fannio of Faenza, the son of obscure and humble parents. He was early familiar with the Scriptures, and began to speak to various persons on the doctrines of Christ. At first he seemed to the priests only an ignorant man, but they found he was too wise in the gospel to be tolerated. He was cast into prison, and when thrown off his guard by the entreaties of his wife and children, he yielded, recanted, and was set at liberty. No sooner was he free than his conscience led him to amend his fault by preaching Christ with more zeal than before. He travelled about Romagna, declaring the good tidings openly in every city. If he found but two or three con-

---

[*] According to Scaliger, the first martyr of Italy in the times of the Reformation, was a man named Jacobin. He was not a protestant, but differed a little from the Romish church, for as a journalist declared, "in those days they burnt for a small matter."

verts he was exceedingly happy. One day he was arrested, and told that he was to be cast into the flames; he smiled and said, that his hour was not yet come. He was correct, for he was taken to Ferrara, and he gained many souls in that city. At the pope's order, he was imprisoned for eighteen months in a castle, where his voice was still heard. His wife and sisters visited him, but he would not again yield to their dishonorable proposals. He sent them away in peace, and devoted himself to the conversion of his fellow-prisoners.

Olympia visited him, and was earnest in her entreaties with the governor and other influential persons, but she could not secure his release. Pope Julius III. made it one of his first official acts to order Fannio to be put to death. A messenger came one evening telling him that he was to die. He embraced the bearer of the tidings and thanked him for the message. He spoke to his companions about the happiness of such a death. One said to him, "Whom have you left guardian of your children? have some compassion on them and on your loving wife." He replied, "I have left them in the hands of the best of guardians." "Who is he?" "Our Lord Jesus Christ."

Just then he was bound for the torture. He firmly endured it all, through almost a night of agony. Towards the dawn he was taken to the public square. A crucifix was held up; he said, "Pray do not take the trouble to remind me of

Christ by a bit of wood, for I hold him with lively faith in my heart." He died like Stephen, with the name of Jesus on his lips. He left some writings, almost every sentence of which had a gem of Scripture in it. At the head of all that he wrote was this inscription, "I shall not die but live and declare the works of the Lord."

The signal was given, and soon persecution raged at Ferrara, but Olympia was beyond the reach of the inquisitors. In 1550 she set out with her husband for Germany, after parting in tears from her mother and sisters and taking with her an only brother, Emilio, but eight years old, to support and educate him. We find her at Schweinfurt, the native place of her husband, where he was acting as physician to the Spanish troops. As he had some private fortune, they settled down in a home of their own, little dreaming of a storm. But Maurice of Saxony, under colour of defending the protestants, raised the standard of war. He made a treaty securing his objects, but Albert of Brandenburg, a ferocious bandit warrior stood out against him, made Schweinfurt his strong-hold and sent out his soldiers to pillage the neighbouring country. Maurice and his allied princes resolved to unkennel him, and the place was attacked. Andrew Grunthler had been near to death from a pestilence, but he and his little family concealed themselves in a winecellar while the town was besieged and while the fires and the plague were raging fearfully. The soldiers entered and the pillage began: the hidden ones could save nothing but their lives, and poor Olympia saw her husband twice taken by the soldiers. She ran barefoot and in tattered garments, making ten miles the first day, and suffering from the tertian fever. "But God did not forsake us," she wrote, "for he sent us, while on the way, fifteen crowns in gold by a gentleman whom we did not know, and then led us to other gentlemen who clothed us in a suitable manner. At last we came to this town of Heidelberg where my husband has been made professor of medicine, and we have now as much furniture in the house as we had before."

A few years of sorrow passed, during which many touching letters and poems were written, and Olympia's life was soon to close. The ties between her own and the Curioni family grew bright as golden threads. Violante, the eldest and the highly accomplished daughter of Curioni, had married the worthy Jerome Zanchius, an Italian refugee, now a professor at Strasburg and a distinguished theologian.* Her father, scarcely recovered from a severe illness, wrote to Olympia that Violante had been near to the grave. But she rallied so that she was carried upon a litter all the way from Strasburg to Basle, (ninety miles,) and stayed some months with her parents. These trials called from the pen of the gifted Olympia her last letter. "I

---

* Author of the Treatise on Predestination, translated by Augustus Toplady.

wept for joy," said she, "that you were rescued from the grave. May God preserve you for the service and advantage of the church. I grieve to hear of your daughter's illness, but my grief is diminished by what you say of there being some hope of her recovery. As for me, dear Celio, know that I have no thought of surviving long. I am beyond the reach of medicines. . . . Nothing remains for me but to expire. But as long as my heart beats, I will remember my friends and the benefits I have received from them. I commend the church to your care: let all you do be for its benefit. . . . Heidelberg is deserted; many have fled on account of the plague. I send you the poems which I have been able to recollect and write out since the ruin of Schweinfurt: all my other writings perished. You must be my Aristarchus and polish them. Again farewell."

Before this letter reached Basle, the eyes of Olympia Morata had closed in death, and her spirit had joyfully triumphed in Christ. Her happy departure was described to Curioni, and this bright example was soon a comfort to Violante, who was already in "the valley of the shadow of death." The plague was carrying off its thousands in Strasburg and Basle. In the latter city one street is still called *Todtengasse*, Death street. While Violante lay dying, John Sleidan,* the historian, was dangerously ill of the plague at Strasburg. She

---
* His real name was John Philipson of Sleidan.

thought of him, and said, "Tell Sleidan to take courage and die with joy; I shall soon follow him. If we should be joined by Peter Martyr, what a joyous company to meet Christ!" With a smile on her face, she finally said, "To heaven, to heaven!" and expired.

Her father, who had called her the tenderest names—his little queen, the hope and comfort of his last days—was now in deepest grief. He turned for consolation first to heaven, and then to his household, from which death had already taken several of his thirteen children. The plague carried three other daughters to the tomb; they left behind the clearest evidence of their victory in the Lord.

To this day there hangs in the museum at Basle, a small unartistic picture of a little girl holding a letter in her hand, on which one may read the name, *Dorothea*. Few that pass it by think or know what a chapter of the Italian reformation gathers around it. Dorothea was the second daughter of Celio and Carlotta Curioni. She was born in 1542. When her father came from Lausanne for his family, and had the opportunity of frightening a band of armed inquisitors with a carving knife, and then escaping, this child must have been too young for such a perilous journey as her mother must take. Perhaps this was the chief reason why she was left behind with some kind friends at Lucca. The friendly family adopted her as their own daughter. She became well known to Paleario. He seems to have made her a special favourite while he was absent from his own children. When she was ten years old, her father expressed a wish to have her portrait. Paleario sent it with a letter, in which he says, "a silent picture cannot portray a living soul. If I had been present when it was first begun, I would have had it done in profile, as we see in the ancient coins. . . Physical philosophers declare the countenance to be an index of the mind; so here you see an admirable modesty and a matronly gravity in the expression of the eyes, far beyond her age; this serious look is conjoined with singular gentleness and beauty. . . . I never saw parents more affectionate than they (the family) are to your child. It would pain them to hear her called yours, for they look upon Dorothea as a daughter; not having any children of their own, they vie with each other in loving, educating, and adorning this young girl. May God, the ruler and king of all ages, preserve them, for in these times there are not many who so abound in love, but it seems rather to languish and become extinct among all people. May our Lord Jesus Christ, who only can, sustain us."

Curioni collected and edited the writings of Olympia Morata; paraphrased the gospel of John; edited the works of the eminent William Budæus of Paris; and wrote various works, of which the best was one upon "The Extent of the Kingdom of

God," a work that contained some views which the reformers did not all approve. He felt the greatest anxiety about the conduct and sufferings of the Italian converts, and he addressed them a circular letter, sympathizing with them while under the tyranny of Rome, and counselling them to remain firm in their Christian faith. It was needed, and it may have given many of the martyrs courage. He also published the *One Hundred and Ten Considerations* of Jean Valdes.

This good man lived to weep for the death of two sons who gave promise of eminence, one of whom wrote a history of America. His youngest son, Leo, a scholar and diplomatist, was doing much for the protestants in Poland, when his father wrote him that sorrow and age were pressing him toward the grave. Leo cheerfully gave up a splendid position, and hastened to Basle to comfort his parents in their decline. On the 18th of November, 1569, at the age of sixty-six, Curioni went to the college to deliver his last lecture. Seeing his friend Stefano he said, "What a wretched set of beings we are!" His friend, thinking that he spoke of literary men, replied, "We are more favoured than others." "I do not mean that;" said the venerable professor. "I allude to the infirmity of human nature, and the various miseries to which it is exposed; this makes me rejoice that I shall soon be free." The next Sabbath he partook of the Lord's supper, declared again his faith in Christ, and his agreement with the reformed church, and four days later he ceased to breathe. He was followed to the tomb by a weeping train of students and scholars, and laid in the crypt of the cathedral at Basle, by the side of his three young daughters and his son Augustine. Eighteen years later his wife was laid by his side.

We have dwelt at some length upon the Curioni and Morati families, because they furnish us a picture of the literary character, the heroism, the trials, and the Christian devotion of many of the Italian reformers. We can almost wish that Aonio Palear"io and his family had joined them, before he took such an interest in sending forward the portrait of little Dorothea.

CHAPTER X.

PALEARIO AT MILAN.

(1555-1566.)

It was the custom for every newly-elected pope to change his name on taking the crown and the holy chair; it was well; for when the old name was laid aside there was often one less word to suggest the former wickedness of the "holy father." The name Caraffa was execrable, but the title Paul IV., might secure some reverence towards an aged man, who did not bring to the papal throne a single quality befitting the assumption that he was the "vicar of Christ." What would do for the popes would not, however, do for the people. A loud cry was raised against Conti, the professor of eloquence at Milan, because he changed his name to Majoragio, deriving it from the property that had once belonged to his father. It was imputed to him as a crime; he defended himself, lived it down, passed through a brilliant career, lost his health by severe study, died at forty-one, and left behind him an extraordinary number of writings on various subjects.

To this vacant chair of eloquence at Milan, Paleario was elected, first for one year and afterwards for ten. His friend, Francesco Crasso, whom he had relied upon in defeating the Sienna conspiracy, and of whom he said, "if ever there was a wise man, he is one," was at Milan. To him, probably, the appointment was owing, and to his hospitality Paleario was invited on his arrival in that city. It seems to have been in 1556, for Charles V. had lately resigned his kingdoms to his son, Philip II., and retired to the convent of Yuste. The new professor describes his reception, and gives much good advice to "Lampridio, Doroteo and Fedro T. Paleario, his children and his heart's delight."

"I arrived at Milan on the 17th of October. I am much pleased with the appearance of the city, so much so that if I had not such precious pledges as you to recall me, I might fall in love with this place, and quite forget Tuscany. But there is no place, no assembly, however celebrated, which, without you all, does not appear to me desert and solitary. Crasso received me in the most courteous manner; I am now staying with him. Acting by his advice, I went to visit all the senators at their own houses, to pay them my respects. These great men received me with the utmost politeness and attention. On the 29th, I recited an oration in the temple of the Virgin, at La Scala, in presence of a full assembly of the senate, the governors and the prætors, the treasurers, the professors of the law college, the philosophers, and the people of all ranks. The concourse of people was so great, that not only was the temple overflowing, but all the avenues of the few streets which led to it were filled with crowds of citizens. . . . . I write you all this that you may inform any friends who are interested in our affairs, and that you may be incited to virtue and the love of study. Literature is the only patrimony that I shall be able to give you. Our property is small, our fields are more for beauty than profit. Devastated by the late Siennese war, and without cattle, they scarcely maintain the family. The municipal taxes are doubled, and we are often required to pay tribute beyond our means. See to what a pass our affairs have arrived! What shall I say about your sisters? They are growing up, and will soon become members of other families. They will require a dower, but we have not a penny laid by. If the harvest fails, we shall have no resource but great economy. I shall also restrict myself that I may save a part of my salary, though, indeed, this is not very easy. The long duration of the French war has made everything dearer. If we find such sons-in-law as we wish, some of the Lucchese merchants will furnish us with money, that we may not be altogether unprovided; they are more generous than mighty kings. If you perceive any diminution of friendship on account of my absence, it is your part, my dear Lampridio, as the eldest, to revive and confirm their good-will by writing to them. As flowers are preserved fresh by the falling of the dew, so friendship is kept alive by communication and contact.

"Console, if necessary, your mother; she has great fortitude of mind, and is a truly excellent person, but still she is a woman. Take care of the girls, and watch over that dear boy Fedro, and do not let evil companions spoil him; nor do you let their advice prevail with you, that I may not feel unhappy by being from home while you are so young. If you, as the eldest, govern the house well, I shall, indeed, esteem myself fortunate; for I shall see with my own eyes that which others desire to see after their death. Take your mother's advice . . . . for she is dearer to me than life. Your progress in study gives me very great pleasure, for I wish you, my dear Lampridio, to devote yourself to philosophy, and particularly to Greek literature. Fedro, who I hope will study law, should rather take up Latin, so that every one may know that I am not only so happy as to have good sons; but also sons brought up in my own line of study."

To another friend he wrote, "I am tied here with a very moderate stipend, occupied in public lectures on Latin and Greek. I do not say how much I dislike this work. But I have noble and distinguished scholars, and my labour is not thrown away." He was burdened with pecuniary difficulties and in reference to some aid received, probably from Tuscan friends, he said, "If God had not helped me to get this money, I should have been lost." The senate also came to his aid, and he was able to remove his family to Milan, during the third year of his professorship.

The Milanese authorities had already voted certain privileges to "the most eloquent orator and celebrated poet, Aonio Paleario," who had "brought both honour and distinction" to the city, and who was "eminently deserving of being relieved from every burden and inconvenience, and of being gratified by every favour and honour, in consideration of his virtue and learning, and of the well-proved and singular assiduity with which he instructs the Milanese youth, daily rendering them more noble and accomplished." He therefore had a good foundation for the following appeal to them: "Aonio Paleario, invited some years ago to teach the Milanese youth, lived with one servant only at an inn, and would not make use of the diploma of Privileges, in order to avoid burdening the state for his private advantage. But now he has taken a house and brought his family from Tuscany and has to support them at great expense and inconvenience, in consequence of the extreme scarcity of provisions. He begs that those privileges, which were given him without asking, may now be confirmed." The councillors, in March 1559, ordered to be granted him, "a sum of money sufficient for the support of seven persons, both for wine, corn and meat." This was to be paid him every year dating from the first of January last."

Paleario had met with prejudice at Sienna and Lucca, while labouring to cultivate a taste for the higher branches of knowledge, and he knew the danger of urging his students to explore the rich mines opened to them in the word of God. He had not the full courage of Curioni or Morato Fulvio, or he would already have been driven from his country or crushed by the inquisition. At Milan he had to struggle against the same prejudices and be exposed to the wayward caprices of unlearned men. In those days, philosophy, or as we would say science, was almost a forbidden subject. Paleario dared to say something, and he advised his hearers to press their inquiries into the sciences, for, "while searching out the secrets of nature, they may elevate their thoughts to heaven, and contemplate the divine mind which presides over the stars and rules the world; thus in this extensive sphere of knowlege, imitating the Divinity, that we may also live a heavenly life, not existing for ourselves alone, but for our country, our relations and friends, and for the whole human race."

He looked forward to a congress of sovereigns at Milan, and wrote an oration on peace, which he never delivered, for the congress was not held. Among other things, he referred to the religious differences then prevailing, and still clung to the hope that a general council would be called to reform abuses and unite all parties in their opinions. He appreciated the importance of the revived doctrines and said that "Every one felt an earnest desire to hear and understand these things. Theologians were sought far and near; the variety of their expositions and their popular eloquence in public preachings gave rise to so many sects, that in the towns and villages and in the country, there was scarcely a house or assembly where there was not a difference of opinion about religion." The fact of such divisions might well be deplored as an evil, but he did not clearly perceive the remedy. It was not to be cured by articles of agreement framed in a council of princes and scholars, but by a more thorough knowledge of the Scriptures.

In a letter to the new Emperor Ferdinand, to whom he had dedicated his poem on the Immortality of the Soul, he wrote, as having "grown old together" with him, and rejoicing that the nations under his rule were also under the government of "our Lord and Saviour Jesus Christ." Nobly does he say, "My mind is still impressed with the ideas of my youth, and the expectation of great things from you, in whose hand God, the Father of our Lord Jesus Christ, has placed so many kingdoms and people. . . . one to whom God has finally assigned the care of the empire, so that it is not I but Christ who speaks. Endeavour, O Ferdinand, pious emperor of the Romans, to meditate on these things, and prepare so to act that the heavenly kingdom of Christ, disturbed by hatreds, divided by parties of evil men and the licentiousness of those from whom it was least expected, may be restored to peace."

The invasion of the Turks created a panic in the cities and universities; many fled to safer regions. At first Paleario thought it unmanly to flee, and said, "that as good always follows exertion, I would have followed the example of those who know how to die in a holy manner for Christ." But it seems that prudence was finally considered the better part of valour, and he sought a cool retreat somewhere on the Adriatic shores. One motive may have been to enjoy a summer's vacation. To some friend he wrote in playful style, congratulating him on the birth of a son, "Imagine myself in your place, would I not have rejoiced? Your joys are mine. . . As there are great meetings of matrons on the first birth in a family, I mean to send you some pictures to ornament your house. I take pleasure in the muses as connected with my studies. . . . Tell me what you like best, for in these things I am a true Damasippus [a virtuoso, or dealer in antiques.] If you give a dinner, I will send you some oysters and delicious fish from our villas, which are near the sea, if the sumptuary law is not passed. If so, it must be obeyed; but I will at least send you what is not forbidden by law; apples, mushrooms, grapes, sweet herbs, pinks, roses, and other flowers, of which our gardens are as full as yours in spring, though now a rose is as rare with you as a white bird. Everything I have is yours as well as mine."

This touch of generosity and good-humour was no unusual impulse with Paleario; it was a trait of his nature. He began to feel that he could afford to be generous. He was appreciated at Milan. With his family around him in a pleasant home, he enjoyed his comforts with gratitude. He could say to the senate, "Nothing is wanting to our city; placed as the light of Italy, it shines with brilliance, and is distinguished for its courtesy and magnificence. It is now ten years, senators, that I have lived among you. Not a year has passed without my being laden with your benefits. First, I was invited by royal letters to come into Tuscany, and an ample stipend assigned me. Then I was honoured with privilege, and immunities were granted me; afterwards my salary was increased. Finally, you have taken into consideration my old age and failing health, and have arranged for me to live here comfortably with my family. . . . Never will your favours be forgotten, and meanwhile, neither fatigue nor idleness shall ever prevent me from fulfilling the public duties appointed me, and I shall continue to instruct the rising youth in the purest literature. . ."

He had leased a house for nine years, but the heirs of the original owner sought to take the house from him after he had made various improvements. He appealed to the senate, saying, "All this expense and trouble Aonio incurred, in the hope of making the house useful in his profession of teaching, and of being able to use the garden for instructing the youth who came to him." The senate may have imagined that Aristotle was on earth again, when they learned of his habit of walking with students in the garden; but whether they confirmed his right to the lease does not appear.

In the meantime Paleario kept up an active correspondence with the reformers at Basle, for Curioni was still living. A certain Bartolomeo Orello, a simple, honest man, went back and forth as a carrier, trading perhaps a little along the way to make good his expenses. From the presses at Basle many works were sent forth into Italy. Paleario was having a book printed by Thomas Guarini; three hundred copies were sent to him, so badly printed that he sent the money to pay for the labour, and said, "As I do not choose my book to circulate in Italy with so many mistakes and errors, I make you a present of the volumes and the money also." Guarini had inserted a statement, contrary to orders, that the whole work had been revised and authorized by Paleario. "This," says the author, "gives occasion to the Inquisitor to read the book and carp at it. . . . You are happy in your country, but we poor wretches get into such trouble for the most trifling thing, that we are quite weary of life."

The little book on the "Benefit of Christ's Death" had been making no small stir in the world. As early as 1544, Catarino of Sienna, changing the law for a monk's cowl, turning from being an admirer of Savonarola to an accuser, and devoting himself to writing violent philippics against heretical works, came across the "Beneficio." He honoured it by exposing those precious doctrines which he called heresy. It was placed in the "blessed catalogue" of prohibited books. The excellent bishop Vergerio wrote in its defence, saying, "Many are of opinion that in our day nothing has ever been written in Italian, so sweetly pious and simple, or so calculated to instruct the weak and ignorant, especially in the article of justification. I may add, that Reginald Pole, an English cardinal, the intimate friend of Morone, was thought to be the author of this book, or at least to have had a considerable share in its composition. It is, however, certain that he both defended it and promoted its diffusion, in unison with his friends Flaminio, Priuli, and others of his school."

The first biographer of Paul IV. (Caraffa, the originator of the Inquisition,) mentions "a pedant called Angelo, who stayed a long time at Venice, and from that city sent to his accomplices the pestiferous books, *del Beneficio di Christo;*" also, "a Modenese bookseller, Antonio Gadaldino, a thorough heretic, with all his family; he sold a great many copies of the *Beneficio di Christo*, a most pernicious book, which taught in the Lutheran style, justification by faith alone, imputed through the merits of Christ. . . . This same book was so precious to the heretics that they printed it many times.* . . . Cardinal Cortese of Mordena, though a Benedictine monk, and highly esteemed for his learning and excellence, was called to account for having read and approved the book. . . . It was printed repeatedly by order of (Cardinal) Morone, and deceived many because it treated of justification in an attractive but heretical manner, attributing it all to faith. . . . It made light of works and merits, and this being the article on which so many prelates and friars of that age stumbled, it spread very widely, and was by many approved; in Verona alone it was understood and disapproved."

This writer in guessing at the author, ascribes it to "a monk of San Severino in Naples, a Sicilian, and a disciple of Valdes." This was coming somewhere nearer the mark than many others, for Paleario was doubtless of San Severino lineage, and he may have been spoken of in that connection. While the "golden little book on the merits of Christ's death" was giving so much trouble to the inquisitors of pope Caraffa, it was affording consolation to the innumerable readers of the forty thousand copies which were in circulation during the life-time of the author.

The bookseller, Gadaldino, who was such a "heretic with all his family," was considered worthy

* In six years 60,000 copies were printed at Venice alone. Large editions were published elsewhere. . . In Rome piles of it as high as houses were burnt." *Kurtz's Church History.*

of persecution in his old age. He was "one of the first to introduce forbidden books in the mother-tongue." At Modena he was one of the "literati," who took delight in hearing the friar Pergola, described by a Romanist as one who "preaches the gospel, and never mentions male or female saints, nor the fathers of the church, nor Lent, nor fasting, nor many other things; which preaching was much to the taste of the academicians." Many an "heretical Lutheran book" was found in the houses of the citizens, and traced to the shop of the old book-seller. He began to be widely known and bitterly hated, for if his books were burned, he bought and printed new editions, especially of the "Beneficio," which was a great favourite with him. The pope had him arrested, when he feared that Gadaldino could not be removed, on account of "his age and decrepitude." His sons went to the Duke of Modena, fell at his feet bathed in tears, pleading for "their poor infirm old father," and asking that the pope would allow him to be tried in his own city. It was all in vain. The venerable man was taken to Bologna, kept in prison for several years, and finally released. He died at the age of ninety years.

CHAPTER XI.

MARTYRDOM OF PALEARIO.
1566–1570.

WHEN Paleario seemed happily settled at Milan, he was startled to learn of the arrest of a noble friend, by the Inquisitors. This opened his eyes to the perils in which he was placed.

Pietro Carnesecchi was a Florentine, descended from a noble family. He was, from youth, a man that none could fail to notice on account of his fine appearance, his elegant manners, his liberal education and his generous spirit. He was secretary and then apostolic notary to Clement VII., and so great was his influence that it was often said, " the church is governed by Carnesecchi rather than by Clement." Yet his modesty and kindness insured him against the jealousy of the papal court. The pope gave him an abbey at Naples and another in France. After the death of Clement he was arrested in his worldly career (for it was *worldly*) by the true light from heaven.

He went to Naples and heard Valdes interpret the Scriptures. There he formed a lasting friendship with Flaminio, each of them a poet. Others of that Christian band held a large place in his heart. He received the reformed or rather the *revived* doctrines, and was willing to follow Christ with all his soul. His aim seemed to be "the discovery of truth, in spite of all obstacles which we find in custom, antiquity or human authority." He severely felt the death of Valdes (1540,) and when far away from Naples, must have shed tears when reading the following words from a friend, " Would to God we could return (to Naples.) But I keep thinking, where should we go, now that Valdes is dead? This has been a great loss for us and for the world; because Signor Valdes was one among the rare men of Europe. The writings which he has left us on the Epistles of St. Paul and the Psalms of David give full proof of this. He was undoubtedly, both in words and deeds, a most accomplished man."

Carnesecchi travelled through Italy, forming the acquaintance of various persons, who were seeking the same rest for the soul that he was seeking. He met Paleario at Venice. He became a guide to many who were halting between the Roman church and the Divine Christ. He extended the most generous hospitalities to all who visited him, gave money to those in need, and encouraged the youth in their study of the Scriptures. There was one lady who corresponded with him, and if their letters could be found they would, no doubt, throw increasing light upon the reformation in Italy. But the Inquisition took care that this source of information should be destroyed or locked up in the Vatican.

This lady was the beautiful and accomplished Julia Gonzaga. In early life she had married Vespasian Colonna, an aged widower with one daughter, a brave warrior with but one leg and one arm, and an invalid in need of tender handling. His moral qualities were worthy of her, and he regarded her as nearly angelic. When he died she was the Duchess of Trajelto and Fondi. She was living in retirement at Fondi on the Calabrian coast, when the Turkish pirates landed one night, pushed on to the town and prepared for their work of plunder. A faithful servant heard them at the walls, gave the alarm and she escapèd through a window, barefoot and hoodless. Mounting a horse, she made her way across the mountains to a refuge. Her house was burned, and the rich tombs of her kindred despoiled. Amid these adversities she married Ippolito de Medici, and her step-daughter Isabella became the wife of the strong Luigi Gonzaga, Julia's brother. Lawsuits grew out of these marriages, and in 1537, the lady Julia went to Naples to secure her rights. There she heard of the little gatherings where Valdes presided and taught the Scriptures, and instead of troubling herself with the law she consoled herself with the gospel. She met some of the most eminent of those inquirers who afterwards were the shining lights of Italy. Among them was Carnesecchi. She cast in her lot with those reformers, and was ready for the trial by persecution. Isabella lost in battle her husband, to whom she had given a gem set in a gold ring on which were engraved two eyes that were to charm him when in war. This ring was a theme for six poets, one of whom was Paleario.

Carnesecchi fell under suspicion of heresy, was summoned to Rome, examined and absolved. He prudently went to France, where he read the writings of the reformers, confirmed his faith, and returned to Venice. He was there cited before the Inquisition,* but declined to appear. Then came excommunication and orders for his arrest. He remained fearless; he had counted the cost, and was prepared for it. He supplied the "heretics" with money, the reformed books, and sent aid to the refugees at Geneva. Among the books which he was accused of reading, was the "Benefit of Christ's death."

He went to Florence, where he put himself under the protection of Duke Cosmo, his intimate friend and former companion. Soon immense bonfires of books were seen blazing in public squares; troops

---

* Certain Romish writers extol the Inquisition for proving so efficient in crushing out the Reformation in Italy. Caracciola, in his Life of Paul IV. (the cruel Caraffa) says, of the Inquisition: "Before its institution in various cities of Italy, and particularly at Florence, there were so many Macchiavelli and Carnesecchi that scarcely a vestige of the Catholic faith remained." This horrid engine of cruelty saved Romanism from being almost extinguished! The weapons of Rome were carnal. She was afraid of the truth.

of monks were shouting their triumphs and uttering their threats. Cardinal Alessandro was the chief Inquisitor, a man whom the aged pope had threatened to imprison, and who was determined to make an example of Carnesecchi. The inquisitor suddenly became the pope, (Pius V.,) and he at once sent orders to the duke for the surrender of his friend. One day Carnesecchi was the guest of his sovereign, and when at dinner the orders came, with an officer to execute them. The duke permitted the capture—perhaps was in the plot. This Christian gentleman was conveyed to Rome, and put in prison.

It seems that Julia Gonzaga was in danger of being cited before the Inquisition; but her brothers were her defenders. The Gonzaga family were hard to manage. They were of the emperor's party, and opposed to the pope. Ferrante had helped to capture and sack Rome, and was disposed to do the like again if there was occasion. Moreover, death released her from peril, but her correspondence with Carnesecchi was brought forward as evidence against him. Of the trial we should know little, had not a Florentine ambassador at Rome, kept a journal, in which there are references to Carnesecchi from July 5th, 1566, to October 3d, 1567. The prisoner was so steadfast in his faith that the ambassador thought him beside himself. The pope was unyielding, although the journalist kissed his toe, and urged every plea that he could for mercy. He tells how the martyr was deprived of his honours, property and benefices; degraded by having his fingers and brow scraped, for they had been touched with the oil of consecration; clad with "an overcoat painted all over with flames of fire," and ten days afterwards, "beheaded on the bridge and then burned." The ambassador then exclaims, "May it have pleased God to compassionate him in the moment of death; for before it, by what I can learn, he had not laid aside any of his previous opinions."

After this martyrdom, terror and alarm prevailed throughout Italy. The new pope had signified to all the faithful what they might expect. It was a crime to read Paleario's book, the *Beneficio di Christo*. The author of it had cause for alarm. He had written another book of a more fearful tendency, as long ago as 1542. It bore the title of, "A Testimony and Accusation against the Popes." It had not been published, and he sought a safe place for the manuscripts. He carefully made up his package, gave his faithful messenger Orello due cautions, and sent it to Theodore Zuinger, a learned physician of Basle. In a new preface to it he said: "If hitherto the most highly-gifted or most holy persons could not escape danger and reproach, unless they conformed to the will of the popes, how could I, who am humble and needy, oppose myself to the papal wrath? I perceived that I was likely to lose every comfort in this world, except Christ; that every access to worldly honour and prosperity would be closed; that I would utterly alienate kind friends from the pope's party; that I should lose in a moment the fruit of years of study and diligence, and not only be deprived of my little tract of land, but be forced also to separate myself from my friends, my excellent wife and my dear children, to leave Italy and live in solitude, or be the inmate of a prison and finally be put to death. . . . I have undertaken to defend a cause against which nothing true can be said. What then have I to fear?"

In a few months he received a letter from Zuinger, saying, "That the literary world was under great obligations to Paleario for the number of eminent scholars he had made; that he would benefit the church by his writings; that the manuscript brought by Orello, could easily be put into a chest with two locks; but that Zuinger did not feel himself competent to bring it before a general council, as Paleario intended should be done. He advised the author to entrust it to some eminent divines, such as professors Sulzer and Cocceius."

Paleario replied, "The letter sent to you by Orello being full of theology, in which I now take more delight than in oratory, I feared would be tedious to you. Your kindness has comforted me. I am growing old, my dear Theodore; I often think of my departure to Christ, and occupy myself in whatever I think most pleasing to him to whose service I have dedicated myself from my youth up.

For when the Emperor Charles V. and the German princes resolved to hold a general council at Mantua, (1542,) I wrote, at the peril of my life, a testimony to be read there in the presence of the pope. As this council never met, I also wrote an accusation (*actio*.) This work, now entrusted to you, I am anxious should not be utterly lost; but that in due time it may appear with advantage. . . . In this paper there is nothing monstrous, nothing impious, nothing contrary to religion. Every word is corroborated by the word of God, and approved by your own theologians. In order not to give offence, I have cautiously avoided touching those points which have given rise to such controversy between the Swiss and German churches. Let each remain in his own opinion until all are united in one body. Oh! may God, the Father of our Lord Jesus Christ, grant that all may be of one mind. When, at the request of pious nations, the emperor, the kings and Christian princes, shall assemble in one place with the pastors of the churches, and the most distinguished theologians, to regulate all things according to the gospel, I desire that these, my writings, may be presented as possessing the power to slay the evil genius of the churches. Wherefore, though the author's name be suppressed, it may not please the senate to have them speedily published. . . . They will give too much room to cavillers, sophists, and enemies of the gospel. If we are to fight face to face, it is better that the enemy should not know what weapons we have. It would be madness to communicate our arguments to those whom we are about to combat."

In imagination Paleario had such a council before him, and he says, "The time is come to give a firm and holy testimony for Christ. For in years past, when we were threatened with rods, fire, and other horrors, we were unable to declare our faith, piety or devotion to Christ: we had then perhaps some excuse for silence: for had we then braved every danger, we would not have materially assisted our brethren. But now when the opportunity is offered us by this same God and Father . . . why should we refuse to be mocked and scourged of men or thrown into the fire? It is not the first time that these things have happened to the followers of Christ. . . . We shall suffer all things willingly by taking courage, and thinking, not whether we can keep hold of life, but how we can die for him and go to him; and thus, not with words but with blood, leave a witness to posterity. I, Aonio, servant of Jesus Christ, here depose a firm testimony that if necessary, I do not refuse to die for that faith which I owe to Christ as the author of my peace and salvation."

Paleario had some expectation of being driven out of Italy as appears from the new preface to the Testimony. The seizure of Carnesecchi had involved many persons, although the tortures could not draw from him the name of any one then living in Italy, who held the true faith. The times grew worse. 'Reports of arrests came from all quarters. The archbishop of Milan was putting his foot upon the necks of the laymen, who like Paleario dared to think for themselves and to believe in Christ. Inquisitors, who knew every hiding-place, were scouring the north of Italy, and many victims were hurried to Rome.

It was soon the turn of another eminent scholar, our heroic veteran Paleario. It seems that he was thinking of removing to Bologna, when the Friar Cremona accused him of heresy. He passed through twelve months of perplexity, during which he doubtless might have fled from Milan, but he remained upon the ground. He then addressed a letter to the Senate.

"A year has now passed, O Senators, since I was accused by the Reverend Father Inquisitor, a Milanese. Nothing more distressing has happened to me during my whole life. A most extraordiary conspiracy has been formed against me, on account of a Latin oration which I wrote more than twenty-five years ago. By this accusation I am obliged to separate myself from your young men, whom you invited me from Tuscany to instruct. Now the Inquisitor lays before me an edict, and orders me in the shortest possible time to remove to the city of Rome, and until he can name the day, he retains me in the college of the Holy Roman Inquisition. . . . I am advanced in age and my health is uncertain, yet I make no difficulty in undertaking the long journey: but I wish to finish the last months of my annual occupation, and then receive my salary. If the Inquisition will not allow this, I must nevertheless pay a debt contracted in your city, and have money for the journey, and for my maintenance in Rome. May it please God to grant my desire of being liberated from this unworthy accusation, and of returning to the office of lecturer assigned to me by you. I beg of you . . . to grant me one of the quarters of my pension, which from no fault of mine has been retained. Then I may obey the orders of the Father Inquisitor." Whether this request was granted is not known.

On what were the suspicions against him founded? The oration mentioned was that written in his own defence in 1542, twenty-five years before. The Jesuit Laderchi says that the chief cause was, his having published "a little book, in which he artfully concealed the mortal poison of heresy, and had on this account been persecuted by two friars, and threatened by the Inquisition. This 'poison' had taken such hold of him, that in an oration, written for the fathers of the Siennese republic, he repeated the same things without shrinking from making them public." This little book was the *Beneficio;* the "poison" was the doctrine of justification by faith.

Did Paleario reflect with sorrow upon the mysterious influences of early friendships? Did he bitterly recall the little disappointments of his early life, out of which had gradually grown his exposures to death? The friendship of Cincio Phrygipani had led him to rely on him for means to go from Sienna to Padua: but it ended in disappointment. He prepared to start, but must delay, for Cincio had disappointed him. Then he met Bellanti, and formed a new and lasting friendship. This led him into the courts, where he incurred the wrath of Cotta and his band. Ten years later Cotta attempted to crush him, and he wrote an oration in self-defence. The restless Cotta gloried in seeing him disappointed in his request for a professorship at Sienna, and Paleario seemed afterwards to find disappointments even from the good offices of his friends, and now the long series of influences culminates; he is arrested for the sake of his old friendships, his defence of his friends, his defence of himself, and his defence of the gospel. But perhaps Cincio and the Bellanti family had been brought to a true faith through his instrumentality. At least their love had long been a comfort to him. He had no disposition to regret those influences, for they were a cord in which was clearly visible one bright thread wrought in it by the hand of God.

From his enemies we have but slight notices of his trial. Had he recanted they would have given a fuller record to the world. His journey to Rome, his imprisonment, his examination, his sufferings are all wrapt in obscurity. Whether he was tortured we know not. The secret archives may one day reveal the desperate revenge of his enemies upon a layman who had been the friend of the best cardinals, and who had dared to show forth the benefits of Christ's death. From these archives a popish annalist says he drew the following chief heads of the accusation:

I. He denied the existence of purgatory.

II. He disapproved of burying people in churches.

III. He despised all religious orders and dresses, which distinguished the monks.

IV. He attibuted justification and the remission of sins solely to Jesus Christ, through faith in him.

Laderchi declares that "he fully approved of all the heretical doctrines written in various commentaries, and that there was no error of Œcolampadius, Luther, Bucer or other heretics, which he had not embraced. Like Erasmus he denied the studies of our (Romish) divines, and asserted that the Scriptures through their neglect, had been laid aside, and that it was owing to heretics (Reformers) that they were drawn from obscurity and studied afresh in new translations. Besides the expressions in his oration, he in fact confessed his heresies. More are to be found in the original trial, words pronounced by himself, which prove that he was a thorough heretic worthy of the severest punishment."

The venerable old man, who had long before

thought that his were not the "times for a Christian to die in his bed," saw that there was no hope of deliverance from martyrdom. No mercy was to be expected from those who were eager to dip their hands in his blood. No judge was there to give him a fair hearing if he should hold up the Scriptures and prove that he simply held the faith of the apostles and early martyrs. No law was there but that of the pope, and that pope was the terrible Pius V. He therefore could only say to the judges, "If your eminences have so many credible witnesses aganst me, there is no need of giving yourselves or me any farther trouble. I am resolved to act as the blessed apostle Peter* advises, when he says, 'Christ suffered for us, leaving us an example that we should follow his steps; who did no sin neither was guile found in his mouth; who when he was reviled, reviled not again; when he suffered he threatened not; but committed himself to him that judgeth righteously.' Judge therefore and condemn Aonio, satisfy my adversaries, and fulfil your office."

This speech, so full of heroic Christianity, is described by his enemies as a "burst of fury." Every Christian will rather exclaim with Schelhorn, "Here is the patience and the faith of the saints!" Laderchi says, "Not all the pains bestowed could reclaim him from the darkness of error to the light

---

* A most severe rebuke inasmuch as the popes claimed to be the successors of Peter in the papal chair.

of truth. He richly merited not only to be destroyed by fire here below, but to be devoted to eternal flames." Words lose their meaning when they come from such a cruel heart.

It was the custom to send a condemned heretic to the prison of Torre di Nona, belonging to the city. Carnesecchi was ten days there before his execution. How long Paleario was there cannot now be ascertained. He was probably three years in his entire imprisonment at Rome. There was a society of Florentines in Rome, named the *Misericordia*, organized for the merciful purpose of visiting and comforting persons condemned to death. It was established in 1488, and it still exists; at their anniversary they bury all the halters used during the year in the cloisters of their church. When informed that their services were needed, they sent four of their most devoted brethren to pass the night with the condemned person, exhort him to penitence and patience, and to set before him the sufferings of Christ as an example—perhaps not as an atonement. They assisted him in writing letters, in making a will, and in preparing for death. It may have been their privilege to attend upon Paleario during his last days. At least, by some means, he wrote the following letters from his prison, where he dare not give a full account of his views and hopes, lest his last messages of affection should not be allowed to pass out of the inquisitor's hands.

"My Dearest Wife:—I would not have you to be sorrowful at my happiness, or to take ill my good. The hour is come in which I shall pass from this life to my Lord and Father and God. I go there as willingly as to the marriage of the Son of the great King, which I have always entreated my Lord, in his great goodness and infinite liberality, to grant me. So, my beloved wife, console yourself in the will of God, and in my satisfaction, and devote yourself to the disconsolate family which remain; bring them up and keep them in the fear of God, and be to them both father and mother. I am already past seventy years old and useless. My sons must strive by virtue and by toil to live honourably. God the Father, and our Lord Jesus Christ, and the communion of the Holy Ghost be with your spirit.
Rome, 3d *July*, 1570."

"To Lampridio and Fedro, my beloved sons:— These most courteous gentlemen do not fail in their kindness to me to the very last, and they allow me to write to you. It has pleased God to call me to himself in the manner which you will hear, and which will appear to you hard and bitter; but if you consider it well, and that it is my greatest pleasure to conform myself to the will of God, you also must be satisfied. I leave you for patrimony, virtue and diligence, as also the little property which you possess. I do not leave you any debts; many ask sometimes who ought to give. You were freed more than eighteen years ago; you are not bound for my debts. If you are called upon to pay them, have recourse to his excellency, the duke, who will not see you wronged. I gave Lampridio the account of debt and credit; with your mother's dower bring up your little sister as God shall give you grace. Salute Aspasia and sister Aonilla, my beloved daughters in the Lord. My hour approaches. May the Spirit of God console you and preserve you in his grace.

Rome, 3d July, 1570."

It appears that Paleario had seven children, five of whom were living when he wrote from his prison; two sons and three daughters. Aspasia was married to Fulvio della Rena, a physician. Aonilla became a nun in a convent at Colle. Aganippe was, probably, the little sister whom her father wished to see "brought up as God should give grace." His sons had grown up and entered upon a learned profession. They could inherit nothing; the very property which should pay his debts was forfeited. By a refinement of cruelty, the children of heretics were made beggars, and branded with ignominy. It appears, from a somewhat doubtful authority, that Fedro Paleario had a daughter Sofonisba, who shone with brilliance at the court of Florence, and was educated and given an inheritance by Duke Cosimo. No direct descendants of Aonio Paleario are known, except through this grand-daughter.

Paleario had made several draughts of his will in

different years. He first left "all his writings and expositions of the Holy Scriptures" to members of the Bellanti family. But some of them went to Basle. One article inserted in 1550, reads like irony: "he leaves to the most holy nail of Colle the devotion which he bears to this relic." In another, he charges the parish and council of Colle, if they should finally become his heirs, " to see that every Sunday in the parish church of Colle the gospel of Jesus Christ, in the four Evangelists and the Epistles of St. Paul, and the canonical Epistles, be read and explained in the vulgar tongue. If this should be suspended for a year, then he substitutes the hospital of St. Maria Nuova at Florence, as his heir." In the registers of Colle there are entries concerning Paleario and his sons, showing that they had filled certain municipal offices.

There has been found a paper which assumes to be a report of the Misericordia society, and which reads thus: "On Sunday night our company was summoned, and on Monday, the 3d of July, 1570, Messer Aonio Paleario of Veroli, an inhabitant of Colle di Val d'Elsa, was consigned to us in Tordinone, as condemned and sentenced by the ministers of the holy Inquisition. Who confessed and penitently asked pardon of God and of his glorious mother, V. Maria, and of all the court of heaven, and said he wished to die as a good Christian, and that he believed all that the holy Roman church believes. He did not make any will except giving us the two letters below, written with his own hand, entreating us to send them to his wife and children at Colle di Val d'Elsa. The holy mass was then celebrated, and at the usual hour he was taken to the bridge, where he was hanged, and then burned."

We can believe all this except the statement of his returning to the Roman church. Under the cowl of those friendly monks there was, perhaps, a heart that loved the church more than the truth. Forgeries have been often put forth concerning the last hours of those who died by torture in Rome. If he recanted or made such concessions, why was he "hanged and then burned?" Why was not the report published at once, so as to prevent the many friends of this distinguished man, and the thousands who were reading his little book, from circulating their opinion that he died true to his faith? Why did his enemies themselves declare that he died "hardened and obstinate," and that "nothing could reclaim him?" Why did those Romanists who searched the archives of the Inquisition find nothing to prove, or even hint his recantation? Had he conceded to the views of his attendants, his last two letters would have contained something quite different from what we read in them.

It has been said that Paleario differed in two points from most Protestants: the first, that marriage was a sacrament; but M'Crie says, "He appears to me merely to mean that it was a divine or sacred ordinance;" the second, that he considered it unlawful to take an oath on any occasion in a court of justice, thus anticipating the view now held by the Society of Friends.

The writings of Paleario were various, and appeared in many editions. The "Testimony against the Papacy," sent in manuscript to Basle, seems not to have been disclosed there, or was sent back to Sienna, when it was found in 1596, in the author's hand-writing. It was printed at Leipsic in 1606. So great an impression did it make that a Romish writer declared, that Paleario was condemned to be burned, not chiefly for his "simple piety," but for having written "the Accusation against the Popes," and for his letter to Calvin, Luther and others, in reference to the Council of Trent. But "the Accusation" was not known for a long time after his martyrdom. It is gratifying to learn that it has recently been translated into Italian by two ex-priests of Rome.

The eminent historical advocate for civil and religious liberty, De Thou (Thuanus,) says that "the writings of Paleario show his great erudition" and that "he was put to death at Rome, because he had said that the Inquisition was a deadly weapon for literary men." Saxi, in 1780 described Paleario as "an orator, poet, philosopher and philologist cruelly put to death by Pius V.," and cites a large number of writers who mention him with honour. McCrie says, "When we take into consideration his talents, his zeal, the utility of his writings and the sufferings which he endured, Paleario must be viewed as one of the greatest ornaments of the Reformed cause in Italy."

THE
BENEFIT OF CHRIST'S DEATH,

OR

THE GLORIOUS RICHES OF GOD'S FREE GRACE, WHICH EVERY TRUE BELIEVER RECEIVES BY JESUS CHRIST, AND HIM CRUCIFIED.

BY

AONIO PALEARIO,

FIRST WRITTEN IN ITALIAN, AND NOW REPRINTED FROM AN ANCIENT ENGLISH TRANSLATION.

EDITED BY THE
Rev. WM. M. BLACKBURN,
AUTHOR OF
"AONIO PALEARIO AND HIS FRIENDS," &c.

PHILADELPHIA:
PRESBYTERIAN BOARD OF PUBLICATION,
No. 821 Chestnut Street.

CONTENTS.*

CHAPTER I.

	PAGE
Of original sin, and man's wretchedness	15

CHAPTER II.

How the law was given by God, to the end that we, knowing our sin, and not having any hope of ability to make ourselves righteous by our own works, should have recourse to God's mercy, and unto the righteousness of faith......... 18

CHAPTER III.

How the forgiveness of our sins, justification, and salvation, depend only on Jesus Christ......... 22

CHAPTER IV.

Of the effects of lively faith, and of the union of man's soul with Christ......... 34

CHAPTER V.

In what wise the Christian is clothed with Jesus Christ............ 67

CHAPTER VI.

Certain remedies against distrust......... 78

* This table of contents is taken from the edition of 1638.

PALEARIO AND HIS BOOK.

THE learned layman, Aonio Paleario, has been recognized for nearly three centuries as one of the eminent reformers and martyrs of Italy. He was born about the year 1500, at Veroli, where the Roman Campagna borders on the kingdom of Naples. He was left an orphan at an early age, with a small property, which he sold after it was desolated by the armies that aided in the sack of Rome, A. D. 1527. He applied a generous part of the proceeds to restore his mother's tomb, and inscribe upon a monument the names of his family. From this we learn that Matteo Paleario and Clara Janarilla were his "most excellent parents," and that he had three "most honest sisters."

When his native town and his bishop, Filonardi, had done all they could for his education, he went to Rome, studied in one of the colleges, and became the private secretary of a nobleman—probably Cardinal Cesarini. He stored his mind with the new classical learning, and secured the friendship of some of the greatest men of his country and of the Roman church. But he was of too independent a spirit to be the menial of a cardinal; perhaps, also, he was disgusted with the papal court, and he went northward, seeking for teachers who could instruct him in philosophy.

Little events often determine human destiny. Aonio, a young man of thirty, was at Sienna, waiting impatiently for his rich young friend Cincio to join him, and go with him to Padua. Cincio had promised to pay all expenses. They were to study together in the university. After many disappointments, Paleario was about to go alone, when he met Antonio Bellanti, visited him in his castle and won his heart. Then one year was spent at Padua. Bellanti, a tribune of the people, was arraigned before the senate of Sienna, and he summoned Paleario as his lawyer, to defend him. The triumph over the accusers was complete. But one of them, Ottone Melio Cotta, determined to have his revenge upon the eloquent champion.

Paleario bought the ancient villa of Ceciniano, near Colle and Sienna, married, taught, practised law, published a poem on Immortality, and wrote a little book on the benefits which Christians receive from the death of Christ. This book was published anonymously about the year 1543. It became known to certain monks of Sienna. They were angry because he had aided the heirs of Bellanti in prosecuting them for having robbed their grandmother of a sum of money. Three hundred conspirators banded together, twelve of whom swore not to eat nor drink until Paleario was destroyed. Chief of them all was Cotta. Paleario was in danger of death for heresy. He wrote an oration, which his devoted friend, Cardinal Sadolet, declared to be "highly polished and dignified, and of thundering eloquence." It is not known whether the trial was instituted, for there are no records of it to be found, but Paleario in some way gained his cause. The oration was not to be forgotten.

There can be no reasonable doubt that the book which Paleario wrote, and described in his oration, is the same book which had such an immense circulation, and bore the title of "The Benefit of Christ's Death."*

We here insert the description which Paleario gave of his own book, in his oration at Sienna. It goes far to prove him the author of the book now reprinted. He says, "In it (the book) I spoke of that order and series of things which has its origin from eternity; of the kingdom prepared and established by God before the foundation of the world, of which Christ is the only head, author and governor; of the abrogated law and of the heavy yoke of bondage: I said as much on this point as these wretched times would permit, not indeed all I would have wished to say, for to enter fully on this subject there is no place exempt from peril. . . . It was made a subject of accusation against me, that in this same year, [1542,] I had written in Italian *on the great benefits* which accrue to mankind from his [Christ's] death. . . I said that, since he in whom divinity resided has poured out his life's blood so lovingly for our salvation, we ought not to doubt the goodwill of heaven; but may promise ours s the greatest tranquillity and peace. I affirmed, agbly to the most unquestionable monuments of antiquit, that those who turn with their souls to Christ crucified, commit themselves

---

*The original title was, *Trattato utilissimo del beneficio de Giesu Christo crucifisso verso i Christiani.*

to him by faith, acquiesce in the promises, and cleave with assured faith to him who cannot deceive, are delivered from all evil, and enjoy a full pardon of all their sins."

"Volaterna, in producing the accusation about *the book on the death of Christ*, repeated the evidence. It was found to be false. What followed? Nothing. I, for having exalted Christ have been often accused, summoned to justice, expelled, and all but condemned to death. Volaterna suffered no punishment for his wickedness."

Forty thousand copies are said to have been sold in six years. It was translated into several languages, and circulated throughout Europe. One writer says, that sixty thousand copies were scattered in Italy, and that finally piles of them as high as houses were burned in Rome. Such a book could not escape the destructive wrath of the Inquisition. It was forbidden to be read by the papal "indexes," and to be sold by the booksellers. One of the charges against Cardinal Morone was, "Inasmuch as he took pains to distribute a little book, entitled *The Benefits of Christ*." Morone was cleared, but there were many martyrs to the "Benefits."

The book was attributed to various persons. It called forth "confutations" and "defences." We cannot enter into the arguments that go to prove Paleario the author. The claim is generally admitted, as urged by Schelhorn,[*] Gerdes, Bayle and Tiraboshi. The Romish annalist,

---

[*] "I am of opinion that the author of this highly-lauded book was not [Cardinal] Pole, but that pious martyr of Jesus Christ, Aonio Paleario . . . . . who was intimately acquainted with Pole, and much beloved by him." *Schelhornii Amœn. Hist. Eccl.*

Laderchi, says, "Paleario published a book, in which he craftily infused the mortal poison of heresy, and on that account, by means of two monks, he had been exposed to some trouble and annoyance from the office of the inquisition."

While the "golden little book" was winning souls and making martyrs, Paleario was filling the professorship of eloquence and the classics successively, at Lucca and Milan. He held some correspondence with Calvin, Luther, and other reformers. Perhaps, if he had not felt so strongly the ties of family and fatherland, he would have followed such Italians as Ochino and Peter Martyr in their flight to protestant countries. His toils and trials make a touching story, and he struggled on against debt, envy, suspicion and persecution, determined to raise the standard of scholarship and incite young men to liberal studies.

Paleario had less than most of his fellow-reformers to fear from the popes, for he either knew them personally, or had powerful friends at the papal court. When Cardinals Bembo and Sadolet died, he felt less secure; but he took no special alarm until the cruel inquisitor, Ghislieri, was elected pope, taking the name of Pius V. This man gave the signal for the martyrdom of the most enlightened scholars, by putting the noble Carnesecchi* to death. As soon as Paleario heard of it, he sought to protect a work of his against the papacy, from the hands of the inquisi-

---

* One of the charges against Carnesecchi was, that " he believed all the heresies of the book called 'Benefit of Christ's death.'" If he had been the author as a few have supposed, he would, most likely, have been accused upon that ground.

tion. When writing the "Benefit of Christ's Death" he had refrained from making any special allusion to the great errors of popery. But about the same period he had written "An Act and Testimony against the Popes." This work he committed to the reformers of Basle for preservation. He seems to have thought of removing to Bologna.

The Inquisition laid the net, and, about the year 1568, Paleario was arrested at Milan, conveyed to Rome, and shut up in the prison of Torre di Nona. The principal charges against him were four: 1. That he denied purgatory. 2. That he disapproved of burying the dead in churches. 3. That he ridiculed the monastic life. 4. That he ascribed justification solely to faith in the merits of Christ. The oration in his self-defence at Sienna was produced against him. The evidences of his "heresy" were overwhelming, but he exhibited great firmness before the inquisitors. Laderchi, an enemy, reports that the aged man turned to his judges and said, "Seeing that your eminences have so many creditable witnesses against me, it is unnecessary for you to give yourselves or me longer trouble. I am resolved to act according to the advice of the blessed apostle Peter, when he says, 'Christ suffered for us, leaving us an example that we should follow his steps; who did no evil, neither was guile found in his mouth; who, when he was reviled, reviled not again, when he suffered he threatened not, but committed himself to him that judgeth righteously.' Proceed, then, to give judgment: pronounce sentence on Aonio, and thus gratify his adversaries and fulfil your office." He was condemned to death by the gibbet, and his body to be burned. Some authorities assert that he was burned alive. The Romanists, as usual, pretend that Paleario was repentant, and that he died in the papal communion. But if he recanted, why was he destroyed? Laderchi, a Romanist, asserts that he held all the heresies of Erasmus, Luther, "and other heretics," and confessed them. "More are to be found in the original trial, words pronounced by himself, which prove him to have been a thorough heretic, and worthy of the severest punishment." This annalist further says, "When it appeared that this son of Belial was obstinate and refractory, and could by no means be recovered from the darkness of error to the light of truth, he was deservedly delivered to the fire, that, after suffering its momentary pains here, he might be found in everlasting flames hereafter." On the morning of his martyrdom he was permitted to write two letters to his wife and children, and he certainly is farthest from expressing anything like a recantation. One of these letters is as follows:

"My Dearest Wife:—I would not wish that you should receive sorrow from my pleasure, nor ill from my good. The hour is now come when I must pass from this life to my Lord, and Father and God. I depart as joyfully as if I were going to the nuptials of the Son of the great King, which I have always prayed my Lord to grant me through his goodness and infinite mercy. Wherefore, my dearest wife, comfort yourself with the will of God and with my resignation, and attend to the desponding family

which still survives, training them up and preserving them in the fear of God, and being to them both father and mother. I am now an old man of seventy years, and useless. Our children* must provide for themselves by their virtue and industry, and lead an honourable life. God the Father, and our Lord Jesus Christ, and the communion of the Holy Spirit, be with your spirit! Thy husband,
"AONIO PALEARIO.
"ROME, *July* 3, 1570."

We cannot but believe that the venerable man of seventy years died a witness for the truth, as it is in Christ, and receiving the benefits derived from his death. His memory seems to be reviving in Italy. In 1851, the city of Colle did itself the honour of placing on one of its houses the inscription, "*Aonio Paleario lived here.*"

The Inquisition waged a fierce war against the "Benefit of Christ's Death." It passed out of sight. In later times Bayle declared, "The work is lost." Macaulay, following Ranke, said in the Edinburgh Review, 1840, "The inquisitors proscribed it; and it is now as utterly lost as the second decade of Livy."

The honour of leading to its discovery belongs partly to Dr. Thomas M'Crie of the Scottish Presbyterian Church, the first historian who brought to light a large amount of facts pertaining to the Reformation in Italy. He found in an old will that the book had been translated and read

---

* His two sons had already entered upon a learned profession; two daughters were married, and one was in a convent. They were no doubt deprived of their property, as the children of a heretic. There is now a family at Veroli which claims to be descended from the martyr.

PALEARIO AND HIS BOOK. 13

in English as early as 1577. His notice* of it caught the eye of several scholars, who made a search for it. The Rev. John Ayer of Hampstead, found three copies of the fourth English edition at Cambridge, and republished it. This version had been made by A. G., who probably was Arthur Golding, a translator of several works written by foreign reformers. In his preface he said, "Thou hast here delivered to thee, good reader, a little treatise, first written in the Italian tongue, and printed at Venice; after that translated into the French language, and printed at Lyons; and now translated and printed for thee to read in the English tongue. Inquire not of the author—he is unknown; and to know him would do thee little good. Read the book devoutly, regard the matter of it attentively; it may do thee much good in these evil days."

In those "evil days" Edward Courtenay, the twelfth earl of Devonshire, lay a prisoner in London Tower, and made a translation from the Italian. This has been found in manuscript at Cambridge, having two notes on the margin written by Edward VI. Other versions have been discovered in other languages. An Italian copy, supposed to be the original, has been reprinted under the editorship of the Rev. Churchill Babington.

The present edition is a faithful reprint of that republished by the Rev. John Ayer, or the fourth edition of the translation made about the year 1573, soon after Paleario's

* "That it was translated into English, and read in Scotland, appears from the following notice: 'Item, foure, Benefite of Christ, the piece 2 shs. (Testament of Thomas Bassinden, printer in Edinburgh, who deceased 18th October, 1577.') M'Crie's *Reformation in Italy*, *Presbyterian Board of Publication*, page 132, *note*.

martyrdom. The spelling and a few obsolete words have been modernized, such as *since* for *sith*, *neither* for *nother*. Some of the unimportant side-headings have been omitted, as they do not belong to the text. Most of the Scripture quotations have been conformed to the authorized English version, so that the author's proofs might bear a familiar face to the reader; but no substitution has been made in cases where the change would affect the author's argument. Those which remain as in the old edition, are dated (1573.) The anachronism of substituting texts from the version of 1611, for those in a translation of 1573, will not be considered serious, when those texts will thus be rendered more agreeable and convincing to English readers. Care has been taken not to add a word to the text, nor to take away one thought from the rich casket of truth. Except the citation of Scripture texts and a few definitions, the notes are all those of the present editor. Most of them are intended to illustrate the experience of Paleario.

This edition is so prepared that it may be bound with the editor's work, entitled "Aonio Paleario and his Friends," or issued separately as a tract. May the Lord so bless it that all readers will derive from Christ the great benefits purchased by his death! Those who profit by it will appreciate the saying of bishop Vergerio, who saw with delight its first popularity in his native Italy; "Many are of opinion that in our day nothing has ever been written in Italian so sweetly pious and simple, or so calculated to instruct the weak and ignorant, especially in the article of justification." W. M. B.

TRENTON, N. J.

OF THE

BENEFIT THAT CHRISTIANS RECEIVE

BY

JESUS CHRIST CRUCIFIED.

CHAPTER I.

OF ORIGINAL SIN, AND OF MAN'S WRETCHEDNESS.

THE holy Scripture saith that God created man after his own image and likeness, making him, as in respect of his body, impassible,* and, as touching his soul, righteous, true, good, merciful, and holy. But, after that he, being overcome with desire of knowledge, had eaten of the apple that God had forbidden him, he lost the said image and likeness of God, and became like the brute beasts, and like the devil who had abused him. For as touching his soul, he became unrighteous, untrue, cruel, pitiless, and the enemy of God; and, as touching his body, he became passible,† and

The state of man before and after that he had sinned.

---
* Impassible : free from suffering.
† Passible : subject to suffering.

subject to a thousand inconveniences and diseases, and not only like, but also inferior to brute beasts. And even as, if our forefathers had obeyed God, they should have left us their righteousness and holiness as an heritage; even so, by being disobedient unto God, they have left us the inheritance of unrighteousness, wickedness, and God's displeasure, in such sort as it is unpossible for us (through our own strength) to love God, or to frame ourselves unto his holy will. Nay, we be enemies unto him, as to one that must punish our sins, because he is a just judge; and therefore can we not any more trust wholly to his holy mercy. To be short, our whole nature was corrupted by Adam's sin. And, like as erst* it had superiority above all creatures, so became it an underling to all, the bond-slave of Satan, sin, and death, and condemned to the miseries of hell. Also he lost his judgment altogether, and began to say that good was evil, and evil good; esteeming false things to be true, and true things to be false. Which thing the prophet considering, saith that "all men are liars,"† and that "there is not one that doeth good;‡ because the devil, like a stout man of arms, ruleth his palace, that is to wit, the world, whereof he became the prince and lord. There is no tongue that can express the thousandth part of our misery, in that we, being created by God's own hand, have lost the said image of God, and are become like the devil, and too like to him

---

* Erst: originally.   † Psalm cxvi. 11.   ‡ Psalm xiv. 3.

in nature and condition, willing whatsoever he willeth, and likewise refusing whatsoever he misliketh. By reason whereof, being given up for a prey to that wicked spirit, there is no sin so grievous which every one of us would not be ready to do, if the grace of God stay us not. And this our deprivation of righteousness, and this forward {Original sin.} inclination to all unrighteousness and naughtiness, is called original sin; the which we bring with us from out of our mother's womb, so as we be born the children of wrath; and it hath had his first spring from our first fathers, and is the cause and fountain of all the vices and iniquities that we commit; wherefrom if we will be delivered, and return again to our first innocency, to recover the image of God, first of all it standeth us on hand to know our own wretchedness. For, like as no man will ever seek to the physician, except he know himself to be diseased, or acknowledge the excellency of the physician, and how much he is bound unto him, except he know his own disease to be pestilent and deadly; even so no man acknowledgeth Jesus Christ the only Physician of our souls, except he first know his own soul to be diseased: neither can he perceive the excellency of him, nor how much he is bound unto him, except he first enter into the knowledge of his own outrageous sins, and of the incurable infirmity, which we have received through the infection of our first fathers.

CHAPTER II.

HOW THE LAW WAS GIVEN BY GOD, TO THE END THAT WE, KNOWING OUR SIN, AND HAVING NOT ANY HOPE OF ABILITY TO MAKE OURSELVES RIGHTEOUS BY OUR OWN WORKS, SHOULD HAVE RECOURSE TO GOD'S MERCY, AND UNTO THE RIGHTEOUSNESS OF FAITH.

Our God, therefore, minding of his infinite goodness and mercy to send his only Son to set free the wretched children of Adam, and knowing that first of all it behoved him to make them understand their own misery, chose Abraham (in whose seed he promised to bless all nations,) and accepted his offspring for his peculiar people, unto whom (after their departure out of Egypt, and deliverance from the bondage of Pharaoh) he, by the means of Moses, gave the law; which forbiddeth all lusting, and commandeth us to love God with all our heart, with all our soul, and with all our strength, in such wise as our whole trust be reposed in him, and we ready to leave our life for his sake, to suffer all torments in our members, and to be bereft of all our goods, dignities and honours, for the love of our God, choosing to die rather than to do any thing that may mislike him, be it never so little, and doing all things in that behalf with a merry heart, and with all forwardness and cheerfulness. Moreover, the law commandeth us to love our neighbour as ourself, meaning by the neighbour all manner of men, as well friends as foes; and it willeth us to do to every man as we would be done unto, and to love other men's cases as our own. And so, by looking in this holy law, as in a clear looking-glass, man doth out of hand espy his own great imperfection and unableness to obey God's commandments, and to render him the honour and love which he ought to yield to his Maker. The first office of the law, then, is to make sin known;* as St. Paul affirmeth. And in another place he saith, "I had not known what sin is but by the law."† The second office of the law is to make sin increase,‡ forasmuch as we, being quite gone from the obeying of God, and become bound-slaves to the devil, being full of wicked works and inordinate affections, cannot abide that God should forbid us to lust, which increaseth so much the more as it is the more prohibited; by reason whereof St. Paul saith that sin was dead, but the law came and raised it up again, and so it became out of

<small>The first office or duty of the law.</small>

<small>The second office of the law.</small>

* Rom. iii. 20 : " By the law is the knowledge of sin."

† Rom. vii. 7 : (translation of 1573.)

‡ Probably the author had in mind Rom. v. 20 ; vii. 5. The *design* of the law was not merely to check transgressions but to make the knowledge and conviction of sin increase. The *result* is to call forth the opposition of the depraved man so that he multiplies his transgressions.

measure great. The third office of the law is to show the wrath and judgment of God, who threateneth death and everlasting punishment to such as keep not the law throughout in all points. For the holy Scripture saith, "Cursed be he that confirmeth not all the words of this law to do them."* And, therefore, St. Paul saith that the law is a ministry [of death,]† and that it bringeth forth wrath.‡ The law, then, having discovered sin, and increased it, and showed forth the wrath and indignation of God, who threateneth death, executeth his fourth office, which is to put a man in fear; who thereupon falleth into sorrowfulness, and would fain satisfy the law; but, forasmuch as he seeth clearly that he is not able, he waxeth angry against God, and would with all his heart that there were no God, because he feareth to be sore chastised and punished by him; according as St. Paul saith, that "the carnal mind is enmity against God; for it is not subject to the law of God, neither indeed can be."§ The fifth office of the law (which is the principal end, and the most excellent and necessary office of it) is to constrain a man to go unto Jesus Christ; in like wise as the Hebrews, being dismayed, were constrained to appeal unto Moses, saying, "Let not the Lord speak unto us, lest we die; but speak thou unto us, and we will obey thee in all things." And the Lord answered, "Verily they have spoken ex-

side notes: The third office of the law. The fourth office of the law. The fifth office of the law.

* Deut. xxvii. 26.   † 2 Cor. iii. 7.   ‡ Rom. iv. 15.   § Rom. viii. 7.

ceeding well."* Yea, they were not praised for any other thing than for their desiring of a mediator betwixt God and them, which was Moses, who represented Jesus Christ, that should be the Advocate and Mediator between God and man. In respect whereof, God said unto Moses, "I will raise them up a Prophet from among their brethren, like unto thee, and I will put my words in his mouth; and he shall speak unto them all that I shall command him. And it shall come to pass that whosoever will not hearken unto my words which he shall speak in my name, I will require it of him."†

* Exod. xx. 19, with Deut. v. 28; xviii. 17; (translation of 1573.)
† Deut. xviii. 18, 19.

CHAPTER III.

HOW THE FORGIVENESS OF OUR SINS, OUR JUSTIFICATION, AND OUR SALVATION, DEPEND UPON JESUS CHRIST.

WHEN as our God then had sent the said great Prophet which he had promised us (who is his only Son,) to the end that he should set us free from the curse of the law, and reconcile us unto our God; that he should make our will fit for good works, healing our free-will, and repairing in us the foresaid image of God, which we had lost through the fault of our first parents; forasmuch as we know that "there is none other name under heaven given among men, whereby we must be saved,"* but the name of Jesus Christ, let us run unto him with the feet of lively faith, and cast ourselves between his arms, since he allureth us so graciously, crying, "Come unto me all ye that labour and are heavy-laden and I will give you rest;"† what comfort or what joy in this life can be comparable to this his saying there, when as a man, feeling himself oppressed with the intolerable weight of his sins, understandeth so sweet and amiable words of the Son

---

* Acts iv. 12.   † Matt. xi. 28 : "I will refresh you," (1573.)

of God, who promiseth so graciously to refresh and rid him of his great pains? But all the matter lieth in acknowledging our own weakness and misery in good earnest. For he shall never know what is sweet, who hath not tasted of the sour. And therefore Jesus Christ saith, "If any man thirst, let him come unto me, and drink;"* as if he had meant to say, If a man know not himself to be a sinner, nor thirst after righteousness, he cannot taste of the sweetness of Jesus Christ; how sweet it is to talk of him, to think of him, and to follow his most holy life. But, when we once thoroughly know our own infirmity by mean of the law, let us hearken to St. John Baptist, who pointeth us to the Sovereign Physician with his finger, saying, "Behold the Lamb of God, which taketh away the sin of the world."† For he it is that delivereth us from the heavy yoke of the law, abrogating and disannulling the curses and sharp threatenings of the same, healing all our infirmities, reforming our freewill, returning us to our ancient innocency, and repairing in us the image of our God; insomuch that (according to St. Paul's saying,) "like as by Adam we be all dead, so by Jesus Christ we are all quickened."‡ And it is not to be believed that the sin of Adam, which we have by inheritance from him, should be of more force than the righteousness of Christ, the which also we inherit by faith. It seemeth that man hath great cause to complain,

* John vii. 37.   † John i. 29.   ‡ 1 Cor. xv. 22, (1573.)

that (without any reason why)* he is conceived and born in sin, and in the wickedness of his parents, by means of whom death reigneth over all men. But now is all our sorrow taken away; inasmuch as by a like mean (without any occasion given on our behalf) righteousness and everlasting life are come by Jesus Christ, and by him death is slain; whereof St. Paul maketh a very goodly discourse, which I purpose to set down here following:— "Wherefore (saith he) as by one man sin entered into the world, and death by sin: and so death passed upon all men, for that all have sinned. For until the law sin was in the world; but sin is not imputed where there is no law. Nevertheless death reigned from Adam to Moses, even over them that had not sinned after the similitude of Adam's transgression, who is the figure of him that was to come. But not as the offence, so also is the free gift. For if through the offence of one many be dead, much more the grace of God, and the gift by grace, which is by one man, Jesus Christ, hath abounded unto many. And not as it was by one that sinned, so is the gift. For the judgment was by one to condemnation, but the free gift is of many offences unto justification. For if by one man's offence death

---

* Without any reason in his own personal conduct, for he could not commit actual sin before he was born. The reason lies in the fact that Adam was his federal representative. The author evidently meant that as a man's natural and original sinfulness does not come from his individual acts, so his justifying righteousness does not come from his personal conduct.

reigned by one; much more they which receive abundance of grace, and of the gift of righteousness, shall reign in life by one Jesus Christ. Therefore as by the offence of one judgment came upon all men to condemnation, even so by the righteousness of one the free gift came upon all men unto justification of life. For as by one man's disobedience many were made sinners, so by the obedience of one shall many be made righteous. Moreover the law entered that the offence might abound. But where sin abounded grace did much more abound; that as sin hath reigned unto death, even so might grace reign through righteousness unto eternal life, by Jesus Christ our Lord."*

By these words of St. Paul, we manifestly perceive the thing to be true, which we have said heretofore: that is to wit, that the law was given to make sin known; which sin we do also know not to be of greater force than Christ's righteousness, where-through we be justified before God. For, even as Jesus Christ is stronger than Adam was, so is his righteousness more mighty than the sin of Adam. And, if the sin of Adam was sufficient enough to make all men sinners and children of wrath, without any misdeed of our own, much more shall Christ's righteousness be of greater force to make us all righteous, and the children of grace, without any of our own good works; which cannot be good, unless that, before we do them, we our-

* Rom. v. 12-21.

selves be made good; as Austin* also affirmeth. Hereby a man may know in what an error they be, who, by reason of some great offence, despair of God's good-will, imagining that he is not willing to forgive, cover, and pardon all sin, having already punished and chastised all our sins and iniquities in his only-begotten and dear-beloved Son, and consequently granted† a general pardon to all mankind; which everybody enjoyeth that believeth the gospel, that is to say, which believeth the happy tidings that the apostles have published through the whole world, saying, "We beseech you for Jesus Christ's sake, Be ye reconciled unto God; for he that never knew sin was made a sacrifice for our sin, that we might become righteous in him."‡ The prophet Isaiah, foreseeing this great goodness of God, writeth these heavenly words, which do so well paint out the passion of our Lord Jesus Christ, and the cause thereof, as it is not to be found better described, even in the writings of the apostles. "Who (saith he) hath believed our report? and to whom is the arm of the Lord revealed? For he shall grow up before him

The greatness of sin ought not to cause despair.

---

* Augustine was born 353; died 429. It is not known what particular passage the author intended to quote. The doctrine runs through all the writings of Augustine, that the tree must be good before the fruit can be good. He says, "He who is a child of God must feel himself impelled by the Spirit of God to do right; and having done it he thanks God, who gave him the power and the pleasure of so doing." "Good works follow justification; they do not precede it."

† Offered.   ‡ 2 Cor. v. 20, 21, (1573.)

as a tender plant, and as a root out of a dry ground; he hath no form or comeliness; and when we shall see him, there is no beauty that we should desire him. He is despised and rejected of men; a man of sorrows, and acquainted with grief: and we hid as it were our faces from him; he was despised, and we esteemed him not. Surely he hath borne our griefs, and carried our sorrows; yet we did esteem him stricken, smitten of God and afflicted. But he was wounded for our transgressions, he was bruised for our iniquities; the chastisement of our peace was upon him; and with his stripes we are healed. All we like sheep have gone astray; we have turned every one to his own way; and the Lord hath laid on him the iniquity of us all. He was oppressed, and he was afflicted, yet he opened not his mouth; he is brought as a lamb to the slaughter, and as a sheep before her shearers is dumb, so he opened not his mouth."*

O great unkindness! O thing abominable! that we, which profess ourselves Christians, and hear that the Son of God hath taken all our sins upon him, and washed them out with his precious blood, suffering himself to be fastened to the cross for our sakes, should nevertheless make as though we would justify ourselves, and purchase forgiveness of our sins by our own works; as who would say that the deserts, righteousness, and bloodshed of Jesus Christ were not enough to do it, unless we

* Isaiah liii. 1–7.

came to put to [it] our works and righteousness; which are altogether defiled and spotted with self-love, self-liking, self-profit, and a thousand other vanities, for which we have need to crave pardon at God's hand, rather than reward. Neither do we think of the threatenings which St. Paul useth to the Galatians; who, having been deceived by false preachers, believed not that the justification by faith was sufficient of itself, but went about still to be made righteous by law. Unto whom St. Paul saith, " Christ is become of no effect unto you, whosoever of you are justified by the law; ye are fallen from grace. For we, through the Spirit, wait for the hope of righteousness by faith."*

Now, if the seeking of righteousness and forgiveness of sins, by the keeping of the law which God gave upon Mount Sinai, with so great glory and majesty, be the denying of Christ and of his grace, what shall we say to those that will needs justify themselves afore God by their own laws and observances? I would wish that such folks should a little compare the one with the other, and afterward give judgment themselves. God mindeth not to do that honour, nor to give that glory to his own law; and yet they will have him to give it to men's laws and ordinances. But that honour is given only to his only-begotten Son, who alone, by the sacrifice of his death and passion, hath made full amends for all our sins, past, present, and to come; as St. Paul

* Galatians, v. 4, 5.

and St. John declare.* Wherefore, as often as we apply this satisfaction of Jesus Christ's unto our souls by faith, out of all doubt we obtain forgiveness of our sins, and become good and righteous before God, through his righteousness. And therefore, after that St. Paul hath said that, as touching the righteousness of the law, he had lived unblamable, he added, " And yet, whatsoever I have gained by it, I have accounted it in all respects to be but loss, for the love of Christ. And specially I esteem all things to be loss for the excellent knowledge of Jesus Christ my Lord; for whom I have counted all things to be loss, and deem them but as dung, so I may win Christ, and be found in him, not having mine own righteousness which is of the law, but the righteousness which is by the faith of Jesus Christ, which righteousness is given of God, I mean the righteousness of faith, that I may come to the knowledge of Jesus Christ."† Oh most notable words, which all Christians ought to have engraven in their hearts, praying God to make them to taste it perfectly. Lo! how St. Paul showeth plainly that whosoever knoweth Christ aright esteemeth all the works of the law to be hurtful; forasmuch as they make us to swerve from our trust in Jesus Christ; to whom every man ought to impute his salvation, and to trust only unto him alone. And, to enforce this sentence the more, he added further,

* Heb. vii. 27; John xii. 32. Heb. x. 12, 14; 1 John i. 7, ii. 2.
† Phil. iii. 6-10. (1573.)

that he esteemeth all things but as dung, so he may gain Christ and be found incorporated in him; declaring thereby that whosoever trusteth in his own works, and pretendeth to justify himself by them, getteth not Jesus Christ, neither is engrafted into him. And, forasmuch as the whole mystery of our faith consisteth in the truth hereof, to the end we might the better understand what he meant to say, he addeth and repeateth oftentimes, that he had nothing to do with all the outward justification, and all the righteousness that is grounded upon the keeping of the law; but that he would clothe himself with the righteousness which God giveth by faith to all them that believe that all our sins are fully chastised and punished in Jesus Christ, and that Jesus Christ (as St. Paul saith,) "is made unto us wisdom, and righteousness, and sanctification and redemption; that, according as it is written, He that glorieth, let him glory in the Lord."* Very true it is, that in the holy Scriptures there are some texts to be found, which, being misunderstood, seem to gainsay this holy doctrine of St. Paul's, and to attribute justification and remission of sins unto works and to charity. But those authorities have already been well expounded by some, who have showed plainly that such as have understood them in the sense aforesaid understood them not aright. Wherefore, my dear-beloved brethren, let us not follow the fond opinion of the bewitched

* 1 Cor. i. 30, 31.

Galatians; but rather let us follow the truth which St. Paul teacheth us, and let us give the whole glory of our justification unto God's mercy and to the merits of his Son; who by his own bloodshed hath set us free from the sovereignty of the law, and from the tyranny of sin and death, and hath brought us into the kingdom of God, to give us life and endless felicity. I say, yet further, that he hath delivered us from the dominion of the law, insomuch as he hath given us his Holy Spirit, who teacheth us all truth, and that he hath satisfied the law to the full, and given the same satisfaction unto all his members (that is to wit, to all true Christians) so as they may safely appear at God's throne, because they be clothed with the righteousness of his Christ, and by him delivered from the curse of the law. <sidenote>How man is delivered and set free from the curse of the law.</sidenote>

Then cannot the law any more accuse us or condemn us, nor move our affections or appetites, nor increase sin in us. And therefore St. Paul saith that the obligation which was against us is cancelled by Jesus Christ, and discharged upon the tree of the cross, insomuch as he hath set us free from the subjection of the law, and consequently from the tyranny of sin and death, which can no more hereafter hold us oppressed, because it is overcome by Jesus Christ in his resurrection, and so consequently by us, which are his members; in such manner that we may say with St. Paul, and with the prophet Hosea, "Death is swallowed up in victory. O death! where is thy sting? O grave! where is thy victory? The sting of death is sin; and the strength of sin is the law. But thanks be to God, which giveth us the victory, through our Lord Jesus Christ."* He is the blessed Seed that hath crushed the head of the venomous serpent, that is to wit, of the devil; insomuch that all those which believe in Jesus Christ, reposing their whole trust in his grace, do overcome sin, death, the devil, and hell; as Christ hath done. He is that blessed Seed of Abraham, in the which God hath promised blessedness to all nations. It behoved every particular person to fight with the said horrible serpent, and to deliver himself from that curse.

But that enterprise was so great, that all the force of the whole world knit together was not able to go through with it. Wherefore our God, the Father of mercy, being moved with compassion of our miseries, hath given us his only-begotten Son, who hath delivered us from the venom of the serpent, and is himself become our blessedness and righteousness, conditionally that we accept the same, renouncing all our own outward justification. Then, my dear brethren, let us embrace the righteousness of our Lord Jesus Christ, and let us make it ours by means of faith: let us assure ourselves that we be righteous not for our own works, but through the merits of Jesus Christ, and let us live merrily†

---

* Hosea xiii. 14. 1 Cor. xv. 55–57.

† Merrily, *i. e.* cheerfully.

and assured that the righteousness of Jesus Christ hath utterly done away all our unrighteousness, and made us good, righteous, and holy before God; who, beholding us ingrafted into his Son by faith, esteemeth us not now any more as the children of Adam, but as his own children, and hath made us heirs of all his riches, with his own begotten Son.

CHAPTER IV.

OF THE EFFECTS OF LIVELY FAITH, AND OF THE UNION OF MAN'S SOUL WITH JESUS CHRIST.

THIS holy faith worketh after such a sort in us, that he, which believeth that Jesus Christ hath taken all his sins upon him, becometh like unto Christ, and overcometh sin, the devil, death, and hell. And the reason thereof is this; namely, that the church (that is to wit, every faithful soul) is Christ's wife, and Christ is her Husband. For we know how the law of marriage is, that of two they become one self-same thing, being two in one flesh, and that the goods and substance of either of them How our sins are taken away by Christ. become common to them both; by means whereof the husband saith that the dowry of his wife is his, and likewise the wife saith that her husband's house and all his riches are hers; and of a truth so they are; for otherwise they should not be one flesh; as the Scripture saith. After the same manner hath God married his only-begotten and dear-beloved Son to the faithful soul, which hath not any other thing peculiar of her own, save only sin; and yet the Son of God hath not disdained to take her for his well-beloved spouse, together with her peculiar dowry, which is sin. And now, by reason of the union which is in this holy marriage, look, what the one hath is also the other's. Jesus Christ therefore saith thus: The dowry of man's soul, my dear wife, that is to wit, her sins and transgressings of the law, God's wrath against her, the boldness of the devil over her, the prison of hell, and all other her evils, are become mine, and are in my power to do what I list with them. Wherefore it is at my choice to deal with them at my pleasure; and therefore I will put out the hand-writing which is against the soul my wife; I will take it out of the way; I will fasten it to my cross in mine own body, and in the same will I spoil principalities and powers, and make a show of them openly, and triumph over them, and consume them utterly unto nothing.

Now, when God saw his Son, who knew no sin, neither had any sin in him, thus willingly taking on him the foulness of our iniquity, he made him to be sin for us, even the very sacrifice for our sin, and did sharply punish our sin in him, putting him to death, even the death of the cross. Howbeit, forasmuch as he was his well-beloved and obedient Son, he would not leave him in death, nor suffer his Holy One to see corruption, but raised him up from death to life, giving him all power in heaven and earth, and set him at his right hand in glory. Now, then, the wife likewise, with exceeding great joy, doth say: The realms and kingdoms of my most dear Husband and Saviour are mine: by him I am an heir of heaven: my Husband's riches, that is to wit, his holiness, his innocency, his righteousness, and his Godhead, together with all his virtue and might, are mine, and for me; and therefore in him I am holy, innocent, righteous, and godly, and there is not any spot in me. I am well-favoured and fair; inasmuch as my lawful Husband hath not any blemish in him, but is altogether goodly and fair. And, since that he is wholly mine, and so, consequently, all that he hath is mine, and all that he hath is pure and holy; it followeth that I also am pure and holy. Therefore, to begin at his most innocent birth, he hath thereby sanctified the birth of his spouse conceived in sin. The godly childhood and youth of the Bridegroom hath justified the childish and youthful life of his dear-beloved bride. For the love and union that is betwixt the soul of a true Christian, and the Bridegroom Jesus Christ, maketh all the works of either of them to be common to them both. By reason whereof, when a man saith, Jesus Christ hath fasted, Jesus Christ hath prayed, Jesus Christ was heard of the Father, raised the dead, drave devils out of men, healed the sick, died, rose again, and ascended into heaven; likewise, a man may say that a Christian man hath done all the self-same works; forasmuch as the works of Christ are the works of the Christian; because he hath done them for him. Verily a man may say that the Christian hath been nailed to the cross, buried, raised again, is gone up into heaven, become the child of God and made partaker of the Godhead. On the other side, all the works that a Christian man doeth are Christ's works; because it is his will to take them for his. And, forasmuch as they be unperfect, and he thoroughly perfect, and cannot away with any unperfect thing, he hath made them perfect, with his virtues; to the end that his wife should be always joyful and well-contented, and not be afraid of any thing, assuring herself that, although there be yet still some default in her works, yet, notwithstanding, they be acceptable to God in respect of his Son, upon whom he hath his eyes always fastened. Oh the unmeasurable goodness of God! How greatly is the Christian bound unto God! There is no love of man, be it never so great, that may be compared with the love that God beareth to the soul of every faithful Christian, whereof Christ is the Bridegroom. Whereupon St. Paul saith that Jesus Christ hath so loved his wife, the church, which is builded of living stones (that is, of the souls of the believing Christians,) "that he might sanctify and cleanse it with the washing of water by the word, that he might present it to himself a glorious church, not having spot or wrinkle or any such thing; but that it should be holy and without blemish,"* (that is to wit, like unto him in holiness and innocency,) and also be the true and lawful daughter of God, who hath loved the

* Eph. v. 25, 27.

world so well, that, as Jesus Christ himself saith, "He hath given his only-begotten Son, to the end that every one which believeth in him should not perish, but have life everlasting. For God sent not his Son into the world to condemn the world; but to the end that the world might be saved by him, insomuch that he which believeth in him shall not be damned."*

Some man might demand after what manner the union of this holy marriage is made, and how the soul, which is the bride, and her Bridegroom Jesus Christ, are knit together? What assurance can I have that my soul is united unto Jesus Christ, and become his spouse? How can I assuredly glory that I am queen and mistress of his great riches, as a wife may? I can easily believe that other folks shall receive this honour and glory; but I cannot persuade myself that I am one of those same to whom God hath given so great grace. For I know mine own wretchedness and imperfection. My dear-beloved brother, I answer thee, that thine assurance consisteth in true and lively faith, wherewith, as St. Peter saith, God cleanseth men's hearts.† And this faith is grounded in the believing of the gospel, that is to say, in the believing of the glad tidings which hath been published on God's behalf through the whole world; which tidings containeth in effect, that God hath used the rigorousness of his justice

marginal note: How the faithful man's soul is assured of his being married unto Christ.

---

* John iii. 16, 17, (1573.)   † Acts xv. 9.

against Jesus Christ, chastising and punishing all our sins in him. And whosoever receiveth this good tidings, and believes it steadfastly, hath the true faith, and doth enjoy the forgiveness of his sins, and is also reconciled unto God, and of the child of wrath is become the child of grace, and, recovering the image of God, entereth into the kingdom of God, and is made the temple of God; who marrieth man's soul to his only Son, by the mean of this faith, which faith is a work of God, and the gift of God; as St. Paul saith oftentimes. And God giveth it unto those whom he calleth to him, of purpose to justify them, and to glorify them, and to give them everlasting life; according as our Lord Jesus Christ witnesseth, saying, "This is the will of him that sent me, that every one which seeth the Son and believeth on him may have everlasting life; and I will raise him up at the last day."* "And as Moses lifted up the serpent in the wilderness, even so must the Son of man be lifted up; that whosoever believeth in him should not perish, but have eternal life."† Also he saith to Martha, "I am the resurrection and the life; he that believeth in me, though he were dead, yet shall he live; and whosoever liveth and believeth in me, shall never die."‡ And to a company of Jews he saith, "I am come a light into the world, that whosoever believeth on me should not abide in darkness."§ And

* John vi. 39. † John iii. 14, 15. ‡ John xi. 25, 26.
§ John xii. 46.

St. John in his [first] Epistle saith, "In this was manifested the love of God towards us, because that God sent his only-begotten Son into the world that we might live through him. Herein is love, not that we loved God, but that he loved us, and sent his Son to be the propitiation for our sins."* And moreover, he sent him to destroy our enemies. For the bringing whereof to pass, he made him partaker of our flesh and of our blood, as saith St. Paul, "that through death he might destroy him that had the power of death, that is the devil, and deliver them, who, through fear of death, were all their life-time subject to bondage."† Seeing then that we have records of the holy Scriptures concerning the promises, whereof we have spoken heretofore, and concerning many other promises that are dispersed in divers places of the same, we cannot doubt of it. And, forsomuch as the Scripture speaketh to all in general, none of us ought to distrust in himself, that the self-same thing which the Scripture saith should not belong particularly to himself.

And, to the end that this point, wherein lieth and consisteth the whole mystery of our holy faith, may be understood the better, let us put the case, that some good and holy king cause proclamation to be made through his whole realm by the sound of a trumpet, that all rebels and banished men shall safely return home to their houses, because that at the suit and desert of some dear friend of theirs it

* 1 John iv. 9, 10.   † Heb. xi. 14, 15.

hath pleased him to pardon them; certainly none of those rebels ought to doubt of the obtaining of true pardon of his rebellion, but rather ought assuredly to return home to his house, to live under the shadow of that holy king. And, if he will not return, he shall bear the penalty of it, because that through his own unbelief he dieth in exile, and in the displeasure of his prince. But this good king is the Lord of heaven and earth; who, for the obedience and desert of our good brother, Jesus Christ, hath pardoned us all our sins, and, as we have said afore, hath made open proclamation through the whole world, that all of us may safely return into his kingdom. Wherefore he that believeth this proclamation doth straightways return into God's kingdom, (whereout of we were driven by the offence of our first parents,) and is blessedly governed by God's Holy Spirit.* And he that giveth no credit to the said proclamation shall never enjoy the said general pardon, but for his unbelief's sake shall abide in banishment under the tyranny of the devil, and live and die in extreme misery, living and dying in the displeasure of the King of heaven and earth —and that justly. For we cannot commit a greater offence against this good God, than to account him

---

* To invoke the Holy Spirit means that we do not wish to be governed by our own spirits. Thus it often happens that men do not approve what they have done by the Holy Spirit. . . This is because they have not really invoked the Holy Spirit, but only desired to be assisted in carrying out their own will." *Paleario's Letter to Bishop Martelli.*

as a liar and deceiver; which verily we do, in not giving credit to his promises.

O how passing heavy is this deadly sin of unbelief! which, so far forth as is possible, bereaveth God of his glory and perfection; besides the great harm that it doeth to a man's self, which is his own damnation and the endless torment of his soul, which the miserable conscience feeleth even in this life. But, on the contrary, he that cometh unto God with assuredness of this faith, believing him without any mistrust or doubt of his promises, and warranting himself for a certainty that God will perform all that ever he hath promised him, giveth all the glory unto God, and liveth continually in rest and endless joy, evermore praising and thanking the Lord God for choosing him to the glory of the eternal life.

And hereof they have an assured earnest-penny and gage, that is to wit, the Son of God whom they take for their most loving Bridegroom, the blood of whom hath made their hearts so drunken,* that, through this passing holy belief, there is in the Christian heart engendered so lively a hope, and so certain a trust of God's mercy towards us, and such an operation is wrought in us, as we rest ourselves wholly upon God, leaving the whole care of us unto him in such wise, that, being thoroughly assured of God's good-will, we are not afraid, neither of the devil, nor of his ministers, nor of death. Which holy and

* Exhilerated.

steadfast trust of God's mercy enlargeth our heart, cheereth it up, and with certain marvellous sweet affections directeth it unto God, filling it and setting it on fire with an exceeding fervent love. And therefore Paul encourageth us to " go with all boldness to the throne of grace ;"* and he counselleth us that we should not shake it off, nor " make light of our trust, which hath great recompense and reward."†

But this so holy and divine affiance is gendered in our hearts by the working of the Holy Ghost; who is communicated unto us by faith, which never goeth without the love of God. And hereof it cometh that we be provoked to do good works with a certain liveliness and effectual cheerfulness; whereby we gather such a strength and inclination to do them, as we be thoroughly ready and forward to do and suffer all intolerable things for the love and glory of our most gracious and merciful Father; who hath enriched us with so abundant grace through Jesus Christ, and of his enemies made us his most dear children. This true faith is no sooner given a man, but he is by-and-by endued and imprinted with a certain violent love of good works, to yield right sweet and amiable fruits both unto God, and likewise to his neighbour, as a very good and fruitful tree. And it is no more possible that he should be otherwise, than it is possible that a faggot should be set on fire, and not cast light immediately.

* Heb. iv. 16, (1573.)   † Heb. x. 35, (1573.)

This is the holy faith, without the which it is impossible that any man should please God,* and whereby all the holy men (as well of the Old Testament as of the New) have been saved, according as St. Paul witnesseth of Abraham; concerning whom the Scripture saith, that "Abraham believed God; and it was counted unto him for righteousness."† And therefore he saith a little before, "We conclude that a man is justified by faith without the deeds of the law."‡ And in another place he saith, "there is a remnant [saved] according to the election of grace; and if by grace, then it is no more of works; otherwise grace is no more grace,"§ and to the Galatians he saith, "that no man is justified by the law in the sight of God, it is evident; for the just shall live by faith. And the law is not of faith; but, the man that doeth them shall live by them."|| And further he saith, that "a man is not justified by the works of the law, but by the faith of Jesus Christ;" and he adds that, "if righteousness come by the law, then Christ is dead in vain."¶

Moreover to the Romans, making comparison between the righteousness of the law, and the righteousness of the gospel, he saith that the one consisteth in the doing of works, and the other in believing: "For, if thou confess our Lord Jesus Christ with thy mouth, and believe in thy heart

---

* Heb. xi. 6.   † Rom. iv. 3.   Gen. xv. 6.   ‡ Rom. iii. 28.
§ Rom. xi. 56. || Gal. iii. 11, 12.   ¶ Gal. ii. 16, 21.

that God hath raised him up from death, thou shalt be saved. For the belief of the heart maketh a man righteous; and the confession of the mouth maketh him safe."* Lo! how this good teacher St. Paul showeth evidently that faith maketh a man righteous without any works.

And not only St. Paul, but also the holy doctors that came after him have confirmed and allowed this most holy truth of justification by faith; among whom St. Augustine is the chief, who, in his book of Faith and Works, and in his book of the Spirit and the Letter, and in his book of Four-Score and Three Questions, and in his book which he did write to Boniface, and in his treatise upon the xxxi. Psalm, and in many other places, defendeth this article, showing that we become righteous by faith without any help of good works; howbeit that good works are the effects of righteousness, and not the cause of it. And he showeth that the words of St. James, being soundly understood, are nothing contrary to this article. Which thing Origen doth also affirm in his fourth book upon the epistle to the Romans, saying that "St. Paul's meaning is, that faith only is sufficient to make men righteous; insomuch that a man becometh righteous only by believing, although he have not done any good work at all. For so it is, that the thief became righteous without the works of the law; forasmuch as the Lord sought not what good works he

St. Augustine.

* Rom. x. 9, 10, (1573.)

had done in time past, nor waited until he had done any after he had believed, but, having accepted him for righteous upon his only confession, took him for his companion, even when he should enter into paradise. Likewise, that so renowned woman in the gospel of St. Luke,* while she was yet at the feet of Jesus Christ, heard it said unto her, 'Thy sins are forgiven thee.' And a little after he saith unto her, 'Thy faith hath saved thee: go thy way in peace.'" Afterward Origen saith, "In many places of the gospel, a man may see how our Lord Jesus Christ hath spoken in such wise, as he showeth that faith is the cause of the salvation of the believers. Then is a man made righteous by faith; and the works of the law further him nothing at all. On the contrary, where faith is not, (which faith maketh the believer righteous,) although a man do the works which the law commandeth, yet, notwithstanding, forasmuch as they be not builded upon the foundation of faith, albeit that to outward appearance they seem good, yet can they not justify him that doeth them; because he wanteth faith, which is the mark of them that are become righteous before God. And who is he that can boast himself to be righteous, when he heareth God say by his prophet Isaiah, 'that all our righteousness is as a defiled cloth?'† Then can we not justly glory in ourselves, but in the only faith of the cross of Jesus Christ.

<small>Faith is the mark of those that are justified.</small>

* Luke vii. 48, 50.   † Isaiah lxiv. 6, (1573.)

St. Basil, in his homily of Humility, saith that the Christian ought to hold himself for righteous through belief in Jesus Christ; and his words are these: "The apostle saith that 'he which glorieth should glory in the Lord; in that God hath made Jesus Christ to be our wisdom, righteousness, holiness, and redemption; to the end that he which would glory should glory in the Lord;' because that the perfect and sound glorying is to glory in the Lord. For, in so doing, a man presumeth not upon his own righteousness, but acknowledgeth his want of the true righteousness, and that he is made righteous only by believing in Jesus Christ. And St. Paul glorieth of the despising of his own righteousness and of his seeking of Christ's righteousness, by faith, which cometh of God." St. Hilary, in his ninth canon upon the exposition of St. Matthew, saith these words: "The scribes, considering Jesus Christ but only as a man, were troubled that a man should forgive sins, and pardon that thing which the law could not do, because that only faith justifieth."*

St. Ambrose, in expounding these words of St. Paul ("Unto him that believeth in him which justifieth the ungodly, his faith is accounted for righteousness, according to the purpose of God's grace: like as David also saith that the man is blessed whom God accounteth righteous without works,")† writeth thus: "St. Paul saith, that unto him which believeth in Jesus Christ (that is to wit, to the Gen-

* Comm. in Matt. cap. viii. 6.   † Rom. iv. 5, 6.

tiles) his faith is imputed for righteousness; as it was unto Abraham. In what wise then think the Jews to become righteous by the works of the law, and yet to be righteous as Abraham was; seeing that Abraham became not righteous by the deeds of the law, but only by faith? Then is not the law needful; forasmuch as the sinner becometh righteous before God through only faith, according to God's gracious purpose; as David saith. The apostle confirmeth that which he hath said by the prophet's example, saying, 'Blessed is the man whom God accepteth for righteous without works;'* whereby David meaneth that those men are very happy whom God hath determined to accept for righteous before him, by only faith, without any pains-taking or observation of the law on their behalf. Thus showeth he the blessedness of the time wherein Christ was born; insomuch as the Lord himself saith, 'Many righteous men and prophets have coveted to see the things that you see, and to hear the things that you hear, and have not heard them.'" The self-same thing saith St. Ambrose, in expounding the first chapter of the first epistle to the Corinthians, affirming openly, that "whosoever believeth in Jesus Christ is become righteous without works, and without any desert, and receiveth forgiveness of his sins by faith alone."†

---

* Psal. xxxii. 1, 2.

† It is now conceded that the commentaries on the epistles of St. Paul, here referred to, are not by Ambrose, as was once supposed.

Also he affirmeth the same thing in an epistle which he writeth to Irenæus, saying, "Let no man boast of his own works, for no man becometh righteous by his own works; but he that hath righteousness hath it of free gift, forsomuch as he is made righteous by Jesus Christ. Then is it faith that delivereth by Christ's blood; for happy is he whose sin is forgiven and pardoned." And St. Bernard, in his three-score and seventeenth sermon upon the Ballet of Ballets,* confirmeth the same, saying that our own merits bear no sway at all in making us righteous; which thing must be attributed wholly unto grace, which maketh us righteous freely, and likewise dischargeth us from the bondage of sin. And he addeth that Jesus Christ marrieth the soul, and coupleth it unto himself by faith, without that any desert of our works ought or can come between. But, because I will not be too long, I will make an end of mine allegations, when I have uttered one very notable and good saying of St. Ambrose's in his book intituled, Of Jacob concerning the blessed life.† The said holy man saith that, like as Jacob, having not on his own behalf deserved the birth-right, shrouded himself under the apparel of his brother, and clothed himself with his garment, which yielded a very sweet scent, and in that wise presented himself to his father to receive the blessing under another man's person to his own behoof;

[sidenote: St. Bernard]

---

* Song of Songs.
† The title is, " Of Jacob and the Blessed Life."

even so is it requisite for us to clothe ourselves with the righteousness of Jesus Christ by faith, and to shroud ourselves under the divine pureness of our eldest Brother, if we will be received for righteous afore God.

And certainly this is true. For, if we appear before God unclothed of the righteousness of Jesus Christ, out of all doubt we shall be judged worthy of everlasting damnation. But, contrariwise, if God see us apparelled with the righteousness of his Son, Christ, then will he surely take us for righteous, and holy, and worthy of eternal life. And verily it is a great rashness in such as pretend to attain to righteousness by the keeping of God's commandments, which are all comprehended in loving God with all our heart, with all our soul, and with all our strength, and our neighbour as ourself.

<small>No man can boast of the performance of God's law.</small> But who is so arrogant or so mad as to presume that he is able to perform those commandments to the full? Or who seeth not that God's law requireth perfect love, and condemneth all unperfectness? Let every man consider well his own works, which partly shall seem good unto him, and he shall find that they ought rather to be called transgressions of that most holy law, according also as they be altogether unclean and unperfect; so that he must be fain to utter this saying of David's, "Enter not into judgment with thy servant, O Lord; for no man living shall be found righteous in thy sight."* And Solomon

<small>* Psal. cxliii. 2, (1573.)</small>

saith, "Who is he that may say, My heart is clean?"* And Job crieth out, "What man is he that can be undefiled, and what man born of woman can show himself righteous? Behold, he found no steadfastness among his saints; yea, the heavens are not clean in his sight. How much more abominable and filthy is man, who drinketh iniquity as it were water!"† And St. John saith, "If we say we be without sin, we deceive ourselves."‡ And specially our Saviour Jesus Christ teacheth us to say, as often as we pray, "Forgive us all our trespasses, as we forgive them that trespass against us."§ And hereby may well be gathered the folly of those that make merchandise of their works, presuming to save by them not only themselves, but also their neighbours; as though our Lord Jesus Christ had not said unto them, "When ye have done all that ever is commanded you, say ye, We be unprofitable servants: we have done but as we ought to do."‖ Ye see that, although we had performed God's law to the full, yet nevertheless we should esteem and call ourselves unprofitable servants. Now, then, seeing that men are so far off from this full performance, who is he that dareth be so bold as to glorify himself, that he hath added so great an overplus of deservings above the full

---

* Prov. xx. 9, (1573.) † Job xv. 14–16, (1573.)
‡ 1 John i. 8, (1573.) § Matt. vi. 12, (1573.)
‖ Luke xvii. 10, (1573.)

measure, as he may have to deal abroad unto others?

But, to return to our purpose, I would that the proud sinner, which beareth himself in hand that he maketh himself righteous before God by doing some works which are allowable to the world, would consider that all the works which proceed out of an unclean and foul heart are also unclean and filthy, and consequently cannot be acceptable unto God, nor have any power to make the party righteous. Therefore we must first of all cleanse the heart, if we mind that our works should please God. The cleansing of the heart proceedéth of faith; as the Holy Ghost affirmeth by the mouth of St. Peter.* Then must we not say that the unrighteous person and the sinner becometh righteous, good, and acceptable unto God by his own works; but we must of necessity conclude that faith cleanseth our hearts, and maketh us good, righteous, and acceptable before God, and, furthermore, causeth our works to please him, notwithstanding that they be altogether unprofitable and unperfit.† For, inasmuch, as we become the children of God through faith, he considereth our works, not as a severe and rigorous judge, but as a most merciful Father, having pity of our frailness, and regarding us as the members of his eldest Son; whose perfection and righteousness doth supply all our uncleanness and imperfection, which are not laid to our charge, forsomuch as they

* Acts xv. 9.   † Imperfect.

be covered under the pureness and innocency of Jesus Christ, and come not to judgment before God.

And hereupon it cometh to pass, that all our works which proceed of true faith (notwithstanding that they be wholly sinful and corrupt of themselves) shall nevertheless be praised and allowed by Jesus Christ in the general judgment, because they be the fruits and testimonies of our faith, whereby we be saved. For, insomuch as we have loved the brethren of Jesus Christ, we shall show evidently that we have also been faithful, and brethren of Christ; and therefore by faith we shall be put in full possession of the everlasting kingdom, which our Sovereign Lord God hath prepared for us before the creating of the world,* not for our merits' sakes, but through his mercy; whereby he hath chosen us, and called us to the grace of his gospel, and made us righteous, to the intent to glorify us everlastingly with his only-begotten Son Jesus Christ; who is the holiness and righteousness of us, but not of them which will not confess that faith is sufficient of itself to make a man righteous and acceptable to the Lord God, who, through his fatherly goodness and loving-kindness, offereth and giveth us Jesus Christ with his righteousness, without any desert of our own works.

What thing can work or cause a man to deserve so great a gift and treasure as Jesus Christ is?

Side note: How the works of the faithful, though they be unperfect, please God.

* Matt. xxv. 34.

This treasure is given only through the grace, favour, and mercifulness of God; and only faith is the thing that receiveth such a gift, as to make us enjoy the forgiveness of our sins. And, therefore, when St. Paul and other doctors say that only faith maketh men righteous without works, they mean that it maketh us to enjoy the general forgiveness of our sins, and to receive Jesus Christ, who (as saith St. Paul) dwelleth in our hearts by faith,* and, overcoming and pacifying the troubles of our consciences, satisfieth God's justice for our sins. Furthermore, it appeaseth God's wrath justly moved against us, quencheth the fire of hell, wherein our natural corruption did throw us headlong, and cheerfully destroyeth and overthroweth the devil, together with all his power and tyranny; which things all the works that all men in the world can lay together are not able to deserve nor to bring to pass. That glory and that prerogative is reserved alonely to the Son of God, that is to wit, to the blessed Jesus Christ; who hath power above all the powers that are in heaven, in earth, and in hell, and giveth himself and his merits to all such as, distrusting in themselves, do set their whole hope of being saved in him, and in his merits.

And therefore let no man beguile himself when he heareth it said that only faith justifieth, without works, and think, as false Christians do, (who draw all things to live fleshly,) that the true faith con-

* Eph. iii. 17.

sisteth in believing the bare story of Jesus Christ, after the same manner as men believe the story of Cæsar or of Alexander. Such manner of belief is but an historical belief, grounded merely upon the report of men, and upon their writings, and lightly imprinted in our conceit by a certain custom, and is like to the faith of the Turks, who, for the like reasons, believe the fables of their Alcoran.

And such a faith is but an imagination of man, which never reneweth the heart of man, nor warmeth it with the love of God; neither do any good works ensue, or any change of life which faith should bring forth. And, therefore, they falsely hold opinion, against the holy Scripture, and against the holy doctors of the Church, that only faith maketh not men righteous, but that they must also have works. Unto whom I answer, that this historical and found* belief, and all the works that ensue thereof, are not only unable to make a man righteous, but also do cast the parties headlong to the bottom of hell, like unto those that have none oil in their lamps,† that is to say, no lively faith in their hearts.

The faith that maketh men righteous is a work of God in us, whereby "our old man is crucified,"‡ and we, being transformed in Jèsus Christ, become new creatures, and the dear-beloved children of God. This heavenly faith is it that grafteth us into the

---

* Founded, having a foundation, or fond.

† Matt. xxv. 3.   ‡ Rom. vi. 6.

death and resurrection of Jesus Christ; and, consequently, mortifieth our flesh with the effects* and lusts thereof. For, when we, by the operation of faith, do know ourselves to be dead with Jesus Christ, we are at full point with ourselves and with the world, and are throughly resolved how it is meet that they, which are dead with Jesus Christ, should mortify their earthly members, that is to wit, the sinful affections of their mind, and the lusts of the flesh; and, forasmuch as we know we be raised again with Christ, we bend ourselves to the leading of a spiritual and holy life, like unto that which we shall live in heaven, after the last resurrection.

This holy faith, making us to enjoy the general pardon that is published by the Gospel, bringeth us into the kingdom of our good God, and pacifieth our consciences, maintaining us in continual joy, and holy and spiritual sweetness. This self-same faith knitteth us unto God, and maketh him to dwell in our hearts, and clotheth our soul with himself; so as thenceforth the Holy Ghost moveth us to do the same things whereunto he moved Jesus Christ, while he was in this world and was conversant among men; that is to wit, unto lowliness, meekness, obedientness unto God, lovingness, and other perfections, wherethrough we recover the image of God. For these self-same causes, Jesus Christ did rightly attribute blessedness unto this inspired faith; which blessedness cannot be without

---

* Perhaps affects, *i. e.* affections, may be meant.—*Ayer.*

good works and holiness of life. And how can it be that a Christian should not become holy, seeing that Jesus Christ is become his holiness through faith?

Therefore, by faith we be justified and saved; and therefore St. Paul doth, in a manner, always call those saints whom we call now Christians; who if they have not Christ's Spirit, are none of Christ's, and, consequently, no Christians at all. But, if they have the Spirit of Jesus Christ to rule and govern them, we must not doubt but that, although they know well that they be made righteous through faith only, yet, for all that, they will become never the more slothful to do good works. For Christ's Spirit is the Spirit of love; and love cannot be idle, nor cease from the doing of good works. But, if we will say the truth, a man can do no good works, except he first know himself to be become righteous by faith; for, before he knoweth that, his doing of good works is rather to make himself righteous than for the love and glory of God; and so he defileth all his works with self-love, for the love of himself and for his own profit. But he, that knoweth himself to be become righteous by the merits and righteousness of Christ (which he maketh his own by faith,) laboureth happily, and doeth good works, alonely for the love and glory of Christ, and not for love of himself, nor to make himself righteous. And thereupon it cometh that the true

Sidenotes: St. Paul calleth them saints whom we call Christians. He that believeth cannot be without good works.

Christian (that is to wit, he that accounteth himself righteous by reason of Christ's righteousness) asketh not whether good works be commanded or not; but, being wholly moved and provoked with a certan violence of godly love, he offereth himself willingly to do all the works that are holy and Christian-like, and never ceaseth to do well.

He, therefore, which feeleth not the marvellous effects by his faith, which we have heretofore declared that the inspired faith worketh in the heart of the Christian, let him assure himself that he hath not the Christian faith, and let him pray earnestly unto God to give it him, saying, "Lord, help mine unbelief."* And, when he heareth it said that only faith maketh men righteous, let him not deceive himself, and say, What need I to weary myself in doing good works: faith is enough to send me to paradise? To such a one I answer, that only faith sendeth us to paradise; but yet let him take good heed; for "the devils do also believe and tremble;" as saith St. James.† Oh miserable man! wilt thou go with them to paradise? By this false conclusion thou mayest know, my brother, in what an error thou art; for thou weenest to have the faith that maketh men righteous, and thou hast it not. "Thou sayest thou art rich, and hast no need of any thing; and thou seest not how thou art poor, wretched, blind, and naked. I counsel thee to buy gold of God, that is throughly fixed with fire (that

* Mark ix. 24. † James ii. 19.

is to say, true faith set on fire with good works,) to the intent thou mayest become rich; and to clothe thyself with white raiment (that is to wit, with Christ's innocency,) to the end that the shame of thy nakedness (which is the great filthiness of thy sins) be not seen to the whole world."*

Then is the justifying faith, as it were, a flame of fire, which cannot but cast forth brightness. And, like as the flame burneth the wood without the help of the light, and yet the flame cannot be without the light; so is it assuredly true that faith alone consumeth and burneth away sin, without the help of works, and yet that the same faith cannot be without good works. Wherefore, like as if we see a flame of fire that giveth no light, we know by-and-by that it is but vain and painted; even so, when we see not some light of good works in a man, it is a token that he hath not the true inspired faith which God giveth to his chosen, to justify and glorify them withal. And hold it for certain that St. James meant so when he said, "Show me thy faith by thy works; and I will show thee my faith by my works."† For his meaning was, that he, which is plunged in ambitiousness and worldly pleasures, believeth not, (though he say he believe,) forasmuch as he showeth not in himself the effects of faith.

<small>What St. James meant concerning works.</small>

Also, we may liken this holy faith to the God-

* Rev. iii. 17, 18, (1573.)

† James ii. 18, (1573.) See marginal reading of auth. version.

head which is in Jesus Christ; who, being very man, (but without sin,) did wonderful things, healing the sick, giving sight to the blind, walking upon the water, and raising up the dead unto life again; and yet these marvellous works were not the cause that he was God. For, before he did any of those things, he was God, and the lawful and only-begotten Son of God, and he needed not to work those miracles to make himself God by them; but, forasmuch as he was God, therefore he did them. And so the miracles that Christ wrought made him not to be God, but showed openly that he was God. In like wise, true faith is, as it were, a Godhead in the soul of a Christian, which doeth wondrous works, and is never weary of well-doing; and yet those works are not the cause that a Christian is a Christian, that is to wit, that he is righteous, good, holy, and acceptable unto God; neither needeth he to work all those good works to become such a one. But, forasmuch as he is a Christian by faith, like as Jesus Christ, being a man, was also God by his Godhead, he doeth all those good works, which make not the Christian to be righteous and good, but show him to be good, righteous, and holy. So, then, like as Christ's Godhead was the cause that he wrought miracles; even so faith, working through love, is the cause of the good works that a Christian man doeth. And, like as a man may say of Jesus Christ, that he hath done this miracle or that, and that those miracles, besides that they glorified God, were also a great honour unto Jesus Christ as he was a man, who for his obedience even unto death was recompensed at God's hand in his resurrection, and had given unto him all power both in heaven and earth, which he had not afore as in respect of his manhood, but deserved it by the union which is betwixt the word of God and the manhood of Christ; so doth faith in a Christian; which faith, by reason of the union that it hath with the soul, attributeth that thing to the one which is proper to the other. Whereupon it cometh that the holy Scripture promiseth the Christian everlasting life for his good works; because good works are the fruits and testimonies of lively faith, and proceed of it, as light proceedeth from a flame of fire; according as I have said heretofore. And by this holy faith which embraceth Jesus Christ it cometh to pass that our soul is joined with Christ, and is so united and knit to him that, whatsoever Christ hath merited and deserved, the same is imputed unto the soul, as though it had merited and deserved it. And therefore St. Austin saith that "God crowneth his own gifts in us."

Of this union of the soul with Jesus Christ, Christ himself beareth good record, where he prayeth to his Father for his apostles, and for such as should believe in him by their preaching. "I pray not (saith he) for them only, but also for all those that shall believe in me through their word, to the end they may be all one thing; that, like as thou, my

Father, art in me, and I in thee, so they also may be one in us, and that the world may believe that thou hast sent me, and that I have given them the glory which thou hast given me, so as they should be one self-same thing, like as thou and I are one."* Whereby it appeareth evidently that, if we believe the word of the apostles, (who preached that Jesus Christ " died for our sins, and rose again for our justification,"†) we become all one thing with him; and, forasmuch, as he is all one with God, we also become all one with God, by the means of Jesus Christ.‡ O wonderful glory of the Christian! to whom it is granted through faith to possess the unspeakable benefits which the angels long to behold!

By this present discourse a man may plainly perceive the difference that is betwixt us and them that defend the justification by faith and works together. Herein we agree with them, that we stablish works, affirming that the faith which justifieth cannot be without good works, and that those which are become righteous are they that do the good works that may rightly be called good works.§ But we differ from them in this, that we say that faith maketh men righteous without the help of works. And the reason is ready, namely, because that by faith we "put on Christ,"‖ and make his holiness and righteousness to be ours. And, seeing the case so standeth that Christ's righteousness is given us

* John xvii. 20-22, (1573.) † Rom. iv. 25.
‡ 2 Cor. vi. 16. § 1 Pet. ii. 12. ‖ Gal. iii. 26, 27.

by faith, we cannot be so thankless, blind, and unhappy, as not to believe that he is of sufficient ability to make us acceptable and righteous before God. Let us say with the apostle, "If the blood of bulls and of goats, and the ashes of a heifer, sprinkling the unclean, sanctifieth to the purifying of the flesh: how much more shall the blood of Christ, who through the eternal Spirit offered himself without spot to God, purge your conscience from dead works to serve the living God?*

I pray thee now, thou good and devout Christian, consider well which of these two opinions is the truest, holiest, and worthiest to be preached; ours, which advanceth the benefit of Jesus Christ, and pulleth down the pride of man which would exalt his own works against Christ's glory; or the other, which, by affirming that faith of itself justifieth not, defaceth the glory and benefit of Jesus Christ, and puffeth up the pride of man, who cannot abide to be justified freely by our Lord Jesus Christ, without some merit of his own. But, say they, it is a great quickening up to good works to say that a man maketh himself righteous before God by means of them. I answer, that we also confess that good works are acceptable to God, and that he, of his mere grace and free liberality, recompenseth them in paradise. But we say, moreover, that no works are good, saving those that (as St. Austin saith) are done by them that are become righteous through

* Heb. ix. 13, 14.

faith; because that, if the tree be not good, it cannot yield good fruit.

And, furthermore, we say that such as are become righteous through faith, forasmuch as they know themselves to be righteous through God's righteousness, purchased by Christ, make no bargaining with God for their works, as though they would buy their manner of justification, such as it is, with them; but, being inflamed with the love of God, and desirous to glorify Jesus Christ, who hath made them righteous by giving them his merits and riches, they bestow all their whole study and labour to do God's will, fighting manfully against the love of themselves, and against the world and the devil. And, when they fall through frailty of the flesh, they recover themselves by-and-by, and are so much the more desirous to do good, and so much the more in love with their God, considering that he layeth not their sins to their charge, because they be engrafted into Jesus Christ; who hath made full amends for all his members, upon the tree of his cross, and maketh continual intercession for them to the eternal Father, who, for the love of his only-begotten Son, beholdeth them always with a gentle countenance, governing and defending them as his most dear children, and in the end giving them the heritage of the world, making them like-fashioned to the glorious image of Christ.

These loving motions are the spurs that prick forward the true Christians to do good works, who, considering that they are become the children of God through faith, and made partakers of his divine nature, are stirred up, by the Holy Ghost dwelling in them, to live as it becometh the children of so great a Lord, and are greatly ashamed that they maintain not the beauty of their heavenly noblesse; and therefore they employ their whole endeavour to the following of the first-born Brother, Jesus Christ, living in great lowliness and meekness, in all things seeking the glory of God, giving their lives for their brethren, doing good to their enemies, glorying in the sufferance of reproaches, and in the cross of our Lord Jesus Christ, and saying with Zacharias, "we being delivered out of the hand of our enemies," will "serve him without fear, in holiness and righteousness before him, all the days of our life."* They say with St. Paul that, "the grace of God that bringeth salvation hath appeared to all men. Teaching us, that denying ungodliness, and worldly lusts, we should live soberly, righteously, and godly, in this present world; looking for that blessed hope, and the glorious appearing of the great God and our Saviour Jesus Christ."† These and such other like thoughts, desires, and affections, are wrought by inspired faith in the souls of them that are become righteous. And as for him that either wholly or partly feeleth not these godly affections and operations in his heart, but is given over to the flesh and the world, let him assure himself that he

* Luke i. 74, 75. † Titus ii. 11-13.

hath not yet the justifying faith, nor is the member of Christ; because he hath not Christ's spirit, and consequently is none of his; and he that is none of Christ's is no Christian.

Then let man's wisdom cease henceforth to fight against the righteousness of the most holy faith; and let us give all the glory of our justification to the merits of Jesus Christ,* with whom we be clothed through faith.

* "Cotta asserts that, if I am allowed to live, there will not be a vestige of religion left in the city. Why? Because one day I was asked, what was the chief thing given by God to mankind in which they could place their salvation, I replied, Christ? What the second? Christ! The third, Christ! See then on what times we are fallen. No one was found [in the senate] to rise on my behalf." *Paleario to Fausto Bellanti,* 1542.

CHAPTER V.

IN WHAT WISE THE CHRISTIAN IS CLOTHED WITH JESUS CHRIST.

ALTHOUGH that by the things aforesaid a man may easily and plainly enough perceive how a Christian may clothe himself with Jesus Christ, yet, nevertheless, I mind to speak a little of it, assuring myself that unto the good and faithful Christian it can seem neither grievous nor troublesome to speak thereof, although the thing were repeated a thousand times. Therefore I say that the Christian knoweth that Jesus Christ, together with all his righteousness, holiness and innocency, is his own through faith. And, like as when a man purposeth to present himself before some great lord or prince, he laboureth to array himself in some fair and costly apparel; even so, when the Christian is decked and arrayed with the innocency of Christ and with all his perfection, he presenteth himself boldly before God the Lord of all, assuring himself that, through Christ's merits, he is in as good case as if he had purchased all that which Jesus Christ hath purchased and deserved. And, truly, faith maketh every one of us to possess Christ, and all that is his, as we possess our own garment.

And, therefore, to be clothed with Jesus Christ is nothing else but to believe for a certainty that Christ is wholly ours; and so he is in very deed, if we believe so, and hold ourselves assured that by the same heavenly garment we be received into favour before God. For it is most certain that he, as a most dear Father, hath given us his Son, meaning that all his righteousness, and all that ever he is, can, or hath done, should be in our power and jurisdiction, in such wise as it should be lawful for us to make our boast of them, as if we had done, purchased, and deserved them by our strength. And whosoever believeth this shall find that his belief is good and true; as we have showed heretofore. Then must the Christian have a steadfast faith and belief, that all the goods, all the graces, and all the riches of Jesus Christ are his; for, since that God hath given us Jesus Christ himself, how should it be possible that he hath not given us all things with him?* Now if this be true, as true it is indeed, the Christian may rightly say, I am the child of God; and Jesus Christ is my brother. I am the lord of heaven and earth, and of hell, and of death, and of the law; insomuch as the law cannot accuse me, nor lay any curse upon me, because the righteousness of God is become mine. And this faith is it alone that maketh a man to be called a Christian, and which clotheth him with Jesus Christ; as we have said afore. And boldly may

* Rom. viii. 32.

s be called a great mystery, where-under are
ıtained marvellous things, and things not heard
concerning the great God, which cannot enter
o man's heart, except God do first soften it with
holy grace; as he hath promised to do by his
ly prophet, saying, "A new heart also will I give
u, and a new spirit will I put within you; and I
ll take away the stony heart out of your flesh,
d I will give you an heart of flesh."*

Now then, he, that believeth not after the said
ınner that Jesus Christ with all the goods that he
ssesseth is his, cannot call himself a true Chri-
n, nor ever have a quiet and joyful conscien-
r a good and fervent courage to do good
all easily faint in doing of good works; ye
›reover, he shall never be able to do wo
e truly good. This only belief and trust
ve in the merits of Jesus Christ maketh me,
ıristians, stout, cheerful, merry, lovers of
ady to do good works, possessors of God's k,
m and of God himself, and his right dear-belov
ildren, in whom the Holy Ghost doth truly dwe
hat heart is so cowardly, cold, and vile, which
ısidering the inestimable greatness of the gift that
ɔd hath bestowed upon him, in giving him his own
well-beloved Son with all his perfect- Jesus Christ the
ss, is not inflamed with an exceeding true example of
rnest desire to become like unto him in Christians.
od works? specially seeing that the Father hath

* Ezek. xxxvi. 26.

given him unto us for an example whereon we mus[t]
continually look, framing our life after such a sor[t]
as it may be a true counterpain* of the life of Jesu[s]
Christ; forasmuch as Christ, as saith St. Peter
"hath suffered for us, leaving us an ensample, t[o]
the end that we should follow his footsteps."†

Out of this consideration issueth another kind of
clothing of a man's self with Christ, which we may
term an example-clothing; forsomuch as the Chris[-]
tian must frame his whole life after the example of
Christ, fashioning himself like unto him in all his deeds,
[w]ords, and thoughts, leaving his former wicked life,
[an]d decking himself with the new life, that is to wit,
[wit]h the life of Christ.‡ By reason whereof St.
[Paul s]aith, "Let us cast away the works of dark[ness,
an]d put on the armour of light; not in feast[ing,
n]or in drunkenness, nor in chambering and
[wanto]nness, nor in strife; but put upon you the
[Lord] Jesus Christ, and make no preparation for the
[fles]h, nor for the lusts thereof."§ Hereupon the
[tru]e Christian, being in love with Jesus Christ, saith
[with]in himself, since that Jesus Christ, not having any
[ne]ed of me, hath redeemed me with his own blood,
and is become poor to enrich me; I will likewise
give my goods, yea, and my very life, for the love
and welfare of my neighbour.‖ And, like as I am

---

* Counterpain: counterpart.   † 1 Pet. ii. 21, (1573.)
‡ Eph. iv. 22-24.   § Rom. xiii. 12-14.

‖ Of an affectionate family Paleario writes to his exiled friend
Curioni, in 1552, " In these times there are not many who so abound

THE BENEFIT OF CHRIST'S DEATH.   71.

tothed with Jesus Christ, for the love he hath borne to me, so will I have my neighbour in Christ to clothe himself with me, and with my goods likewise, for the love that I bear him for Christ's sake. He that doth not so is no true Christian, for he cannot say that he loveth Jesus Christ, if he love not the members and brothers of him; and, if we love not our neighbour, for whose sake Christ hath shed his blood, we cannot truly say that we love Jesus Christ; who, being equal with God, was obedient to his Father, even to the death of the cross, and hath loved and redeemed us, giving himself unto us, with all that ever he hath. After the same manner, we, being rich and having abundance of good things at Christ's hand, must also be obedient unto God, to offer and give our works and all that we have, yea, and even ourselves, to our neighbours and brethren in Jesus Christ, serving them and helping them at their need, and being to them as another Christ. And, like as Jesus Christ was lowly and gentle, and far from all debate and strife, so must we set our whole mind upon lowliness and meekness, eschewing all strife and impatience, as well which consist in words and reasoning, as in deeds. And, as Jesus Christ hath endured all the persecutions and spites of the world for the glory of God, so must we with all patientness cheerfully bear the

in love, but it seems rather to languish and become extinguished among all people. May our Lord Jesus Christ, who alone can, sustain us."

persecutions* and reproaches that are done by false Christians to all such as will live faithfully in Jesus Christ; who gave his life for his enemies, and prayed for them upon the cross: and so must we also pray always for our enemies, and willingly spend our life for their welfare.

And this is to follow Christ's steps; according as St. Peter saith. For, when we know Jesus Christ with all his riches to be our own good (which thing is to be clothed with Christ and to become pure and clean without spot,) there remaineth nothing more for us to do, but to glorify God by following the life of Jesus Christ, and to do to our brethren as Christ hath done to us; and specially forsomuch as we be warranted by his word that, whatsoever we do to his brethren and ours, he accepteth it as a benefit done to himself. And, doubtless, seeing that the true Christians are the members of Christ, we cannot do either good or evil to the true Christians but we do it likewise unto Christ; insomuch tha

---

* "However miserable my condition may be, Christ will ever be me the only object of holy hope and veneration." *Palerio to Bailanti,* 1542. Few men ever lived amid more provocations than Palcario, and if he sometimes used strong, severe language toward his persecutors, we can sympathize with him when he says in a letter to Aldelli, "As you wisely advise, I wish to despise honours, to disregard injuries, and to be placable and forgiving, yet while I am striving to draw both from my head and heart, the darts that have been hurled against me, others are being continually thrown. Be not you or my friends surprised therefore, if, while extracting these darts or being attacked afresh, I should call (cry) out in the struggle or groan aloud to express my grief and to frighten my furious enemies." (1543?)

he rejoiceth or suffereth in his members. Therefore, like as Jesus Christ is our clothing by faith, so also must we through love become the clothing of our brethren, and have as good care of them as of our own bodies; for they be members of our body, whereof Christ is the Head.

And this is the godly love and charity which springeth and proceedeth of the true unfeigned faith, which God hath breathed into his elect; which faith, as saith St. Paul, "worketh by love."* Howbeit, forasmuch as the life of our Lord Jesus Christ, wherewithal we must be clothed, was a continual cross, full of troubles, reproaches, and persecutions; if we will fashion ourselves like unto his life, we must continually bear the cross; as he himself saith, "If any man will come after me, let him deny himself, and take up his cross and follow me."†

But the chief cause of this cross is, for that our God purposeth to mortify the affections of our mind, and the lusts of our flesh, by that exercise; to the end we may conceive in ourselves the great perfection wherein we be comprised by our Lord Jesus Christ, by being grafted into him. Also his will is that our faith, being fined like gold in the furnace of troubles, should shine bright to his glory. Moreover, his intent is that we, by our infirmities, should set out his great power, which the world, in despite of it, beholdeth in us; inasmuch as our

* Gal. v. 6. † Luke ix. 23.

frailty cometh strong by troubles and persecutions,* and, the more that it is beaten down and oppressed, so much the more is it strong and steadfast. Whereof the apostle St. Paul saith, "We carry this treasure in earthen vessels, that the excellency of the power might be God's and not ours. On all sides we suffer tribulation, but we are not overcome: we be poor, but not overcome of poverty: we suffer persecution, but yet are we not forsaken: we be despised, but yet we perish not; and so we daily bear about us the dying of our Lord Jesus Christ in our body, that the life of Jesus Christ may also be openly showed in us."†

And, seeing the case is so, that our Lord Jesus Christ and all his dear disciples glorified God by tribulations, let us also embrace them joyfully, and

---

* "I, for having exalted Christ have been often accused, summoned to justice, expelled, and all but condemned to death." *Paleario's oration in self-defence at Sienna.*

"I perceived that I was likely to lose every comfort in the world, except Christ, to whom I had devoted myself. . . . I saw clearly that I should lose in a moment the fruit of years of study and diligence; that I should not only be deprived of my little tract of land, but be forced also to separate myself from my relatives and friends, from my excellent wife and my dear children; that I should be obliged to leave Italy, live in solitude, or be the inmate of a prison, and at length be put to death." Paleario thus describes his risk in writing the "Testimony against the Popes," yet he added, "I have undertaken the defence of a cause against which nothing true can be said. What then have I to fear? Christ has animated my courage."

† 2 Cor. iv. 7–10, (1573.)

ay with the apostle St. Paul, "God forbid that I should glory, save in the cross of our Lord Jesus Christ;"* and let us so deal, as the world may (whether it will or no) perceive and see with his eyes the wonderful effects that God worketh in such as sincerely embrace the grace of his gospel. Let us so deal, I say, as the worldlings may see how with great quietness of mind the true Christians endure the loss of their goods, the death of their children, slanders, the diseases of the body, and the persecutions of false Christians;† and also that they may see how the only true Christians do worship God in spirit and truth, taking in good worth at his hand whatsoever happeneth, and holding all that he doth to be good, rightful, and holy, praising him always for the same, whether it be in prosperity or adver-

---

* Gal. vi. 14.

† "I call my slender means golden poverty, O Conscript Fathers, and in it I truly rejoice. . . . My patrimony is small, but in the secret recesses of my soul, conscience is pure, clear and bright; the furies do not agitate it by day, nor alarm it with burning torches by night. Let them [the conspirators] be crowned with diadems and clothed in purple, and sit enthroned in chains with carpets under their feet. I, with my three-legged stool will retire into my library, and feel content with a woolen robe to protect me from the cold, a handkerchief to wipe my brow, and a couch on which to repose.

"Thou, O Christ, the author, preserver and liberal dispenser of thine own gifts, hast granted me to despise these things, and sufficient firmness of mind to speak, not according to my own sense or will, but according to truth. Do thou please to grant me piety, modesty and temperance, and to add also those things which I think to be agreeable to thee and to thy followers."—*Paleario's oration in self-defence at Sienna.*

sity, thanking him as a most gracious and loving Father, and acknowledging it for a right great gift of God's goodness to suffer any adversity, and chiefly for the gospel and for following the steps of Christ; specially forasmuch as we know that "tribulation worketh patience, and patience experience, and experience hope, and hope maketh not ashamed."*
I say that patience engendereth trial; because that, whereas God hath promised help in trouble to such as trust in him, we find it by experience, in that we continue strong and steadfast all the while, and are upholden by the hand of God; which thing we could not do with all the powers that we have of our own. So then, by patience we find that our Lord giveth us the help that he hath promised us at our need, whereby our hope is confirmed. And it were an over-great unthankfulness, not to trust to such an aid and favour for the time to come, as we have found by experience to be so certain and steadfast heretofore. But what need we so many words? It ought to suffice us to know that the true Christians are through tribulation clothed with the image of our Lord Jesus Christ crucified; which if we bear willingly and with a good heart, we shall in the end be clothed with the image of Jesus Christ glorified. "For as the sufferings of Christ abound in us, so our consolation also aboundeth by Christ;"† and if we suffer with him here below for

---

* Rom. v. 3–5. † 2 Cor. i. 5.

a time, we shall also reign with him there above for ever. *

* "I am growing old, my dear Theodore; I often think of my departure to Christ, and occupy myself in the preparation of what I think most agreeable to him, to whose service I have dedicated myself from my youth up." *Paleario's Letter to Theodore Zuinger of Basle, 1570, shortly before his martyrdom.*

CHAPTER VI.

CERTAIN REMEDIES AGAINST DISTRUST.

But, forasmuch as the devil and man's wisdom labour continually to dispossess us of this most holy faith, where-through we believe that all our sins are chastised and punished in Jesus Christ, and that through his most precious bloodshed we be reconciled to the Majesty of God; it is very needful for a Christian to have his weapons always in a readiness to defend himself from the said most mischievous temptation, which seeketh to bereave the soul of her life. Among the said weapons (in my judgment) the mightiest and best are prayer, the often use of the holy communion, the remembering of holy baptism, and the minding of predestination.

<small>Four remedies against the temptations of distrust.</small>

<small>Prayer.</small> In our prayer we may well say with the father of the poor lunatic person of whom mention is made in the gospel of St. Mark, "Lord I believe; help thou mine unbelief."* Or else we may say with the apostles, "Lord, increase our faith."† And, if there reign in us a continual desire to grow

---

* Mark ix. 24. † Luke xvii. 5.

faith, hope, and love, we will "pray without ceasing,"* as St. Paul instructeth us. For prayer is nothing else but a fervent mind settled on God.   *True prayer.*

By the remembering of baptism we shall assure ourselves that we are at peace with God.   *Baptism.* And, forsomuch as St. Peter saith that the ark of Noah was a figure of baptism; therefore, like as Noah was saved from the flood by the ark, because he believed the promises of God, so also are we by faith saved in baptism from God's wrath.† Which faith is grounded upon the word of our Lord Jesus Christ, who saith that "he that believeth and is baptized shall be saved."‡ And good right it is; for in baptism we put on Jesus Christ,§ as the Apostle St. Paul affirmeth, and consequently we be made partaker of his righteousness, and of all his goods; and under this precious robe the sins, that our frailty committeth, lie hidden and covered, and be not imputed unto us. And so, according as St.

---

* 1 Thes. v. 17.   † 1 Pet. iii. 20, 21.   ‡ Mark xvi. 16.

§ Gal. iii. 27, "For as many of you as have been baptized into Christ, have put on Christ." "To be 'baptized into Christ' obviously means something more than to be baptized in the name of Jesus Christ." . . . It is "to be united or intimately related to Christ by that faith of which a profession is made in baptism. . . that of which external baptism is the emblem—a blessing not necessarily connected with, and in very few instances, if any, conferred simultaneously with the administration of the external rite. . . To 'put on Christ' is to become, as it were, one person with Christ. They are invested, as it were, with his merits and graces. They are treated as if they had done what he did, and had

Paul saith, the blessedness which the Psalm speaketh of appertaineth to us; namely, "Blessed are they whose iniquities are forgiven, and whose s[ins] are covered. Blessed is the man to whom the L[ord] will not impute sin."*

But it standeth a Christian in hand to take go[od] heed that upon these words he take not liberty [to] sin; for this doctrine belongeth to none such [as] honour themselves with the name of Christians, co[n]fessing Christ with their mouth, and yet deny h[im] in their deeds. But it concerneth the true Chr[is]tians, who, though they fight manfully against th[e] flesh, the world, and the devil, do notwithstandi[ng] fall daily, and are constrained to say, Lord, forgi[ve] us our offences. These are they to whom we spe[ak] to comfort them, and to hold them up; that t[hey] fall not into despair, as though the blood of Ch[rist] washed us not from all sin, and that he were [not] our Advocate, and the atonement-maker for [his] members.

And therefore, when we be provoked to doubt the forgiveness of our sins, and that our own co[n]science beginneth to trouble us, then must [we] furnish ourselves with true faith, and out of ha[nd] have recourse to the precious blood of Jesus Ch[rist] shed for us upon the altar of the cross, an[d]

deserved what he deserved. They are clothed with his rig[hteous]ness, and in consequence of this, they are animated by his
Brown on Galatians.

* Rom. iv. 6–8; Psal. xxxii. 1, 2.

THE BENEFIT OF CHRIST'S DEATH.   81

tributed to his apostles at his last supper, The supper of the Lord. under the veil of a most holy sacrament, which was ordained by Christ, to the end that we should celebrate the remembrance of his death, and that by the same visible sacrament our troubled consciences might be assured of our atonement with God. The blessed Jesus Christ made his last will, when he said, "This is my body which is given for you;"* and, "This is my blood of the New Testament, which is shed for many, for the remission of sins."† "We know that a testament" (saith St. Paul) "although it be but a man's testament, yet, nevertheless, if it be confirmed, no man disannulleth or addeth any thing to it;"‡ and that no testament is of force till the testator be dead, but hath full power after the party's decease. Then did Jesus Christ make his testament, wherein he promiseth forgiveness of sins, and the grace and good favour of himself and his Father, together with mercy and everlasting life. And, to the intent that the said testament should be of full force, he hath confirmed it with his own precious blood, and with his own death. By reason whereof, St. Paul saith that Jesus Christ is "the Mediator of the New Testament, that, by his dying for the redemption of those transgressions which were in the former testament, they that are called might receive the promise of the eternal inheritance. For, wheresoever is a testa-

---

* Luke xxii. 19. † Matt. xxvi. 28.
‡ Gal. iii. 15, with marginal readings.

ment, there must also be the death of the testator; for the testament is confirmed by the death of the party, inasmuch as it is of no value so long as the maker of it is alive."* Wherefore we be very certain and assured by the death of Jesus Christ that his testament is available, whereby all our misdeeds are pardoned, and we made heirs of eternal life.

And for a token and faithful pledge hereof, instead of a seal, he hath left us this divine sacrament; which not only giveth our souls assured hope of their everlasting salvation, but also warranteth unto us the immortality of our flesh,† forasmuch as it is even now quickened by that immortal flesh of his, and in a certain manner becometh partaker of the immortality thereof; and he that is partaker of that divine flesh by faith shall not perish for ever.

* Heb. ix. 15, 16, (1573.)

† Irenæus, lib. i. The reference probably is to such words as these, "Our bodies, partaking of the eucharist, are no longer mortal, having the hope of an eternal resurrection." It was held by some of the early fathers that the body of Christ became united with the consecrated bread and wine, and thus entered into the bodily substance of the communicants, through faith, so that they received into themselves a principle of imperishable life. This was mysticism and an error. To sustain it, John vi. 54–56 was quoted, as if our Lord referred to a *bodily* participation of his flesh and blood. We need not prove that this is a perversion of the words of Christ. Our wonder is that this is the only error into which the author of the "Benefit" fell, in regard to the Lord's supper. There is nothing in all his book that furnishes clearer proof of his rejection of all popery, than his views upon this sacrament. On no subject did the reformers of the 16th century come more gradually into the light.

THE BENEFIT OF CHRIST'S DEATH.

unto him that receiveth it without the said [faith], it turneth to a dangerous poison; because that, as when bodily sustenance findeth the stomach [encum]bered with evil humours, it corrupteth like[wise] and worketh great annoyance; even so, if this [spiri]tual food light into a sinful soul that is full of [vic]e and misbelief, it casteth it headlong into [a] greater ruin, not through its own default, but [becau]se that to the unclean and unbeliever all things [are] unclean; notwithstanding that the things be [sanct]ified by the Lord's blessing. For (as saith St. [Paul]) "whosoever shall eat of this bread, and drink [th]is cup of the Lord, unworthily, shall be guilty [of the] body and blood of the Lord," and "he eateth [and d]rinketh damnation* to himself, not discerning [the L]ord's body."† For he maketh no difference‡ [of th]e Lord's body, which presumeth to the Lord's [suppe]r without faith and charity. And, forasmuch [as he] believeth not that body to be his life, and [the cl]eanser of all his sins, he maketh Jesus Christ a [liar, a]nd treadeth the Son of God under foot, and [count]eth the blood of the testament, whereby he [is s]anctified, but as a common or worldly thing, [and d]oeth great wrong to the Spirit of grace, and [shal]l be punished very sore at God's hand, for [h]is unbelief and wicked hypocrisy. For, [where]as he reposeth not the trust of his justifica-[tion i]n the passion of our Lord and Saviour Jesus [Christ], yet nevertheless he receiveth this most holy

* Judgment. † 1 Cor. xi. 27, 29. ‡ Discernment.

sacrament, and maketh protestation that he put
not his trust in any other thing. Whereby he
cuseth himself, and is a witness of his own iniqui
and condemneth himself to everlasting death,
refusing the life which God promiseth him in tl
holy sacrament.

And in this point, when the Christian feeleth tl
his enemies are like to overcome him; that is
wit, when he beginneth to doubt whether he h
received forgiveness of his sins by Jesus Christ, ɑ
that he shall not be able to withstand the devil ɑ
his temptations, and that the accusation of his o
doubtful conscience comes to press him, so as
beginneth to fear lest hell-fire should swallow
up, and death hold him in his everlasting bands
reason of God's wrath; I say, when the good Chi
tian feeleth himself in such agony, let him get h
to this holy sacrament with a good heart and st(
courage, and receive it devoutly, saying in his he;
and answering his enemies thus: I confess I hɑ
deserved a thousand hells, and everlasting deɑ
by reason of the great sins which I have committ
But this heavenly sacrament, which I receive at t
present, assureth me of the forgiveness of all
mis-doings, and of mine atonement with God. F
if I have an eye to my works, there is no doubt
I acknowledge myself a sinner, and condemn n
own self in such wise, as my conscience should nɑ
be quiet, if I should think that my sins are ɟ
doned me for my works' sake. But, when I lool

the promises and covenants of God, who promiseth me forgiveness of my sins by the blood of Jesus Christ, I am as sure that I have obtained it, and that I have his favour, as I am sure that he which hath made the promises and covenants cannot lie nor deceive; and through this steadfast faith I become righteous by Christ's righteousness, wherethrough I am saved, and my conscience quieted. Hath he not given his most innocent body into the hands of sinners for our sins? Hath he not shed his blood to wash away my iniquities? Why then dost thou vex thyself, O my soul? put thy trust in the Lord, who beareth thee so great love, that, to deliver thee from eternal death, it hath pleased him that his only Son should suffer death and passion, who hath taken upon himself our poverty, to give us his riches; laid our weakness upon himself, to stablish us in his strength; become mortal, to make us immortal; come down unto earth, to advance us up to heaven; and become the Son of man with us, to make us the children of God with himself. "Who is he then that shall accuse us? God is he that justifieth us; and who shall condemn us? Jesus Christ is dead for us, yea, and risen again for us, and he sitteth at the right hand of God, making intercession for us."* [Wherefore say with David, "Why art thou heavy, O my soul, and why dost thou trouble me?" dost thou see nothing but the law, sin, wrath, heaviness, death, hell, and the

* Rom. viii. 33, 34, (1573).

devil? Is there not now to be seen grace, remission of sins, righteousness, consolation, joy, peace, life, heaven, Christ, and God? Trouble me no more then, O my soul; for what is the law? what is sin? what are death and the devil in comparison of these things? Therefore, trust in God, who hath not spared his own dear Son, but given him to the death of the cross for thy sins, and hath given thee victory through him.

This is the sweet doctrine of the gospel, which I desire that all Christians could receive with thanksgiving and an assured faith; for then would Christ be nothing but joy and sweetness to them; then would they take heart in the victory of Christ's death, who indeed was made a curse for us, subject to wrath, putting upon him our person, and laid our sins upon his own shoulders, and he hath made with us this happy change, that is to say, he took upon him our sinful person, and gave unto us his innocent and victorious person, wherewith we being now clothed are free from the curse of the law.

And therefore may every poor sinner say, with an assured confidence, Thou, Christ, art my sin, and my curse; or, rather, I am thy sin, and thy curse; and, contrariwise, thou art my righteousness, my blessing, and my life, my grace of God, and my heaven. And thus, if we by faith do behold this brazen serpent, Christ hanging upon the cross, we shall see the law, sin, death, the devil, and hell killed by his death, and so may, with the apostle

Paul, sing that joying-heart ditty: "Thanks be to God which giveth us the victory, through our Lord Jesus Christ."*

And so, with these thanksgivings, with these or such other like thoughts, must we receive the sacrament of the body and blood of our Lord Jesus Christ.]†

After this manner is all fearfulness driven out of the soul of the Christian; and charity is increased, faith strengthened, the conscience quieted, and the tongue never ceaseth to praise God, and to yield him infinite thanks for so great a benefit. This is the virtue, efficacy, and only trust of our soul. This is the Rock whereupon if the conscience be builded, it feareth neither tempest, nor the gates of hell, nor God's wrath, nor the law, nor sin, nor death, nor the devils, nor any other thing. And, forasmuch as the substance of the Lord's supper and table consisteth in this divine sacrament, when the Christian is at it, he must hold his eyes fastened continually upon the passion of our gracious Saviour; beholding him on the one side upon the cross loaded with all our sins, and God on the other side punishing, chastising, and whipping his only-begotten and dear-beloved Son instead of us. O, happy is that man that shutteth his eyes from all other sights, and will neither hear nor see any other thing than

---

* 1 Cor. xv. 57.

† The passage in brackets is from the edition of 1638. In that of 1573, the ciii. Psalm takes the place of it.

Jesus Christ crucified; in whom are laid up and bestowed all the treasures of God's wisdom and divine knowledge! Blessed, say I, is he that feedeth his mind with so heavenly a food, and maketh himself drunken in the love of God with so sweet and singular a liquor.

But, before I make an end of this matter, I will first advertise the Christian that St. Austin hath ordinarily been wont to term this holy sacrament "the bond of charity" and "the mystery of unity." And he saith that "whosoever receiveth the mystery of unity, and regardeth not the bond of peace, receiveth not the sacrament to his own behoof, but as a witness against himself." Therefore we must understand that the Lord hath ordained this holy sacrament not only to make us sure of the forgiveness of our sins, but also to inflame us to peace, unity, and brotherly charity. For in this sacrament the Lord doth after such manner make us partakers of his body, as he becometh all one thing with us, and we with him. By reason whereof, forasmuch as he hath but one body whereof he maketh us partakers, it is meet that we also should by such partaking become all one body together among ourselves. And this union is represented by the bread of the sacrament; which as it is made of many grains mingled and kneaded together, in such wise as one of them cannot be discerned from another; so also must we be joined together after such a sort, and

<small>Christian peace and union are betokened by the bread and wine.</small>

so united together into one agreement of mind as no division may creep in. And this doth St. Paul show us when he saith, "Is not the cup of blessing which we bless the communion of the blood of Jesus Christ? is not the bread that we break the communion of the body of Jesus Christ? Whereas we be many, yet are we but one bread and one body, forsomuch as we be all partakers of one bread."* By these things we understand that, when we receive this holy communion, we must consider that we are all of us ingrafted into Christ, and are all become members of one self-same body, that is to wit, of Jesus Christ, in such wise as we cannot offend, defame, or despise any of our brethren, but we must therewithal offend, defame, and despise our said Head, Jesus Christ; neither can we be at variance with any of our brethren, but in like wise we must be at odds with him. Also we cannot love him, except we love him in our brethren. Look how much care we have of our own body, so much must we have of our Christian brethren, who are the members of our body. And, like as no part of our body feeleth any grief which spreadeth not itself into all the other parts, so ought we to determine with ourselves, that our brother feeleth not any inconvenience which should not move us to compassion. With such manner of thoughts must we prepare ourselves to this holy sacrament, quick-

* 1 Cor. xvi. 17, (1573.)

A preparation to the receiving of the holy sacrament. ening up our spirits with a fervent love to our neighbour-ward. For what greater spur can we have to prick us to love one another than to see that Jesus Christ, by giving himself unto us, not only allureth us to give ourselves one to another, but also, by making himself common to us all, maketh us also to be all one selfsame thing in him? In respect whereof, we ought to covet and procure that in all of us there may be but one mind, one heart, and one tongue, accorded and united together in thoughts, words, and deeds.

And we must mark well that, as oft as we receive this holy and worthy sacrament, we bind ourselves to all the duties of charity; as not to offend any of our brethren, nor to leave any thing undone, that may be profitable and helpful in their necessity. But, if there come any to this heavenly table of the Lord, that are divided at variance with their brethren, the same must assure themselves that they eat unworthily, and are guilty of the body and blood of the Lord, and that they eat and drink their own damnation; for that there wanted nothing on their behalf, but that the body of Jesus Christ was rent and plucked in pieces again, whilst they by hatred are divided from their brethren, that is to wit, from the members of Jesus Christ, and have not any part with him, and yet nevertheless, in receiving this holy communion, pretended to believe that their whole salvation consisteth in the participation and union with Jesus Christ. Then let us go, my brethren, to the receiving of this heavenly bread, to celebrate the remembrance of our Lord's passion, and to strengthen and fortify the belief and assurance of the forgiveness of our sins with the remembrance thereof, and to quicken up our minds and tongues to praise and exalt the infinite goodness of our God, and finally to cherish brotherly love, and to witness the same one to another by the strait* union which all of us have in the body of our Lord Jesus Christ.

Besides prayer, and the remembering of baptism, and the often resorting to the most holy communion, there is one other very good remedy against distrust and fearfulness, which is no less friend to Christian charity; namely, the remembrance of our predestination and election to eternal life, grounded upon the word of God, which is the sword of the Holy Ghost,† wherewith we may beat back our enemies. "Rejoice ye in this (saith the Lord,) that your names are written in heaven."‡ There is no greater joy in this life, nor any thing that more comforteth the Christian that is afflicted, tempted, or fallen into any sin, than the remembrance of predestination, and the assuring of ourselves that we be of the number whose names are written in the book of life, and which are chosen to be fashioned like unto the image of Jesus Christ. Oh how unspeakable is the comfort of him that hath this faith, and museth continually in his heart upon

The fourth remedy against distrust.

---
* Strait: close.   † Eph. vi. 17.   ‡ Luke x. 20, (1573.)

this exceeding sweet predestination, whereby he knoweth that, although he fall often, yet, notwithstanding, God his Father, who hath fore-ordained him to everlasting life, holdeth him up, and reacheth out his hand unto him continually!* And he saith continually in himself, If God have chosen me and predestinated me to the glory of his children, who can hinder me? "If God be for us (saith St. Paul,) who can be against us?"† Nay rather, to the end that the predestination may be accomplished in us, he hath sent his dear-beloved Son, who is a most sure earnest-penny and pledge unto us, that we, which have received the grace of the gospel, are God's children, chosen to eternal life.

<small>The effect proceeding from the knowledge of predestination.</small> This holy predestination maintaineth the true Christian in a continual spiritual joy, increaseth in him the endeavour of good works, and inflameth him with the love of God, and maketh him enemy to the world and to sin. Who is so fierce and hard-hearted, which, knowing that God of his mercy hath made him his child from everlasting, will not by-and-by be inflamed to love God? Who is of so vile and base courage, that he will not esteem all the pleasures, all the honours, and all the riches of the world as filthy mire, when he knows that God hath made him a citizen of heaven? Yea, these are they that worship God rightly in spirit and truth, receiving all things (as well in prosperity as in adversity) at the

* Ps. xxxvii. 24. † Rom. viii. 31.

hand of God their Father, and evermore praising and thanking him for all, as their good Father, who is righteous and holy in all his works. These, being inflamed with the love of God, and armed with the knowledge of their predestination, fear neither death, nor sin, nor the devil, nor hell; neither know they what the wrath of God is; for they see none other thing in God but love and fatherly kindness towards them. And if they fall into any troubles, they accept them as tokens of God's favour, crying out with St. Paul, "Who shall separate us from the love of Christ? Shall tribulation, or distress, or persecution, or famine, or nakedness or sword? As it is written, For thy sake we are killed all the day long; we are accounted as sheep for the slaughter. Nay in all these things we are more than conquerors, through him that loved us."* Wherefore it is not for nought that St. John saith how the true Christians know right well that they must be saved and glorified, and that, by reason of the same affiance, they make themselves holy as Jesus Christ is holy.†

---

* Rom. viii. 35–37. In defending himself against the charges and plots of twelve conspirators, who had sworn not to eat nor to drink until they had destroyed Paleario, (there being three hundred accomplices,) he said, "In such times as these I do not think a Christian ought to die in his bed. To be accused, to be dragged to prison, to be scourged, to be hung up by the neck, to be sewed up in a sack, to be exposed to wild beasts, is little: let me be roasted before a fire, provided only the truth be brought to light by such a death."

† 1 John iii. 2, 3.

And, when St. Paul exhorteth his disciples to a good and holy life, he is wont to put them in remembrance of their election and predestination,* as of a thing of very great force to stir up the minds of the true Christians to the loving of God, and to the performance of good works. And for the same cause our good Lord Jesus Christ speaketh openly of this holy predestination,† as one that knew of how great importance the knowledge thereof is to the edifying of his elect.

But perchance thou wilt say to me, I know well that they whose names are written in heaven have cause to live in continual joy, and to glorify God both‡ in word and deed; but I know not whether I am of that number or no, and therefore I live in continual fear, specially because I know myself to be an exceeding weak and frail sinner, from the violence whereof I am not able to defend myself but that I am overcome of it daily. And furthermore, forasmuch as I see myself continually afflicted and troubled with divers temptations, methinks I do as it were behold with mine eyes the wrath of God scourging me. To answer to these doubts of thine, I say, my right dear brother, that thou must assure thyself that all these are but temptations of the devil; who by all means seeketh to rob us of that faith, and confidence that springeth of faith, and assureth us of God's good will towards us. He laboureth to strip our soul out of this precious gar-

* Eph. i. 4–6. † Luke x. 20. [‡ But, 1573.]

ment; for he knoweth that none is a true Christian, except he believe God's word, which promiseth forgiveness of all sins, and peace to all of them which accept the grace of the gospel. Verily I say that he, which, upon these promises of God, persuadeth not himself assuredly that God is a merciful and loving Father unto him, nor with steadfast confidence looketh to receive the inheritance of the heavenly kingdom at his hand, is not faithful indeed, and maketh himself utterly unworthy of God's grace. In respect whereof St. Paul saith that " Christ as a Son [was faithful] over his house; whose house are we, if we hold fast the confidence, and the rejoicing of the hope, firm unto the end."* And in another place he exhorteth us that we " cast not away our confidence which hath great recompense of reward."† And therefore, my brethren, let us give our whole endeavour to do the will of God as it becometh good children, and beware that we sin not, as near as we can. And, although we fall oftentimes into sin through our own frailty, yet let us not by-and-by surmise that we be vessels of wrath, or that we be utterly forsaken of the Holy Ghost; for we have our Advocate Jesus Christ before God the Father; and he is the atonement-maker for our sins.

Let us bethink us of the opinion of St. Austin, who saith that "none of the saints is righteous and without sin; and yet, notwithstanding that, he

* Heb. iii. 6. † Heb. x. 35.

ceaseth not to be righteous and holy so far forth as he retain his holiness with affection."* And therefore, if we have afflictions and tribulations, let us not think that God sends them because he is our enemy, but because he is our most loving Father. "The Lord (saith Solomon) chastiseth him whom he loveth, and scourgeth every child of his whom he receiveth."† Wherefore, if we have received the grace of the gospel, whereby man is received of God for his child, we must not doubt of God's grace and goodwill towards us. And, when we perceive ourselves to delight in God's word, and to have a desire to follow the life of Jesus Christ, we must steadfastly believe that we be the children of God, and the temple of the Holy Ghost. For those things cannot be done by the power of man's wisdom, but are the gifts of the Holy Ghost, who dwelleth in us by faith, and is as it were a seal of authority, which sealeth up God's promises in our hearts; the certainty whereof is printed aforehand in our minds, and is given us as a pledge to stablish and confirm the same. "After that ye believed," (saith the apostle St. Paul,) ye were sealed with the

Afflictions are no signs of reprobation.

A true mark to know God's children by.

---

* Marc Ant. Flaminio, who probably revised his friend Paleario's book, and who wrote a defence of the "Benefit," says in a letter, "If we read the Scriptures from the beginning to end, we shall see that divine goodness generally leads his children to heaven by a thorny path of sorrow. The most holy man must pass this way to reach the kingdom."

† Prov. iii. 12, (1573.)

Holy Spirit of promise, which is the earnest of our inheritance."* Behold how he showeth us hereby, that the hearts of the faithful are marked with the Holy Ghost, as it were with a seal; in respect whereof he calleth the Holy Ghost the Spirit of promise, forsomuch as he confirmeth the promise of the gospel, the which (as I have oftentimes told you) is a happy tidings that promiseth forgiveness of sins and everlasting life to all such as believe that all their misdoings are blotted out in Jesus Christ. "For ye are all the children of God," (saith St. Paul,) "by faith in Christ Jesus," and "Because ye are sons, God hath sent forth the Spirit of his Son into your hearts crying, Abba, Father."† And to the Romans he saith, "As many as are led by the Spirit of God, they are the sons of God. For ye have not received the spirit of bondage again to fear, but ye have received the Spirit of adoption, whereby we cry Abba, Father. The Spirit also beareth witness with our spirit, that we are the children of God; and if children, then heirs."‡

And we must mark well that, in these two places, the apostle St. Paul speaketh plainly, not of any special revelation, but of a certain record which the Holy Ghost doth commonly yield to all such as receive the grace of the gospel. Then, if the Holy

---

* Eph. i. 13, 14. The old version has "the earnest-penny of our inheritance."

† Gal. iii. 26: iv. 6.   ‡ Rom. viii. 14–17.

Ghost assure us that we be God's children and heirs, why should we doubt of our predestination? The same man saith in the same epistle, "whom he did predestinate, them he also called; and whom he called, them he also justified; and whom he justified, them he also glorified. What shall we then say to these things? If God be for us, who can be against us?" and therefore, if I plainly perceive that God hath called me by giving me faith and the fruits of faith, that is to wit, peace of conscience, mortification of the flesh, and quickening of the spirit, whether it be in whole or in part, why should I doubt that I am not predestinated? And, moreover, we say with St. Paul, that all true Christians (that is to wit, all such as believe the gospel) "have received, not the spirit of the world, but the Spirit which is of God; that we might know the things that are freely given to us of God."* What marvel then is it if we know that God hath certainly given us everlasting life?

But there are some which say that no man ought to presume so far as to boast himself to have the Spirit of God. They speak in such wise as if the Christian should glory of the having of it for his own deserts, and not by the only and mere mercy of God; and as though it were a presumptuousness to profess himself a Christian; or as though a man could be a Christian without the having of Christ's Spirit;† or as though we could without flat hypoc-

* 1 Cor. ii. 12. † Rom. viii. 9.

risy say that Jesus Christ is our Lord, or call God our Father, if the Holy Ghost moved not our hearts and tongues to utter so sweet words.* And yet, notwithstanding, even they that count us presumptuous for saying that God hath given us his Holy Spirit with faith, forbid us not to say every day "Our Father," but rather command us. But I would have them to tell me how it is possible to separate faith and the Holy Ghost asunder; seeing that faith is the peculiar work of the Holy Ghost? If it be presumption to believe that the Holy Ghost is in us, why doth St. Paul bid the Corinthians try themselves whether they have faith or no, affirming them to be reprobates if they know not that Jesus Christ is in them?† But, in very deed, it is a great blindness to accuse the Christians of presumptuousness for taking upon them to glory of the presence of the Holy Ghost; without which glorying there cannot be any Christianity at all. But Jesus Christ, who cannot lie, saith that his Spirit is unknown to the world, and that they only do know him within whom he dwelleth.‡ Then let them begin to become good Christians, and put away their Jewish minds, and embrace the grace of the holy gospel in good earnest; and then shall they know that the good and true Christians both have the Holy Ghost, and also acknowledge themselves to have him.

But some one may say to me, that the Christian cannot by any means know that he is in God's

* 1 Cor. xii. 3.   † [2 Cor, xiii. 5.]   ‡ John xiv. 17.

favour, without some special revelation; and so consequently that he cannot know whether he be predestinated or no. And he may specially allege these words of Solomon: "A man knoweth not whether he be worthy of hatred or of love;"* and also these words of the apostle St. Paul to the Corinthians, "I feel not myself guilty of any thing, and yet feel I not myself justified for all that."† It seemeth to be sufficiently declared by the texts of holy Scripture, that the said opinion is false; and now remaineth only to be showed briefly that these two texts, whereupon the same opinion is chiefly grounded, ought not to be taken in that sense. As touching Solomon's sentence, although it be scarce well and faithfully translated in the common translation;‡ yet is there not any man so dull, who, in reading Solomon's whole discourse, may not plainly perceive that by saying so he meant that, if any man will take upon him to judge by the casualties that happen in this life, who is loved or hated of God, he laboureth in vain, considering that the self-same chances, which light upon the righteous, light also upon the unrighteous; upon him that sacrificeth, as well as upon him that sacrificeth not; and as soon upon the good man, as upon the sinner. Whereof it may be gathered that God doth not always show his love towards those

* Eccl. ix. 1, (1573.) † 1 Cor. iv. 4, (1573.)

‡ Probably the Italian version of the early reformer Antonio Bruccioli, 1530–1532.

whom he endueth with outward prosperities; and, contrariwise, that he showeth not his displeasure towards those whom he punisheth. Then, my right dear brethren in Christ Jesus our Lord, do you think it reason to conclude that a man cannot be sure of God's favour, because the same sureness cannot be perceived by the sundry chances that happen every day in these transitory and temporal things? A little afore, Solomon saith that a man cannot discern any difference between the soul of a man and the life of a beast; for it is seen that both man and beast die after one manner.* Shall we then conclude, by this outward accident, that the persuasion which we have conceived of the immortality of the soul is grounded but only upon conjecture? No, surely; and it were a great folly to stand upon a thing so notably known.

And, as for St. Paul's words, I say that, forasmuch as he was speaking of the administration of the gospel, he meant that his heart misgives him not of any misdealing therein; and yet, for all that, that he is not sure he hath done his whole duty to the full, and therein obtained the praise of righteousness to God-ward, as if he had done all that pertained and was convenient to be done by a faithful steward; and therefore in speaking of his office, like a just and discreet person, he durst not justify himself, nor avow that he had discharged his duty to the uttermost, and satisfied his Lord's will, but re-

* Eccles. iii. 19.

ferred all things to the only judgment of his Lord. And, verily, whosoever readeth these words of the apostle St. Paul, and considereth the words going afore them with some judgment, and likewise the words that follow, will not doubt but this is the true sense of them. I know well that some men, in expounding these words of the apostle St. Paul, say that although he knew himself to be without sin, yet he knew not whether he were righteous to Godward or no; according as David affirmeth that no man can perfectly know his own sins.* But these men perceive not that St. Paul groundeth not righteousness upon works but upon faith,† and that he utterly refuseth his own righteousness, to embrace only the righteousness which God hath given us through our Lord Jesus Christ.‡ Also, they consider not that he was most certain to be accepted for righteous, in maintaining the soundness and pureness of the Christian faith; and that he knew well how the crown of that righteousness was laid up for him in heaven;§ and, also, that he was fully assured that no creature in heaven, earth, nor hell was able to separate him from the love of God;‖ and that he longed to die, because he knew for a truth that after his death he should be with Jesus Christ.¶ All which things should be false, if he had not been well assured that he was righteous, I mean by faith, and not by works. Therefore, my

* Psalm xix. 12. † Rom. iii. 28, v. 1, 18. ‡ Phil. iii. 8, 9.
§ 2 Tim. iv. 8. ‖ Rom. viii. 38, 39. ¶ Phil. i. 20–23.

dear-beloved brethren, let us cease to speak that thing of the apostle St. Paul which he never once thought of himself, but fiercely fought against it continually, in answering such as measured righteousness by works, and not by faith in Jesus Christ.

But, besides these two authorities of Solomon and St. Paul, a man might allege some other places of holy Scripture, which, whereas they warn and encourage men to fear God, seem to be contrary to the assurance of this our predestination. And, if I would declare them all particularly, I should be over-long. But I say generally that the fear of punishment was proper to the Old Testament, and childly love to the New Testament; according as St. Paul witnesseth, when he saith to the Romans, "Ye have not received the spirit of bondage again to fear, but ye have received the Spirit of adoption, whereby we cry, Abba, Father."* And likewise unto Timothy he saith that "God hath not given us the spirit of fearfulness, but of power and of love;"† which Spirit Jesus Christ hath given us according to the promises made by the mouth of the holy prophets, and brought to pass, "that we, being delivered out of the hand of our enemies, might serve him without fear, in holiness and righteousness before him."‡

By these and many other places of the holy Scripture, a man may plainly gather that the painful and slavish fearfulness agreeth not with a Chris-

* Rom. viii. 15. † 2 Tim. i. 7. ‡ Luke i. 74, 75.

tian; and this is already confirmed by this, that such manner of fearfulness is utterly contrary to the spiritual cheerfulness and joy, which is peculiar to the Christian; as the apostle St. Paul showeth openly to the Romans, saying that "the kingdom of God is righteousness, and peace, and joy in the Holy Ghost;"* that is to say, that every man, which entereth into the kingdom of the grace of the gospel, is become righteous through faith; and afterward addeth peace of conscience, which consequently breedeth such a spiritual and holy rest and gladness, in respect whereof the same St. Paul doth oftentimes encourage the Christians to live merrily. And St. Peter saith that all they which believe in Jesus Christ do continually rejoice with an unspeakable and glorious joy, notwithstanding that they be afflicted with divers temptations. And therefore, when the holy Scripture threateneth and frayeth† the Christians, they must understand that it speaketh to such as are so licentious, that, forsomuch as they keep not the thankfulness and honesty that belong to God's children, they must be handled as servants, and held in awe, until they come to taste and feel how sweet and pleasant the Lord is, and until such time as faith work his effects in them, and that they have so much childly love as may suffice to keep and maintain them in honesty of Christian conversation and in following the example of our Lord Jesus Christ. And, when the self-same

* Rom. xiv. 17.   † Frayeth: affrighteth.

Scripture exhorteth the Christians to the true fear, it meaneth not that they should fear the judgment and wrath of God, as though it were presently ready to condemn them; for, (as I have already said,) by the record which the Holy Ghost giveth to their spirit, they know that God hath chosen them and called them, of his own mere mercy, and not for their deserts. By reason whereof they doubt not at all but that, by the self-same goodness and mercy, he will maintain them in the happy state wherein he hath placed them. And after such manner the Scripture exhorteth them not to slavish fear, but to childly fear, that is to wit, that like good children they should be loth to offend against the Christian religion, or to commit anything against the duty and honesty of God's true children, and likewise to grieve the Holy Ghost that dwelleth in them;* to the end that, knowing the corruptedness of our nature, we should always be heedful and diligent, and never have any trust in ourselves; for in our flesh and in our minds do the appetites and affections continually dwell, which, as deadly enemies of the soul, lay a thousand snares and baits for us incessantly, labouring to make us proud, ambitious, lecherous, and covetous. This is the fear whereunto the whole Scripture exhorteth the Christians that have once tasted how sweet the Lord is, and which bestow all their endeavour in following Christ's footsteps, who cast not from them this

* Eph. iv. 30.

holy fear, because they labour to put off the old man.

And the good Christians must never bereave themselves quite and clean of this childly fear, which is the singular friend of Christian charity; like as the slavish fear is such an enemy unto it, as they can by no means dwell together. And by the foresaid things a man may plainly perceive that the good Christian ought never to doubt of the forgiveness of his sins, nor of God's favour. Nevertheless, for the better satisfying of the reader, I purpose to set down here-under certain authorities of the holy doctors, which confirm this foresaid truth.

St. Hilary, in his fifth canon upon Matthew, saith, "It is God's will that we should hope without any doubting of his unknown will. For, if the belief be doubtful, there can be no righteousness obtained by believing." And thus we see that, according to St. Hilary, a man obtaineth not forgiveness of his sins at God's hand, except he believe undoubtedly to obtain it. And good right it is that it should be so. "For he that wavereth is like a wave of the sea driven with the wind and tossed. For let not that man think that he shall receive anything of the Lord."* But let us hear St. Austin, who in his Manual counselleth us to drive away the said foolish imagination, which intendeth to dispossess us of the foresaid good and sage assuredness. "Let such foolish imagination (saith he)

---

* James i. 6, 7.

murmur as much as it listeth, saying, Who art thou? how great is that glory? by what deserts hopest thou to obtain it? I answer assuredly: I know in whom I have believed, and I know that he (of his great love) hath made me his son: I know he is true to his promise, and able to perform his word; for he can do what he will. And, when I think upon the Lord's death, the multitude of my sins cannot dismay me; for in his death do I put all my trust. His death is my whole desert, it is my refuge, it is my salvation, my life and resurrection; and the mercy of the Lord is my desert. I am not poor of desert, so long as the Lord of mercy faileth me not. And, since the mercies of the Lord are many, many also are my deservings. The more that he is of power to save, the more I am sure to be saved." The same St. Austin, talking with God in another place, saith that he "had despaired by reason of his great sins and infinite negligences, if the Word of God had not become flesh." And, anon after, he saith these words: "All my hope, all the assurance of my trust, is settled in his precious blood, which was shed for us and for our salvation. In him my poor heart taketh breath; and, putting my whole trust in him, I long to come unto thee, O Father, not having mine own righteousness, but the righteousness of thy Son Jesus Christ."*
In these two places, St. Austin showeth plainly

---

* The Book of Meditations from which this is extracted, is not now attributed to Augustine.

that the Christian must not be afraid, but assure himself of righteousness, by grounding himself not upon his own works, but upon the precious blood of Jesus Christ, which cleanseth us from all our sins, and maketh our peace with God. St. Bernard, in his first sermon upon the Annunciation, saith most evidently that "it is not enough to believe that a man can have forgiveness of his sins but by God's mercy, nor any one good desire or ability to do so much as one good work, except God give it him; no, nor that a man cannot deserve eternal life by his works, but if God give him the gift so to believe. But, besides all these things (saith St. Bernard,) which ought rather to be counted a certain entrance and foundation of our faith, it is needful that thou believe also that thy sins are forgiven thee for the love of Jesus Christ." See how this holy man confesseth that it is not enough to believe generally the forgiveness of sins; but he must also believe particularly that his own sins are forgiven him by Jesus Christ; and the reason is ready at hand, namely, forasmuch as God hath promised thee to accept thee for righteous through the merits of Jesus Christ, if thou believe not that thou art become righteous through him, thou makest God a liar, and consequently thou makest thyself unworthy of his grace and liberality.

But thou wilt say to me, I believe well the forgiveness of sins, and I know that God is true; but I am afraid that I am not worthy to have so great a gift. I answer, that the forgiveness of thy sins shall not be a gift of free grace, but a wages, if God should give it thee for the worthiness of thy works. But I reply unto thee, that God accepteth thee for righteous and layeth not thy sin to thy charge, because of Christ's merits which are given unto thee and become thine by faith. Therefore, following the counsel of St. Bernard, believe thou not only the forgiveness of sins in general, but also apply the same belief to thine own particular person, by believing without any doubt that all thy misdoings are pardoned thee through Jesus Christ. And so thou shalt give the glory unto God, confessing him to be merciful and true, and shalt become righteous and holy before God ; for by the same confession the holiness and righteousness of Jesus Christ shall be communicated unto thee.

But to return to our purpose of predestination : I say that, by the things above mentioned, a man may evidently perceive that the assurance of predestination doth not hurt, but rather greatly profit, the true Christians. And I think not that it can hurt the self* Christians and reprobates. For, albeit that such manner of folk would bear themselves in hand, and pretend to the world-ward to be of the number of predestinate, yet can they never persuade their own consciences, which will ever be gnawing and crying out to the contrary. But yet it seemeth greatly, that the doctrine of predestina-

* Self-righteous men who think they are Christians.

tion may hurt them. For they be wont to say, If I be of the number of the reprobates, what shall it avail me to do good works? And, if I be of the number of the predestinate, I shall be saved, without any labouring of mine to do good works. I answer thee at few words, that by such devilish arguments they increase God's wrath against themselves; who hath disclosed the knowledge of predestination to the Christians, to make them hot and not cold in the love of God, and to set them forward and not backward unto good works. And therefore the true Christian on the one side holdeth himself assuredly predestinated unto everlasting life, and to be saved, not at all by his own merits, but by God's election, who hath predestinated us not for our own works'. sakes, but to show the greatness of his mercy; and on the other side endeavoureth himself to do good works after the example of Jesus Christ, as much as if his salvation depended upon his own policy and pains-taking. As for him that ceaseth to do good, because of the doctrine of predestination, saying, If I be predestinated, I shall be saved, without straining of myself to do good works; he showeth evidently that his travailing is not for the love of God, but for the love of himself. By reason whereof, the works that he doth may perhaps be good and holy to the sight of men, but they be wicked and abominable before the Lord God, who hath an eye to the intent. And hereupon it may be gathered, that the doctrine of predestination worketh rather good than harm to the false Christians. For it discovereth their hypocrisy; which cannot cure itself so long as it lieth hidden under the mantle of outward works.

But I would have them that say, I will not strain myself to do well; for if I be predestinated I shall be saved without tiring of myself so much; I say, I would have them tell me, how it happeneth that, when they be diseased, they say not also, I will have neither physician nor physic; for look, what God hath determined upon me cannot but come to pass. Why eat they? why drink they? why till they the ground? why plant they vines? and why be they so diligent in doing all things convenient for to sustain the body? Why say they not, also, that all these turmoilings, policies and travails of ours are superfluous; forasmuch as it is not possible but that whatsoever God hath foreseen and determined, concerning our life and death, must needs come to pass? And, therefore, if God's providence make them not negligent and idle in things pertaining to the body, why should it make them more slothful and negligent in that which concerneth the Christian perfection, which without all comparison is far nobler than the body? But, as we see that neither Jesus Christ, nor St. Paul, for any doubt of offending reprobates, have forborne to preach the truth, which is necessary to the edifying of the chosen, for the love of whom the everlasting Son of God became a man and was put to death upon the cross, we also in like wise ought not to forbear the preaching of predestination, forasmuch as we have seen that it importeth great edification.

Now are we come to the end of our purpose, wherein our chief intent hath been (according to our small power) to magnify the wonderful benefit which the Christian man hath received by Jesus Christ crucified, and to show that faith of herself alone justifieth, that is to wit, that God receiveth and holdeth them for righteous, which believe steadfastly that Christ hath made full amends for their sins; howbeit, that, as light cannot be separated from fire, which of itself burneth and devoureth all things, even so good works cannot be separated from faith, which alone by itself justifieth.

And this holy doctrine (which exalteth Jesus Christ, and represseth and abateth the pride of man) hath and always shall be rejected and fought against by such Christians as have Jewish minds. But happy is he who, following the example of St. Paul, spoileth himself of his own righteousness, and would have none other righteousness than that which is of Jesus Christ, wherewith if he be clothed and apparelled, he may most assuredly appear before God, and shall receive his blessing and the heritage of heaven and earth, with his only Son Jesus Christ our Lord; to whom be all honour, praise, and glory, from this time forth for evermore.—AMEN.

Christ is the End of the Law.

Printed in Dunstable, United Kingdom